VAXclusters

ISBN	AUTHOR	TITLE
0-07-002467-7	Aronson	*SAS: A Programmer's Guide*
0-07-002673-4	Azevedo	*ISPF: The Strategic Dialog Manager*
0-07-005075-9	Berson	*APPC: Introduction to LU6.2*
0-07-006533-0	Bookman	*COBOL II for Programmers*
0-07-006551-9	Bosler	*CLIST Programming*
0-07-007248-5	Brathwaite	*Analysis, Design, and Implementation of Data Dictionaries*
0-07-007252-3	Brathwaite	*Relational Databases: Concepts, Designs, and Administration*
0-07-009816-6	Carathanassis	*Expert MVS / XA JCL: A Complete Guide To Advanced Techniques*
0-07-009820-4	Carathanassis	*Expert MVS / ESA JCL: A Guide to Advanced Techniques*
0-07-015231-4	D'Alleyrand	*Image Storage and Retrieval Systems*
0-07-016188-7	Dayton	*Integrating Digital Services*
0-07-016189-5	Dayton	*Telecommunications: The Transmission of Information*
0-07-017606-X	Donofrio	*CICS: Debugging, Dump Reading and Problem Determination*
0-07-017607-8	Donofrio	*CICS Programmer's Reference*
0-07-018966-8	Eddolls	*VM Performance Management*
0-07-032673-8	Johnson	*MVS: Concepts and Facilities*
0-07-033571-0	Kavanagh	*VS COBOL II For COBOL Programmers*
0-07-034242-3	Kessler	*ISDN: Concepts, Facilities, and Services*
0-07-010071-0	McGrew, McDaniel	*In-House Publishing In a Mainframe Environment, Second Edition*
0-07-040666-9	Martyn, Hartley	*DB2 / SQL, A Professional Programmer's Guide*
0-07-044129-4	Murphy	*ASSEMBLER For COBOL Programmers: MVS, VM*
0-07-050054-1	Piggot	*CICS: A Practical Guide To System Fine Tuning*
0-07-050686-8	Prasad	*IBM Mainframes: Architecture and Design*
0-07-051265-5	Ranade et al.	*DB2 Concepts, Programming and Design*
0-07-051143-8	Ranade, Sackett	*Advanced SNA Networking: A Professional's Guide For Using VTAM / NCP*
0-07-051144-6	Ranade, Sackett	*Introduction To SNA Networking: A Guide To VTAM / NCP*
0-07-054528-6	Samson	*MVS Performance Management*
0-07-054594-4	Sanchez, Canton	*IBM Microcomputers Handbook*
0-07-054597-9	Sanchez, Canton	*Programming Solutions Handbook for IBM Microcomputers*
0-07-071136-4	Wipfler	*Distributed Processing In The CICS Environment*

VAXclusters

Architecture, Programming, and Management

Jay Shah

McGraw-Hill, Inc.

New York St. Louis San Francisco Auckland Bogotá
Caracas Hamburg Lisbon London Madrid Mexico
Milan Montreal New Delhi Paris
San Juan São Paolo Singapore
Sydney Tokyo Toronto

Library of Congress Cataloging-in-Publication Data

Shah, Jay.
    VAXclusters / Jay Shah
        p.   cm. -- (J. Ranade DEC series)
    Includes bibliographical references and index.
    ISBN 0-07-056384-5
    1. VAX/VMS (Computer operating system)   I. Title.   II. Series.
    QA76.76.063s5   1991
    005.4'44--dc20   91-16991
                                                                                CIP

1 2 3 4 5 6 7 8 9 0 DOC/DOC 9 7 6 5 4 3 2 1

ISBN 0-07-056384-5

*The sponsoring editor for this book was Jerry Papke, the editing supervisor was David
E. Fogarty, and the production supervisor was Pamela A. Pelton. Line art composed in
Micrografx Designer and typesetting and indexing composed in Xerox Ventura Publisher
by VisionQuest USA, Inc., Rutherford, NJ 07070.*

Printed and bound by R. R. Donnelley & Sons Company.

The following are trademarks of Digital Equipment Corporation: ALL-IN-1, DEC,
DEC/CMS, DEC/MMS, DECnet, DECwindows, DIGITAL, MASSBUS, MicroVAX,
PDP, Q-bus, ReGIS, ULTRIX, UNIBUS, VAX, VAXBI, VAXcluster, VAX RMS, VMS,
VT, XMI. IBM is a registered trademark of International Business Machines
Corporation. X Window System, VersionII and its derivatives (X, X11, X Version, X
Window System) are trademarks of the Massachusetts Institute of Technology.
TransLAN is a registered trademark of Vitalink Communications Corporation.
Tandem, CLX, GUARDIAN, NonStop, TMF and VLX are trademarks of Tandem
Computer Incorporated.

To my 3-year-old son, Anand,
who may be considered a coauthor because
of his scribbling all over the manuscript

Contents

Preface   xiii

Chapter 1. Introduction to VAX Systems   1

    1.1   VAX Processors   2
    1.2   I/O Buses   4
    1.3   Hardware Components   5
    1.4   Software Components   8
            1.4.1   Digital Command Language   9
            1.4.2   The EVE Editor   10
            1.4.3   Program Development   10
            1.4.4   Layered Products   12
            1.4.5   DECnet   14
            1.4.6   DECwindows   16
    1.5   Summary   17

Chapter 2. The Operating System: VAX/VMS   19

    2.1   Logging in   20
    2.2   Help   20
    2.3   DCL Commands   20
    2.4   The Terminals   23
    2.5   DCL Commands   27
    2.6   Error Messages   31
    2.7   Devices   32
    2.8   Files   33
    2.9   The Process   35
    2.10   Operating System Basics   37
    2.11   Utility Commands   42
    2.12   Logical Names   42
            2.12.1 Device Independence   44
            2.12.2 Using Directories as Devices   45
            2.12.3 Search Lists   45
    2.13   Program Development   46
            2.13.1 Compiler Qualifiers   48
    2.14   LINK   51
    2.15   Summary   55

Chapter 3. VAXclusters and Other High-Availability Systems   57

3.1   **VAXcluster Basics**   57
3.2   **Homogeneous and Heterogeneous Clusters**   61
3.3   **VAXcluster Types: CI-based, NI-based and Mixed Interconnect**   61
3.4   **Parallel Processing and Vector Processing**   64
3.5   **DECnet and Ethernet**   65
3.6   **Networks, Parallel Computers, and VAXclusters**   66
3.7   **High-Availability Systems versus Fault-Tolerant Systems**   69
3.8   **The Fault-Tolerant VAXft System**   70
3.9   **Tandem Non-Stop Computers**   72
3.10   **Stratus Computers**   76

Chapter 4. VAXcluster Components and Terminology   79

4.1   **The System Communication Architecture**   79
       4.1.1   Datagrams, Sequenced Messages, and Data Blocks   80
       4.1.2   System Applications   82
       4.1.3   Cluster Configuration Management   83
       4.1.4   Buffer Management   84
       4.1.5   Connection Management   84
       4.1.6   Directory Services   85
       4.1.7   Datagram and Sequenced Message Services   85
       4.1.8   Named-Buffer Transfer Services   86
4.2   **Hardware Components**   86
       4.2.1   The Computer Interconnect Bus   86
       4.2.2   Star Coupler   88
       4.2.3   CI Controllers   88
       4.2.4   The Hierarchical Storage Controller   88
4.3   **Software Components**   89
       4.3.1   VAXport Drivers   90
       4.3.2   System Communications Services (SCS)   90
       4.3.3   Connection Manager   91
       4.3.4   Distributed File Services   91
       4.3.5   Distributed Lock Manager   93
       4.3.6   Distributed Job Controller   94
       4.3.7   Mass Storage Control Protocol Server   94
4.4   **QUORUMS and VOTES**   95
4.5   **QUORUM Disk**   97
4.6   **Allocation Class**   97
4.7   **Summary**   99

Chapter 5. Creating a VAXcluster   101

5.1   **VAXcluster Hardware Selection**   101
5.2   **A Local Area Network versus a Local Area VAXcluster**   103
5.3   **Installing The Operating System VAX/VMS**   104
5.4   **Serving Local Disks To The Cluster**   106
5.5   **Layout of the Common System Disk**   108

5.6	Adding VAXes To The Cluster	111
5.7	CLUSTER_CONFIG.COM	112
5.8	Satellite Nodes	112
5.9	VAXcluster Password	113
5.10	Summary	114

Chapter 6. Managing a VAXcluster   **115**

6.1	Creating User Profiles (The AUTHORIZE Database)	115
6.2	Creating Batch and Print job Queues	116
6.3	VAXcluster Alias For DECnet Communications	118
6.4	Cluster-Common LAT Service	121
6.5	The VAXcluster Console System	121
6.6	Customizing SYSTARTUP_V5.COM	123
6.7	The Hierarchical Storage Controller	123
	6.7.1 Accessing the HSC from a VAX	127
6.8	The DCL SHOW CLUSTER Command	127
	6.8.1 Using the Command	128
	6.8.2 Output of the SHOW CLUSTER Command	129
	6.8.3 Sending the SHOW CLUSTER Output to a File	131
6.9	The MONITOR Utility	131
6.10	VAX Performance Analyzer	133
	6.10.1 Data Collector	140
	6.10.2 Generating VPA Reports	141
	6.10.3 Advice from VPA and the Knowledge Database	142
	6.10.4 Workloads: System Usage Reports Based on User Groups	144
	6.10.5 Capacity Planning and Modeling	146
6.11	The SYSMAN Utility	148
6.12	Security Audits	150
6.13	Summary	155

Chapter 7. VAXcluster Programming   **157**

7.1	Interprogram Communications	158
7.2	Mailboxes	159
7.3	Logical Names	163
7.4	Global Sections	167
7.5	Synchronization	171
	7.5.1 Event Flags	172
	7.5.2 Locks	177
	7.5.3 The Distributed Lock Manager	181
7.6	Object Libraries	183
7.7	Shared Images	185
7.8	Asynchronous System Traps	188
7.9	Exit Handlers	190
7.10	Distributed Programming Across VAXes	192
	7.10.1 Programming Using DECnet	192

		7.10.1.1	Executing command files over the network	193
		7.10.1.2	Task-to-task communications over the network by command files	193
		7.10.1.3	Task-to-task communications over the network by programs	195
	7.10.2	Task-to-Task Communications within a VAXcluster		199
7.11	**DECdtm — Distributed Transaction Manager**			**199**
	7.11.1	Log Manager Control Program (LMCP) Utility		200
	7.11.2	Monitoring DECdtm Activity		201
7.12	**The Role of Electronic Disks**			**202**
7.13	**The Disk-Striping Driver**			**203**
7.14	**Automatic Failovers**			**204**
7.15	**Redundancy of Printer and Batch Queues**			**204**
7.16	**FDDI and VAXclusters**			**205**
7.17	**Summary**			**207**

Chapter 8. RMS—Record Management Services   **209**

8.1	**Overview**			**209**
8.2	**Record Formats**			**211**
8.3	**Initial Allocation**			**212**
8.4	**Extend Size**			**213**
8.5	**Disk Cluster Size**			**214**
8.6	**I/O Buckets**			**214**
8.7	**Block Spanning**			**215**
8.8	**Files and Records: Sharing and Locking**			**215**
8.9	**Indexed File Parameters**			**216**
	8.9.1	Duplicate Keys		217
	8.9.2	Changeable Keys		217
	8.9.3	Areas		217
	8.9.4	Index Bucket Size		217
	8.9.5	Record Key Fill Factor		218
8.10	**Using RMS Files in C and MACRO-32**			**218**
	8.10.1	RMS Data Structures		218
8.11	**RMS Utilities**			**223**
	8.11.1	FDL		223
		8.11.1.1	EDIT/FDL	224
		8.11.1.2	CREATE/FDL	229
		8.11.1.3	ANALYZE/RMS/FDL	229
	8.11.2	DUMP		230
	8.11.3	CONVERT		231
8.12	**RMS Journaling**			**233**
	8.12.1	RMS Journaling Features		233
		8.12.1.2	Before image journaling	235
		8.12.1.3	Recovery unit journaling	236
	8.12.2	Other Issues		242
8.13	**Summary**			**242**

Chapter 9. Volume Shadowing   245

   9.1   How Volume Shadowing Works   245
   9.2   What Volume Shadowing Cannot Do   247
   9.3   Implementing Volume Shadowing   249
   9.4   Shadowing the VMS System Disk   250
   9.5   Redundant HSCs   251
   9.6   Volume Shadowing on a Cluster   252
   9.7   The DCL Lexical Function F$GETDVI   253
   9.8   Summary   253

Chapter 10. The VAX Architecture   259

   10.1   Overview   260
   10.2   Pages and Memory Management   261
       10.2.1 The Memory Translation Process   261
       10.2.2 Size of Memory   262
       10.2.3 Sharing Memory   264
       10.2.4 Memory Management Details   265
       10.2.5 The Translation Process   266
       10.2.6 The PTE   269
   10.3   Memory-Mapped I/O   271
   10.4   Exceptions and Interrupts   271
   10.5   Registers   273
   10.6   Programming The Machine   276
       10.6.1 The Assembly Language   276
       10.6.2 Assembler Syntax   278
   10.7   Data Types   279
   10.8   Instruction Formats   279
   10.9   The Instruction Set   282
       10.9.1 Arithmetic and Logical Instructions   284
       10.9.2 Character String Instructions   285
       10.9.3 Control Instructions   286
       10.9.4 Procedure Call instructions   287
       10.9.5 Queue Instructions   288
       10.9.6 Variable-Length Bit Field Instructions   288
       10.9.7 Miscellaneous Instructions   289
   10.10 Vector Processing   290
   10.11 Summary   291

Appendix: Relevant SYSGEN Parameters   293
Glossary   297
Bibliography   315
Index   317

Preface

This book describes VAXclusters and shows how to exploit the VAXcluster architecture. A VAXcluster is a collection of VAXes and peripherals connected together to form one synergetic system. Individual VAXes in the cluster run the VAX/VMS operating system. The book also applies to local area VAXclusters (LAVCs) which are VAXclusters using Ethernet as a cluster communications medium. The name VAX/VMS is derived from *virtual address extension / virtual memory system*. The first VAX, VAX 11/780, was introduced in 1977. VAXclusters were introduced in 1983.

The intended audience

This book is for anyone who wants a thorough understanding of VAXclusters. Typical readers would be:

- System managers who currently have or are planning to install VAXclusters
- Software developers and programmers who wish to design high-availability systems
- Programmers who want to understand how a VAXcluster works
- Academicians and students interested in distributed computing architectures

What is the prerequisite?

A prerequisite for understanding the material is basic computer science knowledge. Common terms used by computer engineers are not explained. Since VAXclusters are based on the VAX/VMS operating system, VAX/VMS is also discussed in this book. Nevertheless, familiarity with VAXes and VAX/VMS is beneficial.

Why this book is complete

Just about every bit of information on VAXclusters short of the internal software and hardware design is included here. To start off, VMS and VAXclusters are described in general. Various types of VAXclusters and VAXcluster hardware and software components are discussed. The reader is shown how to create and manage a VAXcluster. Programming issues are covered along with suitable examples so that the cluster architecture can be fully exploited. VAX/VMS features are also described in the book.

What is included?

The VAXcluster design falls in between a loosely coupled system (e.g., one that is interconnected by a network) and a tightly coupled system (e.g., a parallel computer where multiple processors share main memory). A VAXcluster can offer a number of enhancements over a set of independent systems:

- *High availability*. For example: VAXclusters can support "mission critical" applications.
- *Resource sharing*. For example: Disk files can be shared by member VAXes.
- *Common system management*. For example: The cluster can have a common system console.
- *Higher aggregate throughput*. Properly designed applications can take advantage of this feature.
- *Expandability*. For example: New VAXes and devices can be added to the cluster with ease.

VAXes that are cluster members can optionally support parallel processing using multiple processors and hardware-based *vector processors*.

This book

- Explains what VAXclusters are
- Shows various VAXcluster configurations
- Shows how to set up and manage VAXclusters
- Explains VAXcluster terminology
- Discusses the operating system, VAX/VMS
- Discusses VAXcluster programming issues

The book also discusses a number of software and hardware products that facilitate the design of high-availability systems although VAXclusters can operate without these products. Examples of such products are the *electronic disks, volume-shadowing software* and *RMS-journaling software*.

What is the next step?

After reading this book, you should have a thorough understanding of VAXclusters. Depending on your background you may want to:

- Design or modify your applications to exploit clustering features
- Manage a VAXcluster environment
- Understand transaction-processing and distributed-processing systems
- Read some of the books and journals mentioned in the bibliography
- Understand parallel and vector processing on the VAX
- Understand the design of fault-tolerant VAXes (the VAXft series)
- Understand other high availability systems like Tandem and Stratus

Acknowledgments

I worked with Kedar Bhatt at Gujarat University in India, developing courses on assembly language programming. I learned VAX systems programming then. My gratitude to Kedar and Gujarat University.

Jay Ranade was my guide for preparing the book. His advice and opinions strongly influenced the style of the book.

Thanks to my manuscript reviewers, Dave Alquist, Waldo Patton, and Ben Schwartz. Their suggestions improved the technical presentation of the book. Dave's command of the English language was a humbling experience. I rephrased parts of the book at his behest. Special thanks to Carolyn Garbarino of Tandem Computers for helping me with the section on their systems. Finally, thanks to my colleague at Chase Manhattan Bank, Chia Hsu, for technical discussions on VAXclusters.

Introduction to VAX Systems

The VAX architecture is designed by Digital Equipment Corporation (DEC). The company was formed in 1957 with headquarters in Massachusetts. The VAX architecture evolved from DEC's older computer, the PDP (*programmable data processor*). The PDP-11 is a 16-bit computer; the VAX-11 has a 32-bit architecture. "VAX" is derived from *virtual address extension*.

A VAXcluster consists of individual VAX computers running the VAX/VMS operating system. For an introduction to VAXclusters see Chap. 3. To understand VAXclusters, it is necessary to know the VAX architecture and the VAX/VMS operating system. "VAX/VMS" is derived from *virtual address extension/virtual memory system*.

This chapter introduces the software and hardware components of VAX systems. VAX systems are available as micro-, mini-, or mainframe systems. Figure 1.1 shows a VAX 4000 cabinet. The cabinet is called a BA440 enclosure. The option module slots accept *Qbus controllers*. For example, the KRQ50 controller for the RRD40 600-Mbyte CD-ROM reader occupies one slot. The RFxxs are disk drives. For example, the RF71 is a 400-Mbyte disk drive. There are two versions of the RF71: removable and fixed. The TK70 is a 270-Mbyte cartridge tape drive. The TLZ04 is a 4-mm *digital audio tape* (DAT) drive that can record 1.2 Gbytes/tape.

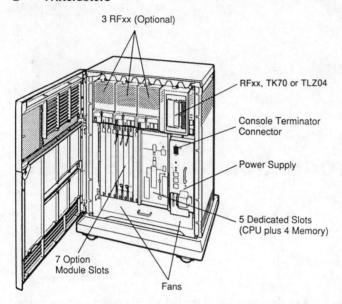

Figure 1.1 A VAX 4000 system. (Copyright © 1990 Digital Equipment Corporation. All rights reserved. Reprinted by permission.)

1.1 VAX PROCESSORS

A typical VAX CPU cabinet contains a card cage. The card cage holds a number of *printed circuit boards* (PCBs). There are three major types of boards: *CPU*, *Memory*, and *Controllers*.

The VAX CPU has 16 *general purpose data registers*, each containing 32 bits. The machine uses 32-bit addressing with a virtual addressing range of *4 Gbytes*. The CPU supports more than *400 instructions*, including character string manipulation, packed-decimal arithmetic, floating-point arithmetic, and variable-length bit field instructions.

The 6000 and 9000 series VAXes support *vector processing* in hardware. The basic instruction set is now extended to perform vector operations. There are about 63 vector-processing instructions. When the vector-processing hardware option is installed, the CPU has 64 vector registers. Each vector register has 64 elements (simple registers), and each element has 64 bits. Various instructions are provided to perform arithmetic in parallel on the contents of these registers.

While the instruction set is (nearly) the same for all VAXes, the hardware technology used to implement the CPU varies among the various VAX models. The VAX models also have different CPU speeds. Figure 1.2 shows the CPU characteristics of some VAX models.

There are four basic families of VAXes: the VAX 9000, VAX 6000, VAX 4000, and MicroVAX 3000 series. The MicroVAX 3000 series will be gradually superseded by the VAX 4000 series computers. VAXes no longer in production (like the 8000 series, MicroVAX II, VAX 11/780, and VAX 11/750) are not discussed explicitly in this book, although many of them are supported by DEC and can be VAXcluster members.

Note that CPU speeds are normally not measured using standard MIPS (*millions of instructions/sec*); rather VUPs (*VAX unit of processing*) and microVUPs are used. DEC believes that MIPS, as a standard of measure, is misleading when applied to the VAX, which has a complex instruction set and a variety of intelligent I/O devices. The throughput of a complete system configuration is more indicative of system performance. One VUP is the speed of a VAX 11/780. Thus, a 3.7-VUP VAX has a CPU that is 3.7 times faster than a VAX 11/780 CPU. One microVUP is the speed of a MicroVAX II. Both the VAX 11/780 and MicroVAX II are no more in production; however, the standards of measure are still in use.

CPU model	CPU speed*	Implementation technology	Maximum memory, Mbytes	I/O bus	Maximum bus I/O throughput, Mbytes/sec
VAXstation 3100	2.7	CMOS	32	SCSI	1.5
MicroVAX 3900	3.8	CMOS	64	Qbus	3.3
				DSSI	4.0
VAX 4000-300	8.0	CMOS	128	Qbus	3.3
				DSSI	4.0
VAX 6000-420	15.0	CMOS	256	VAXBI	60.0
				XMI	80.0
VAX 9000-440	117.0	ECL	512	XMI	320.0

* Notes: CPU speed is relative to VAX 11/780. VAX 6000-520 is a dual-processor. (Some of the VAXes achieve higher I/O rates by using multiple buses.)

Figure 1.2 VAX models.

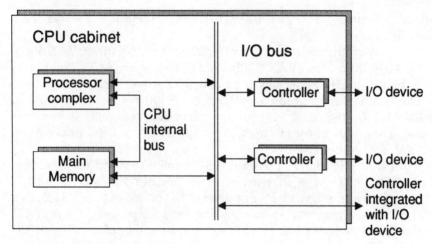

Figure 1.3 The I/O connection.

Memory on the smaller VAXes is 8 bit with 1-bit parity; on the more expensive models ECC (error correcting code) memory is used.

1.2 I/O BUSES

A controller connects the CPU and memory to I/O devices via an I/O bus. Figure 1.3 shows this configuration. Usually, there is a separate internal bus connecting the CPU with memory. This bus has a much higher speed than the I/O buses.

There are six major I/O buses used on VAXes:

XMI   Used on VAX 9000 series; this is the fastest bus to date.

VAXBI   Used on midrange and high-end systems like the VAX 6000series.

UNIBUS   Used on older midrange system; it is being phased out.

Qbus   Used on low-end and midrange systems like the VAX 4000 and MicroVAX 3000 series.

SCSI   Used on VAXstations. SCSI is an acronym for *small computer systems interface* .

DSSI   Used on some of the MicroVAXes and VAX 4000 series computers for disk I/O. Many of the disk controllers on this bus are integrated into the device enclosure rather than in the CPU cabinet. DSSI is an acronym for *digital standard systems interconnect*.

Bus	Speed Mbytes/sec	Supporting VAXes	Sample disk controllers used on the bus
XMI	80.0	6000 and 9000 series	KDM70
VAXBI	10.0	6000 and 9000 series	KDB50
Qbus	3.3	MicroVAX 3000 series	KDA50
SCSI	1.2	VAXstation 3100	SCSI
DSSI	4.0	VAX 4000	DSSI

Figure 1.4 I/O buses on the VAX.

The DSSI bus allows disk drives with integrated controllers to be connected to a VAX. The controllers have software that allows multiple VAXes to communicate with the drive. This allows VAXes in a *computer interconnect* (CI)-based VAXcluster to use common drives without resorting to the use of expensive *hierarchical storage controllers* (HSCs) or, in the case of local area VAXclusters, the use of a VAX to serve a local disk as a cluster common disk.

Some VAXes can have more than one bus of the same type for better I/O performance. Many VAXes support more than one type of I/O bus. Figure 1.4 shows the characteristics of some of the general buses.

Controllers communicate with the CPU using hardware interrupts and *control and status registers* (CSRs). CSRs are registers within the controller that can be accessed as memory locations by the CPU. This implies that the VAX uses memory-mapped I/O. Many controllers have *direct memory access* (DMA) to the main memory.

1.3 HARDWARE COMPONENTS

The VAX supports many I/O devices. Typically, the I/O device communicates with the CPU and memory via a controller. A controller's design depends on the type of bus it can be used with and on the I/O devices it controls. The term "I/O device" is used generically since controllers are also used to communicate with components (like Ethernet) that, technically, are not I/O devices. Figure 1.5 describes some common controllers.

Controller	Bus required	Devices controlled
KDM70	XMI	RA series disk drives like RA92
KDB50	VAXBI	RA series disk drives
KDA50	Qbus	RA series disk drives
DSSI	DSSI	RF series disk drives
DEMNA	XMI	Ethernet interface (DEC LAN controller 400)
DESQA	Qbus	Ethernet interface
CIBCA	VAXBI	VAXcluster Port (CI interface)
CIBCD	XMI	VAXcluster Port (CI interface)
TQK70	Qbus	TK70 cartridge tape controller
SCSI	SCSI	Disk drives like RZ23 and tape drives like TK50 drives
DMB32	VAXBI	Communication lines

Figure 1.5 Some common controllers.

A vast number of devices can be connected to VAX systems. Some of these are:

1. The RA series disk drives are the most common storage device on large systems. The RA92 has a capacity of 1.5 Gbytes and an average seek time of 15.5 msec. The RA90 has a capacity of 1.2 Gbytes and an average seek time of 18.5 msec. The RA70 has a capacity of 280 Mbytes and an average seek time of 19.5 msec. These drives are also packaged as storage arrays in units of four or more. These units are SA550, SA600, SA705, SA800, and SA850.

2. The ESE20 is a *solid state disk*. On the system, the ESE20 works like any RA series disk drive, i.e., the ESE20 is *Digital Storage Architecture* (DSA) compliant. However, instead of rotating magnetic media, the ESE20 is made of volatile semiconductor memory. It has a capacity of 120 Mbytes and an access time of 1.3 msec! Real throughput is at least four times greater than for an RA90 disk.

3. The RF series disk drives have controllers integrated with the disk drives. (The controllers for RA series drives are inside the CPU cabinet of the host system.) The drives use the DSSI bus

and are ubiquitous on MicroVAX 3000s and VAX 4000s. The RF71 is a 5.25-inch drive with a capacity of 400 Mbytes and an average seek time of 21 msec. The RF71 removable drive is similar to the standard RF71 except that it can be removed for safe storage when it is required. The RF72 has a 1.2 Gbyte capacity.

4. The RZ series disk drives are used on VAXes supporting the SCSI bus. The RZ24 has a capacity of 209 Mbytes and an average seek time of 24.3 Msec.

5. The RRD40 is a *compact disk ROM* (CD-ROM) reader. CD-ROM capacity is 600 Mbytes and an average seek time is 500 msec.

6. The TA90 cartridge tape subsystem is an IBM 3480 compatible unit. The cartridge has a capacity of 200 Mbytes. Six cartridges can be stacked for unattended backup of a RA90 drive.

7. A number of 8-mm and 4-mm magnetic tape backup devices are available from DEC and third party vendors. An 8-mm tape can hold more than 2 Gbytes/tape.

8. The TA79 magnetic tape subsystem is an industry standard ½ inch spool tape unit. It has a read and write speed of 125 inches/sec. The TU81-Plus is a standard spool streaming tape drive. It has a *streaming speed* of 75 inches/sec and a *start/stop speed* of 25 inches/sec. Normally, VMS creates ANSI standard tapes. These tapes can be ported to computers of other manufacturers.

9. The TK70 is a *cartridge tape drive system*. The cartridge capacity is 296 Mbytes. The TK50 is similar except that it has a capacity of 95 Mbytes.

10. PrintServer 40 PLUS is a 40 pages/minute laser printer. The LN03 is an 8 pages/minute laser printer. The LN03R is a Postscript laser printer. The LJ250 is an ink jet color printer. The LA75 and LA210 are 250 characters/sec dot matrix printers. The LA75 has a printing width of 80 characters; the LA210 prints 132 columns wide. The LA70 prints at 200 characters/sec. LP29 is a 2000 lines/minute line printer. LG31 is a 300 lines/minute dot matrix printer.

11. The LN03s is being superseded by the DEClaser 2000 family of printers. While both the LN03 and DEClaser 2000 printers are similar in function, they differ in internal design (they are manufactured by different companies). The DEClaser 2000

printer can print 8 pages/minute. The DEClaser 2100 prints single sides, while the DEClaser 2200 prints both sides of pages.

12. MD300 DECimage scanning subsystem is a 300 dots/inch scanner.

13. A number of *synchronous* and *asynchronous* communications controllers are available. Since VAXes are very common in process control and real-time monitoring and control environments, a number of real-time options like A/D and D/A controllers are also available.

We have been introduced to the basic building blocks of a VAX system. Figure 1.6 shows a VAX 6000-520 computer system with associated hardware.

1.4 SOFTWARE COMPONENTS

There are two major operating systems for the VAXes: VAX/VMS and Ultrix. VAX/VMS is DEC's proprietary operating system. Indi-

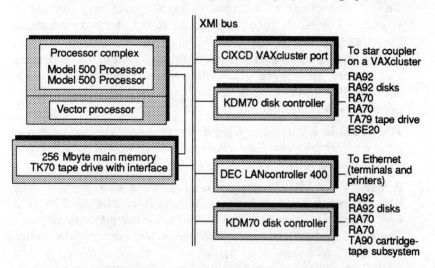

Notes: The TA90 cartridge tapes are IBM 3480 compatible. The RA92 disk capacity is 1.6 Gbytes, while the RA70 capacity is 270 Mbytes. Currently, the Vector Processor speed is 45 MFLOPS (double precision). The two Model 500 processors provide an aggregate CPU speed of 25 VUPs. Each processor has 128 kbytes of cache memory on board.

Figure 1.6 A VAX 6000-520 system.

vidual VAXes in a VAXcluster run VAX/VMS. Ultrix-32 is DEC's implementation of UNIX. Third-party UNIX implementations are also used at many sites. Ultrix is not discussed in this book since a VAX running Ultrix cannot be a VAXcluster member.

VMS is a highly interactive operating system. Program development functions, including compilations, are usually performed on-line. End-user applications also run on-line with the user interface controlled by one of the form management systems on VMS. Programs and commands can also be freely used in submitted batch files. The batch mode is typically used for end-of-day processing of on-line applications and programs that run for a long time without any user interaction.

Terminal interaction is similar to that on PCs. Each character entered at the terminal is sent to the VAX, which in turn echoes it immediately (this is unlike mainframe terminals where characters are buffered in the terminal until a function key is pressed). Currently, VT220 and VT320 are the most common terminals. The newer VT420 terminals offer *dual sessions* and *block-mode data transfers* of data entered in a screen form. Many installations use third-party terminals that normally emulate VT series terminals. The user interface after logging in is also very similar to those of most PCs. In fact, some of the commands like DIRECTORY and TYPE are exactly the same in their basic form.

1.4.1 Digital Command Language

The user interface to VAX/VMS is the *digital command language* (DCL). When a user logs in, a dollar sign prompt is issued by DCL:

```
$
```

DCL then waits for command input. DCL commands are written in a *procedural* language. DCL has a language *interpreter* for executing a string of commands. Powerful programs (procedures) can be written using DCL. A sequence of commands can be stored in a file and executed later. DCL supports parameter substitution, commonly used built-in functions, and conditional execution of commands. Here is an example of a DCL command:

```
$ BACKUP/VERIFY  DUA0:[TEST...]  MUA0:TEST.BCK/SAVE
```

Here is an example of a command file that compiles and links a COBOL program:

```
$! File: COBOL_BUILD_1.COM
$ COBOL PROGA.COB
$ LINK PROGA.OBJ
$ EXIT
```

1.4.2   The EVE Editor

EVE, the *extensible VAX editor*, is now the standard text editor on
VMS. The editor is actually a program written using the *text processing utility* (TPU). Users familiar with the older EDT editor
should learn EVE; it will be worth the effort since EVE is far more
functional than EDT.

The highlights of EVE are:

- *Multiple windows on screen* Multiple files can be displayed and
  edited.

- *Keyboard macros* Keys can be defined that execute as a sequence of other keystrokes.

- *Programmability* The *text processing utility* (TPU) can be used
  to customize EVE to suit individual requirements and taste.

- *Journaling* In case of a system failure, most of the editing that
  was done can be recovered later.

- *Place markers* Positions in the edited files can be marked by
  names. A previously marked position can be restored on the
  screen.

- *DCL commands* These commands can be issued from the editor. Output is captured and displayed on the screen. The output can be edited.

- *Subprocess spawning* This allows temporary exit to DCL to
  execute system commands.

- *Wildcard and fuzzy searches* These features are supported.

1.4.3   Program Development

Languages supported on the VAX/VMS include Ada, APL, BASIC,
BLISS, C, COBOL, DIBOL, FORTRAN, LISP, VAX MACRO,
OPS5, PASCAL, PL/1, RPG II, SCAN, and VAX TPU. Of these,
VAX TPU is the only language that comes bundled with the operat-

ing system. TPU is a programming language for manipulating textual data. Complex applications can be written in multiple languages with calls to programs written in other languages. The *run-time library* and *system services* offer a collection of utility subroutines that can be called from programs. Since VAX/VMS uses virtual memory management techniques, program size is usually not a limitation.

Programs are created using a system editor. EVE is a popular editor. Other editors are EDT and LSE (*language sensitive editor*). EDT was popular in the past, however, EVE is a more modern editor, so EDT is not discussed in this book.

A *symbolic program debugger* aids in program testing. The debugger displays multiple windows. Source code, program output, and user commands are displayed in separate windows. The debugger can be used for testing programs in any language. Conditional execution of statements and other features make the debugger a powerful programming tool.

VAXset is a set of CASE (*computer-aided software engineering*) tools that aid in software project management. The toolkit consists of:

- *Code Management System (CMS)* CMS manages source files for a project. CMS maintains a history of changes made to files by programmers.

- *Language Sensitive Editor (LSE)* The LSE can be used to create or edit programs in any language. The editor provides code templates, which can be useful if you forget the syntax of the statements. The program can be compiled within the editor. Compilation errors can be displayed and the source program corrected from the editor.

- *Source Code Analyzer (SCA)* SCA is a cross-referencing tool for analyzing usage of variables and routines. SCA can be used to search for variable declarations and usage in a set of source programs that constitute a complete application. The source programs are displayed to show the exact occurrence of the variable.

- *Module Management System (MMS)* MMS is used to build a software application from an interdependent set of source programs (which constitute the complete application). Programs can be modified, and then MMS can be used to generate the system. MMS checks revision dates on files and determines which parts of the application needs to be regenerated. MMS can also be used on nonprogram files.

- *DEC Test Manager (DTM)* DTM automates the testing of a software system to determine if the system runs as expected. DTM is a regression analysis tool. The programmer runs the programs under DTM. DTM notes all input given by the programmer and all output generated by the application. This output is a benchmark. Later on, when some programs are modified, DTM can be used to rerun the test to ensure that results are the same as those of the benchmark.

- *Performance and Coverage Analyzer (PCA)* PCA shows how much time is spent by the CPU on each statement of a program during execution. It is an execution profiler that can be used to highlight bottlenecks in an application or optimize programs. Statistics on I/O system calls is also collected.

Files used in programs can be sequential, relative, or indexed. The *record management services* (RMS) is used to manipulate files and is normally available with the operating system. Many languages like COBOL automatically use RMS when files are handled within programs.

DECnet can be used to write distributed applications. Task-to-task communications is supported by DECnet.

1.4.4 Layered Products

Most software products other than the operating system and DECnet are considered *layered products*; "layered" because they reside as a layer above the operating system. VAXset (mentioned above) is a layered product. Some of the other layered products are mentioned here.

ALL-IN-1 is an integrated office automation package supporting word processing, graphics, spreadsheets, and electronic mail. Many of the subpackages used within ALL-IN-1 are also available separately. WPS-PLUS is a word processor. DECspell can be used to check and correct spellings. VAX Grammar Checker proofreads a document for grammatical correctness. VAX DECalc is a spreadsheet package. DECgraph can be used to prepare presentation graphs.

DEC offers a set of packages for application development:

- *Database Management System* Two main DBMSs are available from DEC: VAX DBMS and Rdb. VAX DBMS adheres to the Codasyl standard and has a network architecture. Rdb is a relational DBMS and has an SQL (*structured query language*) interface.

- *Datatrieve* is a report writer and is an interpreter aiding fast program development at the expense of run-time efficiency. It is particularly useful for generating quick reports and graphical output.

- *DECintact* is a high-volume transaction-processing application development software. It supports distributed processing. It can be used for mission-critical applications like electronic funds transfer where transaction integrity is required and where failure of hardware components could be disastrous. DECtp is the generic term for DEC's transaction-processing-oriented products.

- *Applications Control Management System* (ACMS) is another transaction processing application development software that focuses on reduced application development time cycles.

Common data dictionary (CDD/PLUS) is a layered product that centralizes the storage and management of data definitions. CDD/PLUS keeps a description of the data, not the data itself. An application can have a large number of programs accessing a set of files. The record layouts of these files can be defined in a CDD. The definition can be included within programs. The definitions are translated into corresponding program statements by CDD/PLUS depending on the programming language. The advantage of this approach is that changes to record formats (fields) can be made in CDD without having to change the programs. CDD/PLUS also supports database products like Datatrieve, Rdb/VMS, and VAX DBMS. CDD/PLUS will be superseded by a more extensive product called CDD/Repository.

Most end-user applications require forms to be displayed on screen and data to be accepted from fields within the form. While programmers can use standard I/O statements and perform data validation within programs, a number of packages are available for programming ease. *DECforms, terminal data management system* (TDMS), and *forms management system* (FMS) are used to design forms on screen. FMS is the oldest and currently the most commonly used screen design package. TDMS has most of the features of FMS; in addition, TDMS can validate data without any programming. DECforms is the latest package conforming to ANSI/ISO FIMS (*form interface management system*) standard. The DECforms interface is being standardized by DEC for use with their DBMSs and other application development products.

VAX DOCUMENT is an electronic publishing package. Most of the VAX documentation from DEC is created using this package. It is a good tool for producing in-house pamphlets, proposals, and other documents. Graphics can be integrated with text.

The *DECtalk* product consists of a hardware device and software programs. It can be used to create voice output, and, when connected with a telephone system, DECtalk can recognize telephone key presses. Effectively, an automated interactive telephone system can be designed.

VAX *DEC/Shell* is a UNIX interface emulator. It is an alternative to the standard DCL interface.

1.4.5 DECnet

One of the strengths of the VAX/VMS software is DECnet. DECnet is the networking component of VAXes for communications between VAXes (and other computers). For programmers, files residing on devices attached to other VAXes on the network are similar to files on their own computer. Typical uses of a DECnet network are:

- Copying files
- Logging into other VAXes
- Sharing of resources like files and fast line printers
- Running distributed applications

Ethernet technology, though not essential to running DECnet, is extensively used for networking. *Ethernet* is a bus with a rated bandwidth of 10 Mbits/sec. VAXes in the same building are usually interconnected by Ethernet. Ethernet is also used to support terminal servers. *Terminal servers* allow terminals to be logically connected to any VAX on the network. While Ethernet was designed for use in *local area networks* (LANs), Ethernet bridges allow Ethernet to be extended over long distances, even from one continent to another.

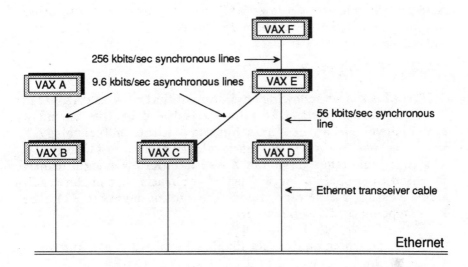

Notes: The Ethernet will usually have other devices like terminal servers, LANbridges, and SNAgateways connected to it. Communications between VAX B and VAX E could be via VAX C or VAX D as determined by DECnet routing layer software. Most of the VAXes will have independent peripherals.

Figure 1.7 A DECnet network.

Thinwire Ethernet is similar to standard Ethernet; the major difference is that the standard coaxial Ethernet cable is replaced by a thinner version. Thinwire Ethernet hardware is more convenient to handle physically. Figure 1.7 shows a DECnet network using Ethernet and point-to-point communications lines.

VAXes can also be interconnected by point-to-point connections. The connections can be synchronous or asynchronous. These connections use the DDCMP (*digital data communications protocol*) protocol under DECnet. Point-to-point connections are normally used when VAXes are far apart or if the connection is for a simple application where the installation of Ethernet products is not cost effective.

DECnet also has SNA connectivity products that allow VAXes to communicate with IBM mainframes. Some of these products are used for *3270 terminal emulation*, APPC LU 6.2 *task-to-task communications*, RJE, and *file transfer*. DECnet also has support for

X.25 connectivity that allows VAXes to communicate with other computers on packet-switched networks like Telenet and Tymnet.

1.4.6 DECwindows

DECwindows is a windowing environment that runs on VAX-based graphics workstations. DECwindows is based on the X-window system developed at the Massachusetts Institute of Technology. X in turn is based on W, which was developed at Stanford University. The first production version of X was X10. X10 was significantly modified to support a large class of applications, and the result was X version 11. Newer versions are enhancements to X11. The key components of X-windows are:

- X server, which handles the display, keyboard, fonts, and so on.
- Xlib, a library of low-level routines.
- Xtoolkit (Xt), which is a library of prepackaged routines that were designed for the convenience of application developers. Xtookit makes use of Xlib. Xt is also known as *Xt intrinsics*. DECwindows uses a toolkit called MOTIF (previously XUI), which is X intrinsics with some enhancements.

DECwindows offers the user a graphics-oriented interaction with the VAX. DCL can be used in terminal-emulation windows. Multiple windows allow multiple sessions to be displayed simultaneously. Currently, a number of VAX software products like VAX MAIL and VAXset software engineering tools have been enhanced to exploit DECwindows features.

MOTIF, a user interface developed using X-windows is being adopted as a standard by many companies. DECwindows supports MOTIF. Currently, without MOTIF, users accustomed to one vendor's products have to learn the new environment when moving over to another vendor's products. With MOTIF, this migration should become easy.

VAXstations are highly suitable for DECwindows applications. In particular, windowing applications are highly graphics oriented; parts of the screen have to be painted very quickly. VAXstations are suitable for this since the CPU is used mainly for handling the screen although it can be used for running other applications. Basically, a VAXstation is a small VAX with a graphics terminal. The VAXstation normally connects to Ethernet and runs standard VAX/VMS. Of course, DECwindows will work on other VAXes also.

1.5 SUMMARY

VAXclusters are made up of individual VAX computers all running the operating system, VAX/VMS. A basic understanding of how VAX/VMS works is required to understand VAXclusters. VAXes and VAX/VMS were introduced in this chapter. VAXes range from small desktop VAXstations to large multi-CPU mainframes with multiple I/O buses and vector processing capabilities. Basic VAX software and hardware building blocks were introduced in this chapter. The next chapter describes VAX/VMS. VAXclusters are discussed in Chap. 3.

2

The Operating System: VAX/VMS

VMS is a highly interactive operating system. Program development functions, including compilations, are usually performed on-line. End-user applications also run on-line with the user interface controlled by one of the form management systems on VMS. Programs and commands can also be freely used in submitted batch files. The batch mode is typically used for end-of-day processing of on-line applications and programs that run for a long time without any user interaction.

Terminal interaction is similar to that on PCs. Each character entered at the terminal is sent to the VAX, which in turn echoes it immediately (this is unlike mainframe terminals where characters are buffered in the terminal until a function key is pressed). Currently, VT220 and VT320 are the most common terminals. Many installations use third-party terminals that normally emulate VT series terminals. The user interface after logging in is also very similar to those of most PCs. In fact, some of the commands like DIRECTORY and TYPE are exactly the same in their basic form. The VAX systems, though, are more functional than ordinary PCs, as will be seen in this book. This chapter introduces the basic operating system features. VAXclusters are introduced in the next chapter.

2.1 LOGGING IN

A *username* and a *password* are required to gain access to a VAX computer. These are supplied by the systems administrator. To log in interactively, hit the RETURN key on the terminal. If the prompt "local>" is displayed then enter "CONNECT nodename" where nodename is the name of the system you want to log into. The "Username: " prompt should be displayed by the operating system, VAX/VMS. Enter your username, followed by the RETURN key. The next prompt will be "Password: ". Enter your password, which is not displayed.

On successfully logging, you should see the "$ " prompt. The prompt is issued by the component of the operating system called *digital command language* (DCL). DCL is your interface to the computer. DCL commands can now be issued. All DCL commands are terminated with the RETURN key.

Terminal servers are described in the chapter on VAX/VMS hardware environment. Here is a sample login from a terminal connected to a terminal server:

```
Local> Connect  MAYUR
        Welcome to VAX/VMS V5.3
Username: SHAH
Password:
        Welcome to VAX/VMS version V5.3 on node MAYUR
Last interactive login on Friday, 28-JAN-1991 12:51
Last non-interactive login on Thursday, 27-JAN-1991 14:04
$
```

2.2 HELP

The HELP command is useful to see the list of commands that are recognized by DCL. HELP also displays usage information on the commands. Figure 2.1 shows an example of how HELP is used.

2.3 DCL COMMANDS

DCL is the interface between users and the operating system. DCL commands are terminated (and executed) by the RETURN key. Parameters for the command can be specified on the command line

```
$ HELP
HELP

    The HELP command invokes the VAX-11 HELP Facility to display
    information about a VMS command or topic. In response to the
    "Topic?" prompt, you can:
        Type the name of the command or topic for which you need
        help.
        Type PROCEDURES for information on commonly performed tasks.
        Type HINTS if you are not sure of the name of the command
        or topic for which you need help.
        Type INSTRUCTIONS for more detailed instructions on how
        to use HELP.
        Type a question mark (?) to redisplay the most recently
        requested text.
        Press the RETURN key one or more times to exit from HELP.
    You can abbreviate any topic name, although ambiguous
    abbreviations result in all matches being displayed.
    Format:
        HELP [topic[subtopic]...]


Additional information available:

ACCOUNTING ADVISE      ALLOCATE    ANALYZE     APPEND
ASCII      ASSIGN      ATTACH      BACKUP      CALL
CANCEL     CLOSE       Command_procedure       CONNECT
CONTINUE   CONVERT     COPY        CREATE      DEALLOCATE
DEASSIGN   DEBUG       DECK        DEFINE      DELETE
DEPOSIT    DIFFERENCES DIRECTORY   DISCONNECT  DISMOUNT
DUMP       EDIT        EOD         EXAMINE     EXIT
Expressions File_Spec  GOSUB       GOTO        HELP
Hints      IF          INITIALIZE  INQUIRE     Instructions
Lexicals   LIBRARY     LINK        LOGOUT      MAIL
MERGE      MESSAGE     MOUNT       New_Features_V44
Numbers    ON          OPEN        PERFORMANCE PRINT
Privileges Procedures  Protection  PURGE       READ
RECALL     RENAME      REPLY       REQUEST     RETURN
RUN        RUNOFF      SEARCH      SET         SHOW
SNA_GM     SNA_Terminals           SORT        SPAWN
SPM        START       STOP        Strings     SUBMIT
SYNCHRONIZE Symbol-assignment      THEN        Time
TYPE       UNLOCK      VPA         WAIT        WRITE
```

Figure 2.1 Sample on-line HELP usage.

```
Topic? time
TIME
        Absolute time:

        dd-mmm-yyyy:hh:mm:ss.ss

        TODAY

        YESTERDAY

        TOMORROW

Delta time:
        dd-hh:mm:ss.ss

Combination time:
        An absolute plus (+) or minus(-) a delta time. Whenever
        a plus sign precedes the delta time value, the entire
        time specification must be enclosed in quotation marks.

        If a description states that a time can be expressed as
        an absolute time, a delta time, or a combination time,
        then you must specify a delta time as if it were part of
        a combination time.

Topic? <Return>
$
```

Figure 2.1 (*Continued*)

separated by spaces and/or tabs. If a required parameter is missing, DCL prompts for the parameter on the next line. For example, the TYPE command is used to display the contents of a file. It requires a file name as a parameter. To type the file STOCKS.DOC, the command is:

```
$ TYPE  STOCKS.DOC
```

  or

```
$ TYPE
_File: STOCKS.DOC
```

The _ indicates a continuation line. Most commands have *qualifiers* (also known as switches) that specify options of the command. Qualifiers that apply to the command can be placed anywhere on the command line, while qualifiers for particular parameters must follow the parameter. Qualifiers start with the slash character /. For example, all of the following commands will copy the file STOCKS.DOC to the file YOUR.DOC and perform a read of the output record after each record is copied:

```
$ COPY/WRITE_CHECK STOCKS.DOC YOUR.DOC
$ COPY STOCKS.DOC /WRITE_CHECK YOUR.DOC
$ COPY STOCKS.DOC YOUR.DOC/WRITE_CHECK
```

If a command takes a long time to execute, entering CTRL/T (control T) will display a status line on the execution, which will not be interrupted. The status line displays the CPU time and I/Os performed. These should increase every time CTRL/T is entered. A command execution can be aborted by CTRL/Y. If CTRL/Y is entered by mistake, execution can be resumed by entering the CONTINUE command.

Here is an example:

```
(Control-t display):
```

```
MAYUR::SHAH 15:07:38 VMSHELP CPU=00:00:21.98 PF=4819 IO=236 MEM=623
```

The parameters displayed are nodename, process name, time, image name, CPU time used by the process, page faults, I/O count, and working set size.

2.4 THE TERMINALS

DEC terminals use the ASCII character set for communication with the host. The terminal-to-host communications protocol is RS232 or RS423. The two major types of terminals are hard-copy terminals like the DECwriter III (LA120) and video terminals like the VT300 series. DECwindow terminals also offer a VT terminal emulator that functions essentially as the standard VT terminals. The VT300 series terminals supersede the older VT200 and VT100 series terminals. The VT420 supports all the features of a VT320 and, in addition, offers dual sessions and block mode data transfers (to reduce the number of interrupts generated on the host VAX). These terminals have a screen display of 80 or 132 columns of 25 lines. The twenty-fifth line is used for status displays. The top 24 lines scroll up when new lines are displayed at the bottom of the screen. The VT1000 series terminals are X-window terminals. Figure 2.2 shows the keyboard of a VT300 series terminal.

(The keys are classified into four groups):

1. *Main keypad.* This is similar to the keyboard on most other computer terminals. Some keys need special mention:

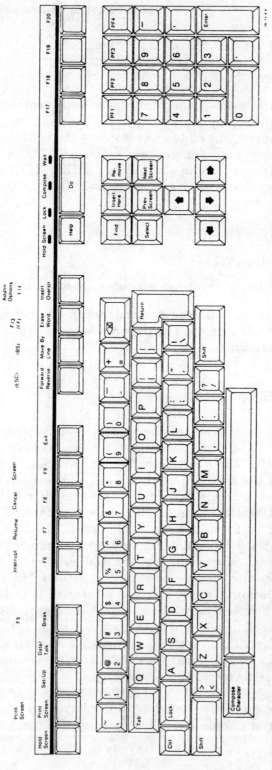

Figure 2.2 Keyboard. (Copyright ©1990 Digital Equipment Corporation. All rights reserved. Reprinted by permission.)

Ctrl   This key generates special codes when it is pressed
              with most other keys . For example, pressing Ctrl,
              keeping it pressed, and then pressing C generates
              the code 03. This two-key combination is written
              here as CTRL/C.

Lock   This key switches between the uppercase and
              lowercase character mode for the alphabetic keys.
              The Lock indicator at the top right of the keyboard
              will be lit when the keyboard is in uppercase mode.

Compose   This key is used to generate extended ASCII
character   characters. Typically, the compose key is pressed
              followed by two other keys to generate a code. It is
              used mainly to generate foreign language
              characters.

<X]   This key is at the top right of the keyboard. It is the
              DELETE key, usually used to delete the last
              character entered.

Conventionally, some of the control keys have special meanings:

CTRL/C   Abort the current application and exit.

CTRL/Q   Continue a display stopped by CTRL/S. An XOFF
              character is sent to the computer by the terminal.

CTRL/S   Stop all display to the terminal. An XON character is
              sent to the computer by the terminal. This is useful
              because the screen is frozen and what is displayed
              can be checked before more information is allowed to
              be displayed. The HOLD-SCREEN key, F1, can also
              be used.

CTRL/T   Display a one line summary of the process. For
              example, if you have issued the COPY command to
              copy a very large file, CTRL/T can be used every few
              seconds to verify whether the CPU time is
              increasing. If the time is not increasing, there may
              be a problem with the copy operation or the
              computer.

CTRL/W   Refresh the screen if disturbed by, say, a power
              fluctuation.

CTRL/Y   Abort (interrupt) the current application and exit to DCL.

CTRL/Z   Exit from the current program.

2. *Editing keypad.* These keys are used by editors and screen-oriented forms and menus. The arrow keys are used by DCL also for command editing.

3. *Numeric keypad.* The keys PF1 to PF4 generate special codes. The other keys normally generate the codes displayed. Normally, the ENTER key is equivalent to the RETURN key. The numeric keypad can be programmed to transform into an application keypad. A different set of codes are generated when the keypad is in application mode. The keys are then interpreted in various ways depending on the application.

4. *Function keys.* There are 20 of these, F1 to F20. F1 is the HOLD-SCREEN key. It is used to stop or continue a display that is scrolling up on the screen. F2 dumps the screen image to the printer port of the terminal. It is used to generate hard copies of displays. F3 is used to enter the terminal SET-UP menu. The SET-UP menu allows you to change terminal characteristics like transmission speed and tab position settings. F4 is used to switch to the other session on dual session terminals like the VT330 and VT340. Note that the keys F1 to F4 do not send any codes to the computer. The F5 key generates the BREAK character that is used by communications equipment. When the terminal is connected to terminal servers like the DECserver 200, 300, or 550, the BREAK key breaks the session temporarily and allows the terminal to issue DECserver commands. The session can be continued by the RESUME command issued to the DECserver.

The keys F6 to F20 generate codes that can be interpreted by the receiving application. Certain conventions are observed by most applications:

F6 is interpreted as CONTROL/C.

F10 is interpreted as EXIT (or CTRL/Z).

F15 is used as a HELP key.

F16 (or DO) is used to temporarily change the mode of operation. For example, the EVE editor changes the mode from text entry to command entry when the key is pressed.

2.5 DCL COMMANDS

The user interface from a terminal with the operating system is via the DCL interface. All DCL command and qualifier names can be abbreviated to the first four characters. Many commands and qualifiers can be abbreviated further if the name does not conflict with the abbreviation of a different command or qualifier. A complete DCL command is entered as:

```
$ cmdname/cmd_qual1/cmd_qual2.. para1/qual1/qual2.. para2...
```

Qualifiers to a parameter or the command name can be specified in any order following the parameter or the command name. Most command name qualifiers can be specified anywhere on the command line. We will look at some commonly used commands.

TYPE is used to display the contents of one or more files. For example, to display files STOCKS.DOC and PAYROLL.DATA, the command is:

```
$ TYPE  STOCKS.DOC,PAYROLL.DATA
```

or

```
$ TY STOCKS.DOC,PAYROLL.DATA
```

The DIRECTORY command is used to see the list of files in a directory on disk or tape. It displays the contents of the default directory on the default disk. If a disk name and/or directory is specified as a parameter, then the contents of that disk and/or directory is displayed. For example, to display the contents of directory [TEST] on the default disk the command is:

```
$ DIR [TEST]
```

The /SIZE qualifier lists the size of the specified files, and the /DATE qualifier displays the creation dates of the files. For example,

```
$ DIR /SIZE /DATE  [BOOK]

Directory DUA5:[BOOK]

BOOK.INDEX;4        12  21-DEC-1988 04:22
SETHOST.LOG;2        7   3-MAY-1989 16:51
SETHOST.LOG;1       13   3-MAY-1989 16:43
START.DOC;3         17   3-MAY-1989 17:43
```

```
START.DOC;2            15    3-MAY-1989 17:32
START.DOC;1             2    3-MAY-1989 16:13
TMP.TMP;1               0    3-MAY-1989 17:44
```

Total of 6 files, 54 blocks.

Note that filenames are sorted in alphabetic order. Also, file-names contain a semicolon followed by a number called version. Typically, when a file is modified and written back by, say, the editor, a new version of the file is created. The new version is one higher than the old one.

The COPY command is used to make additional copies of files on disk or tape. For example, to copy STOCKS.DOC to the directory [TEST] with a new name YOUR.DOC the command is:

```
$ COPY STOCKS.DOC [TEST]YOUR.DOC
```

The RENAME command is used to change the names of existing files on disk. For example, to rename STOCKS.DOC to JAY.DOC the command is:

```
$ RENAME STOCKS.DOC JAY.DOC
```

The rename command is useful to move a file from one directory to another. Move means to place the file in the new directory and remove it from the original directory. For example,

```
$ RENAME [APPLE]STOCKS.DOC [NEWDIR]STOCKS.DOC
```

STOCKS.DOC is removed from the directory [APPLE] and placed in the directory [NEWDIR]. In fact, this feature can be used to move a complete directory and its subdirectories. For example, suppose the directory [BOOK] is under the directory [PETER] and now it is to be removed from [PETER] and placed under the directory [SHANKER.PROJECTS]. The command would be

```
$ RENAME [PETER]BOOK.DIR [SHANKER.PROJECTS]BOOK.DIR
```

Now the directories and files that were under [PETER.BOOK] are accessed via the directory [SHANKER.PROJECTS.BOOK]. Files cannot be moved from one disk to another using this command. The COPY command followed by the DELETE command will have to be used.

The DELETE command is used to delete files. For example, the next command deletes version 2 of the file STOCKS.DOC:

```
$ DELETE STOCKS.DOC;2
```

Files on VAX/VMS have version numbers. When a file is edited, a new version of the file is created. The old version still exists. For example, editing STOCKS.DOC;8 (version 8 of STOCKS.DOC) creates STOCKS.DOC;9. If older versions are not deleted, many versions of files will exist on the disk. Older versions should be periodically deleted to reduce the cluttering of files and also to conserve disk space. The DELETE command can be used to delete files, however, the PURGE command specifically deletes older versions of files. For example, to delete all except the latest version of the file STOCKS.DOC the command is:

```
$ PURGE  STOCK.DOC
```

The /KEEP:n qualifier is used to retain the last n versions of a file. To delete all but the latest three versions of STOCK.DOC the command is:

```
$ PURGE/KEEP:3  STOCK.DOC
```

or even

```
$ PURGE  STOCK.DOC/KEEP:3
```

The SET TIME command is used to change the computer system date and time. The command requires you to have OPER and LOG_IO privileges. The format for specifying time is:

```
dd-mmm-yyyy:hh:mm:ss.cc
```

where cc specifies hundredths of a second. Most of the fields are optional. Date fields not specified are filled in from the current date, while time fields not specified are set to zero. For example,

```
$ SET  TIME=7-SEP-1989:18:30:15.12
$ SET  TIME=21-JAN-1992
$ SET  TIME=18:30
```

SET DEFAULT is used to change your default disk drive and/or directory. The defaults are used when accessing files on disks. For example,

```
$ SET  DEFAULT  DUB0:[TEST]
```

The SHOW commands are used to display process or system characteristics. Commonly used SHOW commands are:

```
$ SHOW  DEFAULT
```
Displays the default disk and directory used when accessing files.

$ SHOW MEMORY	Displays computer memory usage statistics.
$ SHOW NETWORK	Displays names and node numbers of computers that the VAX can communicate with. If the node is not a router only, the current node name and its router node name are displayed.
$ SHOW PROCESS	Displays process name, terminal name, process identification, default disk and directory, user identification code (UIC), and process priority. Additionally, the /ALL qualifier displays process quotas, accounting information, dynamic memory usage, privileges, and rights identifiers.
$ SHOW SYSTEM	Displays all processes running in the system along with their identification and resource usage information.
$ SHOW TIME	Displays system data and time.
$ SHOW USERS	Displays interactive users on the system along with their processes and terminal name.

PRINT is used to queue files for printing. To print the files STOCK.DOC and YOUR.DOC the command is

```
$ PRINT STOCK.DOC,YOUR.DOC
```

The command has a number of qualifiers:

/COPIES=n	Number of printed copies of the file.
/DELETE	Delete the file after printing.
/FLAG	Print a banner page before printing the file.
/FORM=formname	Use a specified form (paper type) to print the file. The list of forms can be seen by SHOW QUEUE/FORM.

/HEADER   Print a header line on every page of output. The header contains the file name and page number.

/PAGE   Print specified pages of the file. For example, to print pages 5 through 20 the qualifier is /PAGE:(5,20).

/QUEUE   Queue the file to a specified queue. Typically, each printer on the system will have one associated queue. To see the queues on the system the command is SHOW QUEUE. If this qualifier is not specified, the file is sent to the queue SYS$PRINT.

An example is:

```
$ PRINT STOCK.DOC/COPIES=3/DELETE/FORM=LONG/QUEUE=LASER$PRINT
```

2.6 ERROR MESSAGES

VAX/VMS software adheres to a convention for displaying error messages. The operating system, compilers, utilities, and most other software display error messages in a uniform format. Here is an example of an error message when the TYPE command is not issued correctly:

```
$ TYPO STOCK.DOC
%DCL-W-IVVERB, unrecognized command verb - check validity
                and spelling
 \TYPO\
```

The syntax for error messages is:

```
%FACILITY-L-IDENT, text
```

The fields are:

FACILITY   The name of the program issuing the message.

L   The severity level of the message is indicated by the single-letter codes:

S, success; I, informational; W, warning; E, error; and F, fatal or severe error.

IDENT   Abbreviated description.

text   Description in plain English.

Here is an example of the TYPE command specifying a file name that does not exist on the disk:

```
$ TYPE ME.DOC

%TYPE-W-SEARCHFAIL, error searching for SYS$SYSDEVICE:
[SHAH]ME.DOC;
-RMS-E-FNF, file not found
```

2.7 DEVICES

Devices are usually attached to *controllers*, which are circuit boards in the CPU chassis (or sometimes built into the CPU board). Devices can also be connected to an *intelligent controller* like the HSC70, which manages I/O to disk and tape devices. A number of devices could be attached to one controller. DUB2: is an example of a device name. A device is identified as:

```
DDCnnn:
```

where DD is the generic device name (sometimes this has 3 characters), C the controller designation, and nnn the specific device on the controller.

The operating system has *software device drivers* that correspond to controllers. For example, the KDB50 disk controller consists of two boards that can be inserted in the backplane of a VAX 8700. This controller can handle up to four RA series disk drives. The generic device name of the disks is DU. The software device driver is called DUDRIVER. The controller is designated as A. The four disks are DUA0:, DUA1:, DUA2:, and DUA3:. If another controller is added to the computer, then it will be designated as B, and the disks attached with this controller are DUB0:, DUB1:, DUB2:, and DUB3:. Figure 2.3 shows some devices and their mnemonic device names.

Device name	Device type	Typical devices
CS	Console floppy	RX02 floppy drive
DJ	Disks	RA60 removable disk
DU	Disks	RA90 fixed disk
DI	Disks	RF71 fixed or removable disk
LI	Line printer	LP25 300 lines per minute line printer
LP	Line printer	LP29 2000 lines/per minute line printer
LT	LAT devices (terminals over Ethernet)	VT420 terminal or DEClaser 2000 printer
MU	Tapes	TA78 125 inch tape drive
MS	Tapes	TU81-PLUS streaming tape drive
MT	Tapes	TE16 tape drives
MB	Mailbox (software device)	MBA12:
NET	Network communications (software device)	NET4:
NL	NULL device (software device)	
OP	Operator console (software device)	
TT	Terminals	VT420 terminal
TX	Terminals	VT420 terminal
VT	Virtual terminal (software device)	VTA2:
XE	Ethernet	DEBNT controller for VAXBI bus connects to Ethernet cable
XQ	Ethernet	DELQA controller for Qbus bus connects to Ethernet cable.

Figure 2.3 Common devices on VAX/VMS.

VAX/VMS also supports software devices. These have device drivers in the operating system, however, there is no hardware corresponding to them. An example is the mailbox device MB, which is used for sending data from one process to another.

Device names on VAXcluster systems are preceded by the name of the computer on which the device resides and a $ sign. For example:

```
MAYUR$DUB6:    !VAXcluster device name for disk DUB6:
```

2.8 FILES

Files can be created on disks and tapes. Examples of disk devices are the RA series drives, *compact disk ROMs* (CD-ROMs), floppy drives and *electronic storage elements* (ESE20); examples of tape devices are TU78 and TU81-PLUS standard tape drives, TK70 cartridge tape drives, and the IBM 3480 compatible TA90 cartridge tape drive. Disks and tapes are known as volumes. Files on disks can have a sequential, relative, or indexed organization, while tapes support sequential files only.

Each file on the disk is owned by one user. Normally, this user is the person who created the file. The owner can allow other users to access the file by specifying the type of protection for the file. Files reside within other files called *directories*. Directories can reside within other directories, effectively allowing a user to maintain a set of logically related files separate from other files belonging to them.

File size is limited by disk space or, if disk quotas are enabled, by disk quota. If a file is modified by, say, an editor, then a new version of the file is created. Older versions remain on the disk until explicitly deleted by the DELETE or PURGE commands. Version numbers start at 1 and can go up to 32,767.

Here are some examples of file specifications:

```
MAYUR::DUA4:[TEST]PAYROLL.COB;27
```

```
MAYUR::PAYROLL.COB
```

```
DUA4:PAYROLL.COB
```

```
[TEST]PAYROLL.COB
```

```
PAYROLL.COB;-2
```

```
123_LONG_FILE_NAME.LONG_FILE_TYPE
```

Files can be created on disk or tape devices. The file specification syntax is:

```
nodename::device:[directory]filename.filetype;version
```

Fields not specified assume default values. Default values depend on the command used to operate on the file. Generally, if the version number is not specified then the latest version is assumed. Nodename is the computer on which the file resides. If it is not specified, the node is assumed to be the VAX you are currently using.

Each process has a default device and directory. These are specified by the system manager in the user authorization file. When specifying file names, if the device and directory are not specified, the default values are assumed. To see the defaults use SHOW

DEFAULT. To change the defaults use SET DEFAULT. For example,

```
$ SET DEFAULT DJA2:[TEST.PROGRAMS]
```

Usually, the file name and file type have no default values. Each of these fields can be up to 39 characters long.

Version numbers start at 1 and can go up to 32,767. When the number is not specified, it is assumed to be the latest version number. Version numbers are an extension of the ".BAK" method used on smaller computers for keeping previous versions of files. The latest version of the file can also be refered to as version 0. Versions can be specified going backwards starting at the latest version by using a minus sign before the version number. For example, if a file has 12 versions, then version -1 is the same as version 11.

2.9 THE PROCESS

A *process* is the environment in which a program image executes. A number of processes are created when a computer is turned on and the operating system is loaded. Normally, the operating system creates a process for each logged in user. Processes can also be created by users.

The operating system maintains a list of parameters that define the environment in which each process is running. The SHOW PROCESS command displays some of the process parameters. The /ALL qualifier displays a more complete list of parameters. Figure 2.4 shows a use of the command.

The display consists of seven groups:

- Summary of process.

- Process quotas for the user. These are defined in the authorization file (UAF) which is usually sys$system:sysuaf.dat.

- Accounting information. This group displays a summary of resource usage.

- Privileges that the process owns. Privileges are generally required to access resources not assigned to the user. For example, the READALL privilege allows the user to read files which are owned by other users. There are about 30 privileges that can be assigned to each user by the system administrator.

```
$ SHOW  PROCESS /ALL

5-DEC-1989 12:44:33.42                        User: ANAND

Pid: 0000023D        Proc. name: ANAND_2        UIC: [BOOKS,ANAND]

Priority:   4        Default file spec: DUA3:[ANAND.MEMO]

Devices mounted: DUB6:

Process Quotas:
  Account name: ANAND
  CPU limit:                      Infinite    Direct I/O limit:       20000
  Buffered I/O byte count quota:    108880    Buffered I/O limit:     20000
  Timer queue entry quota:            1000    Open file quota:          995
  Paging file quota:                 17533    Subprocess quota:           9
  Default page fault cluster:           64    AST limit:                198
  Enqueue quota:                      1000    Shared file limit:        900
  Max detached processes:                0    Max active jobs:            0

Accounting information:
  Buffered I/O count:                  138    Peak working set:         388
  Direct I/O count:                      9    Peak virtual size:       2467
  Page faults:                         373    Mounted volumes:            0
  Images activated:                      1
  Elapsed CPU time:            0 00:00:00.41
  Connect time:                0 00:00:09.05

Process privileges:
  CMKRNL          may change mode to kernel
  DETACH          may create detached processes
  ALTPRI          may set any priority value
  OPER            operator privilege
  EXQUOTA         may exceed quota
  SYSGBL          may create system-wide global sections on a VAX
  SHMEM           may create/delete objects in shared memory
  SHARE           may assign channels to non-shared device
  READALL         may read anything as the owner

Process rights identifiers:
  INTERACTIVE
  LOCAL

Process Dynamic Memory Area
  Current Size (bytes)       25600    Current Total Size (pages)     50
  Free Space (bytes)         21768    Space in Use (bytes)         3832
  Size of Largest Block      21712    Size of Smallest Block         16
  Number of Free Blocks          3    Free Blocks LEQU 32 Bytes       1

Processes in this tree:
  ANAND
    ANAND_2 (*)
```

Figure 2.4 SHOW PROCESS output.

■ Rights identifiers that the process owns. These privileges that allow the user to access objects like files and memory sections that are protected by these rights.

■ Summary of memory use by the process.

■ Subprocesses created by the top-level process using the SPAWN command. These processes normally inherit the parent's process parameters. The ATTACH command can be used to attach the terminal to any one of these processes. In this case, the process ANAND created the subprocess ANAND_2. The symbol (*) indicates that ANAND_2 is the current process.

2.10   OPERATING SYSTEM BASICS

When you log into the computer, a process is created that controls your terminal. The name of the process is the same as your USER-NAME. More than one process in the computer can have the same name. However, each process has a unique identification number called PID. The RUN/DETACH command can be used to create additional processes. The process named JOB_CONTROL on the computer is a detached process that controls batch and print jobs. In fact, your process is a detached process created by the operating system when you log in.

The SHOW SYSTEM command displays the processes on the computer. Figure 2.5 shows a use of the command.

The SHOW USER command displays all the users logged in from all the terminals. Figure 2.6 shows a use of the command.

The SWAPPER process is created by the operating system. SWAPPER handles process swapping to and from disk when there are many processes on the computer and not enough main memory or when it reorganizes processes in memory. ERRFMT formats and logs errors like device malfunctions. EVL (Event Logger) formats and logs network errors. NETACP handles file access on other computers on the network. REMACP controls user logins on the current computer from other computers on the network. VAX-sim_monitor performs system integrity checks and reports a degradation in system performance and in devices. SYMBIONT processes send output from queues to printers connected to the system. OPCOM intercepts output for operators from the operating system and user processes. The output is sent to terminals designated as operator consoles and optionally logged to a disk file. The default disk log file is SYS$MANAGER:OPERATOR.LOG. The only other executable unit on the computer is the operating system.

```
$ SHOW SYSTEM
VAX/VMS V5.3  on node MAYUR 28-AUG-1990 15:33:40.96   Uptime   5 19:18:05
   Pid    Process Name   State Pri    I/O        CPU       Page   Ph.
                                                           flts   Mem

00000081  SWAPPER        HIB  16      0   0 00:01:00.58      0      0
00000084  ERRFMT         HIB   8   5907   0 00:00:13.07     70    100
00000085  OPCOM          LEF   9   3060   0 00:00:08.29  11536    149
00000086  JOB_CONTROL    HIB   9   2983   0 00:00:06.24    129    260
00000087  VAXsim_Monitor HIB   8   1560   0 00:00:03.46    345    204
00000088  NETACP         HIB  10  48295   0 00:12:36.72    401    301
00000089  EVL            HIB   6    293   0 00:00:00.90 123672     54 N
0000008A  REMACP         HIB   9     63   0 00:00:00.11     77     53
0000008B  SYMBIONT_0001  HIB   6     31   0 00:00:00.22    349    306
000001B2  _LTA63:        LEF   7   8486   0 00:02:16.65  77765   1000
000001B4  JANE           LEF   4 246446   0 00:39:15.96 568988    928
000001C1  ANAND_1        CUR   4    148   0 00:00:00.41    355    370 S
000001C2  ANAND          HIB   4  12018   0 00:00:26.42   4222   1271
```

Figure 2.5 SHOW SYSTEM output.

The two commands SHOW SYSTEM and SHOW USERS in Figures 2.5 and 2.6, respectively, have given you some other information. The computer was up for more than 5 days. *Process priority* can be from 0 to 31. Lower priority processes get CPU time only if higher priority processes do not require it. User processes usually execute at priority 4. CPU and I/O utilization is displayed for each process in Figure 2.5. The other columns are explained in later chapters. User ANAND has logged into the computer from two terminals. The first time a user logs in, the operating system creates a process with the USERNAME of the user. Further logins

```
$ SHOW USERS
   VAX/VMS User Processes at 28-AUG-1990 14:24:31.50
Total number of users = 4,  number of processes = 6

Username      Node       Interactive   Subprocess   Batch
JANE          MAYUR           1
ANAND         MAYUR           2              1
```

Figure 2.6 SHOW USERS output.

by the same user create processes with the name of the terminal from where the login is performed preceded by an underscore. The process with PID 000001C1 was created by the SPAWN command issued from the process ANAND. The SPAWN command can be used to create a tree of *subprocesses*. The name of a spawned process is formed by using the process name of the top-level process followed by an underscore and a digit.

The SHOW MEMORY command displays a summary on computer memory usage. Figure 2.7 shows a use of the command.

Of the physical pages in use, about 10620 pages are permanently allocated to VMS.

The display indicates that about 69 percent (45379/65536) of main memory is unused. The *process entry slots* specify the number of processes that can be created on the computer. The *balance set slots* specify the number of processes that can be in memory. If more processes than the maximum are created, some processes will be swapped out onto the disk. Processes may also be swapped out if there is not enough physical memory to accommodate all the processes. The fixed-size pool area contains fixed-size slots of memory that are used when quick allocation and deallocation of small chunks of memory is required. *Dynamic memory* is where the

```
$ SHOW  MEMORY
            System Memory Resources on  4-DEC-1989 16:32:39.67
Physical Memory Usage (pages):      Total       Free      In Use   Modified
   Main Memory (32.Mb)              65536      45379       19891        266

Slot Usage (slots):                 Total       Free    Resident    Swapped
   Process Entry Slots                 70         44          26          0
   Balance Set Slots                   59         35          24          0

Fixed-Size Pool Areas (packets):    Total       Free      In Use       Size
   Small Packet (SRP) List            826         93         733         96
   I/O Request Packet (IRP) List      522        158         364        208
   Large Packet (LRP) List             60          0          60       1584

Dynamic Memory Usage (bytes):       Total       Free      In Use    Largest
   Nonpaged Dynamic Memory        3072000     722528     2349472     703248
   Page Dynamic Memory             276992      59008      217984      55584

Paging File Usage (pages):                      Free      In Use      Total
DISK$MAYURDISK:[SYS0.SYSEXE]SWAPFILE.SYS        39536      10464      50000
DISK$MAYURDISK:[SYS0.SYSEXE]PAGEFILE.SYS        83338       6662      90000

Of the physical pages in use, 10620 pages are permanently allocated to VMS.
```

Figure 2.7 SHOW MEMORY output.

processes and most of the operating system resides. Only a part of the operating system is in static memory. The paging files are used for swapped-out processes and pages. These files must be created using the SYSGEN procedure, and they must be large enough to accommodate any swapping and paging space requirements of the operating system.

The SHOW DEVICES command displays a summary of devices on the computer as shown in Figure 2.8. It is useful to find out which devices are mounted, how much free space each disk has, which devices are allocated to processes, and the number of device malfunction errors on devices.

The error count gives the number of errors that have occurred while accessing the device. Error details can be displayed by creating an error report using the command ANALYZE/ERROR. Devices having the "alloc" status are used exclusively by the process that issued the ALLOCATE command for the device. The devices

```
$SHOW  DEVICES

Device    Device         Error      Volume        Free     Trans    Mnt
Name      Status         Count      Label         Blocks   Count    Cnt
DJA1:     Mounted            0   SYSDEVICE        23697        4      1
DUA3:     Mounted            0   DEVELOP         342270      112      1
DUB2:     On-line            0
DUB3:     Mounted            0   DEVELOP 2      1057755        1      1

Device    Device         Error      Volume        Free     Trans    Mnt
Name      Status         Count      Label         Blocks   Count    Cnt
MUA0:     On-line           92

Device    Device         Error
Name      Status         Count
LTA0:     Off-line           0
LTA23:    On-line            0
OPA0:     On-line            0
TXA7:     On-line alloc      0

Device    Device         Error
Name      Status         Count
LIA0:     On-line alloc      0

Device    Device         Error
Name      Status         Count

ETA0:     On-line            0
PTA0:     On-line            2
PUA0:     On-line            1
```

Figure 2.8 SHOW DEVICES output.

```
$SHOW DEVICE DUB3: /FULL
Disk DUB3:, device type RA82, is on-line, mounted, file-oriented device,
    shareable, available to cluster, error logging is enabled.
Error count                0    Operations completed                64603
Owner process             ""    Owner UIC                   [SYSTEM, TEST]
Owner process ID    00000000    Dev Prot      S:RWED,O:RWED,G:RWED,W:RWED
Reference count            1    Default buffer size                   512
Total blocks         1216665    Sectors per track                      57
Total cylinders         1423    Tracks per cylinder                    15

Volume label       "DEVELOP2"   Relative volume number                  0
Cluster size               3    Transaction count                       1
Free blocks          1057755    Maximum files allowed              152083
Extend quantity            5    Mount count                             1
Mount status          System    Cache name               "_DUA4:XQPCACHE"
Extent cache size         64    Maximum blocks in extent cache     105768
File ID cache size        64    Blocks currently in extent cache    50916
Quota cache size           0    Maximum buffers in FCP cache          273

Volume status:  subject to mount verification, file high-water marking,
    write-through caching enabled.
```

Figure 2.9 SHOW DEVICES/FULL output.

are grouped by disks, tapes, terminals, printers, and others. Further details on devices, like total disk space on a disk, can be displayed by using the /FULL qualifier. Figure 2.9 shows a use of the command.

The /FILES qualifier is useful to find out all the files currently being accessed from a disk. Figure 2.10 shows a use of the command.

The MONITOR utility is a useful tool for observing system behavior. MONITOR sends output to a file or displays the output on your terminal, updating the information at specified intervals (the default is 3 sec). Figure 2.11 shows some examples of MONITOR usage. Qualifiers are:

Qualifier	Description
TOPCPU	Lists the processes that are consuming the most CPU time
TOPDIO	Displays processes performing the most direct I/O, mainly to disks and tapes

TOPBIO   Displays processes performing the most buffered I/O, mainly to terminals, printers, and over the network to other computers

2.11   UTILITY COMMANDS

Standard VAX/VMS comes bundled with a set of commands that can be classified as utilities. Some of these are:

SEARCH   Searches for strings in specified files

DIFFERENCES   Shows the difference between the contents of two files

DUMP   Shows the raw data in a file or tape

MAIL   Provides communications facility for users

PHONE   Provides interactive communications facility for users

SORT   Provides sort-merge capability

BACKUP   Creates tape or disk copies of data

2.12   LOGICAL NAMES

A *logical name* is a variable whose value is a string of characters. The value of a logical name is also known as the equivalent name or translated name. For example, the next command defines the logical name MYDISK as DUB2:

```
$ DEFINE  MYDISK  DUB2:
```

```
$ SHOW  DEVICE  DUB3:  /FILES
Files accessed on device_DUB3: on 5-DEC-1989 12:35:37.46
Process name          PID                    File name
                      00000000    [000000]INDEXF.SYS;1
ANAND                 000001B2    [ANAND.DAT]TST_MESSAGES.DATA;1
ANAND                 000001B2    [ANAND.DAT]SECURITY_FILE.DATA;1
ANAND                 000001B2    [ANAND.TEST]POSITION_FILE.TEST;1
_LTA67:               000001B4    [JANE.DOC]MASTER_TABLE.DOCUMENT;1
```

Figure 2.10 SHOW DEVICES/FILES output.

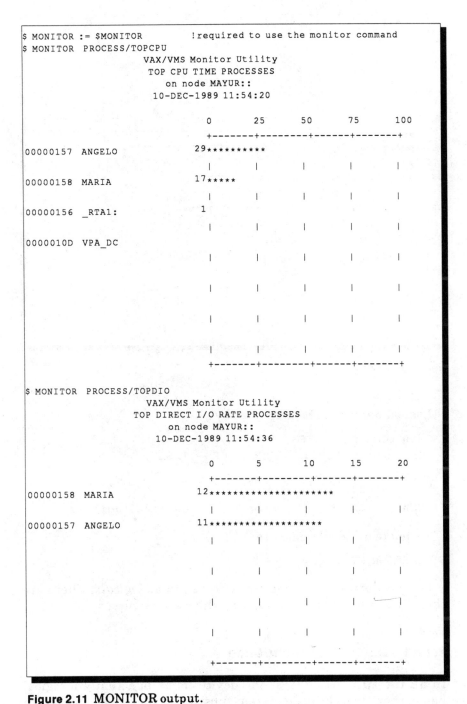

```
$ MONITOR := $MONITOR         !required to use the monitor command
$ MONITOR  PROCESS/TOPCPU
                        VAX/VMS Monitor Utility
                        TOP CPU TIME PROCESSES
                        on node MAYUR::
                        10-DEC-1989 11:54:20


                             0       25      50      75     100
                             +-------+--------+------+-------+
00000157  ANGELO           29**********
                             |       |       |       |       |
00000158  MARIA            17*****
                             |       |       |       |       |
00000156  _RTA1:            1
                             |       |       |       |       |
0000010D  VPA_DC
                             |       |       |       |       |

                             |       |       |       |       |

                             |       |       |       |       |

                             |       |       |       |       |
                             +-------+--------+------+-------+

$ MONITOR  PROCESS/TOPDIO
                        VAX/VMS Monitor Utility
                        TOP DIRECT I/O RATE PROCESSES
                        on node MAYUR::
                        10-DEC-1989 11:54:36


                             0       5       10      15      20
                             +-------+--------+------+-------+
00000158  MARIA            12**********************
                             |       |       |       |       |
00000157  ANGELO           11*******************
                             |       |       |       |       |

                             |       |       |       |       |

                             |       |       |       |       |

                             |       |       |       |       |
                             +-------+--------+------+-------+
```

Figure 2.11 MONITOR output.

```
$ MONITOR PROCESS/TOPBIO
                 VAX/VMS Monitor Utility
               TOP BUFFERED I/O RATE PROCESSES
                    on node MAYUR::
                  10-DEC-1989 11:54:54


                         0      5      10     15     20
                         +-------+--------+------+-------+
00000158 MARIA          12*********************
                         |       |      |      |      |
00000146 _LTA12:         9****************
                         |       |      |      |      |
00000156 _RTA1:          8*************
                         |       |      |      |      |
00000157 ANGELO          2****
                         |       |      |      |      |
00000140 O115            1**
                         |       |      |      |      |
00000106 JOB_CONTROL     1**
                         |       |      |      |      |
                         |       |      |      |      |
```

Figure 2.11 (*Continued*)

Logical names can be displayed by

```
$ SHOW LOGICAL MYDISK
  "MYDISK" = "DUB2:" (LNM$PROCESS_TABLE)
```

or

```
$ SHOW LOGICAL *        !Display all defined logicals
```

To delete a logical name use

```
$ DEASSIGN MYDISK
```

Logical names are sometimes referred to as *logicals*. There are three major uses for logical names, which are discussed here.

2.12.1 Device Independence

In all file specifications, if the device name is actually a logical name, then the operating system substitutes the device name with the value of the translated logical name. For example, the file specification MYDISK:FILE1.DAT is translated as DUB2:FILE1.DAT (using the logical name defined above). If at some later stage files are moved to disk DJA3:, you can still use command files and other programs that reference the files by reassigning the value of the logical name MYDISK as:

```
$ DEFINE MYDISK DJA3:
```

2.12.2 Using Directories as Devices

Consider the logical name assignment,

```
$ DEFINE TEST MYDISK:[SHAH.TST]
```

Here, the logical name TEST refers to a directory. TEST can then be used as a "device." Therefore, the next set of commands are equivalent:

```
$ DIR TEST:*.DAT
$ DIR MYDISK:[SHAH.TST]*.DAT
$ DIR DJA3:[SHAH.TST]*.DAT
```

2.12.3 Search Lists

A logical name can be assigned a list of values. For example,

```
$ DEFINE SLIST MYDISK:[SHAH.TST], -
              MYDISK:[SHAH.DEBUG], -
              MYDISK:[TMP.TST]
```

The list can be used to search through all the directories:

```
$ DIR SLIST:*.COM

    Directory MYDISK:[SHAH.TST]
    DELQUERY.COM;5      1  30-OCT-1987 12:58:01.00
    DIRSEARCH.COM;5     2  29-DEC-1987 12:51:20.00
    DOWN.COM;4          1  27-OCT-1988 14:43:48.56
    Total of 3 files, 4 blocks.

    Directory MYDISK:[TMP.TST]
    MOU.COM;2           1   1-JUN-1989 10:48:00.50
    MYMAILEDIT.COM;2    2   4-JAN-1989 13:44:33.11
```

```
Total of 2 files, 3 blocks.
Grand total of 2 directories, 5 files, 7 blocks.
```

Note that there are no .COM files in [SHAH.DEBUG]. The search list feature can be used for maintaining one logical "device" that is actually a set of subdirectories. Search lists can be used to make one logical device out of a number of devices and directories as exemplified by:

```
$ DEFINE MYDEV  DUB3:, DJA1:, MYDISK:[SHAH]
```

2.13 PROGRAM DEVELOPMENT

Program sources are created using editors like EDT, EVE, and LSE (*language sensitive editor*). *Compilation* of the program creates an object module with a file type of .OBJ. *Linking* this object module by itself or with other object modules creates an executable image with a file type of .EXE. These images are executed by the RUN command. This chapter uses COBOL to demonstrate program development commands. However, the commands for other languages are very similar; wherever the word COBOL is mentioned in a command, it can be substituted by the name of other languages - FORTRAN, PASCAL, CC (for C language), BASIC, and so on.

Here are the basic steps for getting a program to run:

```
$ EDIT/EVE  TEST.COB          !create the file
```

Here is a sample program:

```
Identification division.
Program-id.    sample.
 Date-written.   dec/89.

 * The program:
 *   reads an input file with each record containing a number
 *   followed by textual information, multiplies the input
 *   number by a constant number accepted from the terminal,
 *   writes the new number and the text to the output file
 *   for each record.

 Environment division.
 * Declaration of files and program variables
```

```
    Input-output section.

  File-Control.
      select  test-in  assign to "[test.input]inp.data".
      select  test-out  assign to "duc4:[test.op]out.data".

  Data division

    File section.
    fd  test-in.
    01  test-in-rec.
        03 inp-number              pic 9(4).
        03 inp-text                pic x(53).
    fd  test-out.
    01  test-out-rec.
        03 out-number              pic 9(4).
        03 out-text                pic x(53).

  Working-storage Section.
    77  mult-factor                pic 9(4) usage comp.

Procedure Division.
  * Program execution starts here.
  10-open.
      open input test-in. open output test-out.
      display "Enter multiplication factor: "
                    with no advancing.
      accept mult-factor with conversion.
  20-read-file.
      read test-in at end go to 30-close.
      compute out-number = inp-number * mult-factor.
      move inp-text to out-text.
      write test-out-rec.
      go to 20-read-file.
  30-close.
      close test-in, test-out.
      stop run.
```

The program can be compiled by:

```
$ COBOL  TEST.COB
```

Any error messages, will be listed on the terminal. The output is a file TEST.OBJ. The object file has to be linked to create the executable image:

```
$ LINK  TEST.OBJ
```

The output is TEST.EXE. This file can be executed by the RUN command:

```
$ RUN TEST.EXE
```

Enter multiplication factor: 2

```
$
```

Actually, the file types .COB, .OBJ, and .EXE are optional in these commands.

2.13.1 Compiler Qualifiers

Each language has its own set of compilation switches (qualifiers). Qualifiers are specified after the command as:

```
$ COBOL/LIST/FIPS  TEST.COB
```

Qualifiers common to most languages are:

/LIST	Produces a listing file containing compilation errors, cross reference, and so on.
/DEBUG	Inserts a debugger in the object module. This is done by the compiler.
/CROSS_REFERENCE	Generates a cross reference of symbols and writes it in the listing file.
/DIAGNOSTICS	Creates a special file with file type of .DIA for use by the *language sensitive editor*.
/MACHINE_CODE	Generates assembly language code that is shown in the listing file. The code shows what the machine executes for each source language statement.

Refer to the individual language manuals for qualifiers specific to particular languages. Figure 2.12 shows the listing file generated by the COBOL compilation command:

```
$ COBOL/LIST/CROSS_REFERENCE  TEST
```

SAMPLE   10-Jul-1990 17:02:23   VAX COBOL V3.2-42   Page 1
Source Listing   1-May-1990 15:00:03   [SCOOP.COBOL.TESTING]TEST.COB;1 (1)

```
1         Identification division
2         Program-id            sample
3         Date-written          dec/89
4
5         *  The program:
6         *     reads an input file with each record containing a number
7         *     followed by textual information, multiplies the input
8         *     number by a constant number accepted from the terminal,
9         *     writes the new number and the text to the output file
10        *     for each record
11
12        Environment division
13        *  Declaration of files and program variables
14
15           Input-output section.
16           File-control.
17                  select test-in   assign to  "[test.input]inp.data".
18                  select test-out  assign to "duc4:[test.output]out.data".
19        Data division.
20           File section.
21           fd      test-in.
22           01      test-in-rec.
23                   03  inp-number.        pic   9(4).
24                   03  inp-text           pic   x(53).
25           fd      test-out.
26           01      test-out-rec.
27                   03  out-number         pic   9(4).
28                   03  out-text           pic   x(53).
29
30        Working-storage Section.
31           77      multi-factor           pic   9(4)      usage comp.
32
33        Procedure Division.
34        *  Program execution starts here.
35        10-open.
36                  open input test-in. open output test-out.
37                  display "Enter multiplicationfactor: " with no advancing.
38                  accept multi-factor with conversion.
39        20-read-file.
40                  read test-in at end go to 30-close.
41                  compute out-number = inp-number * mult-factor.
42                  move inp-text to out-text.
43                  write test-out-rec.
44                  go to 20-read-file.
45        30-close.
46                  close test-in, test-out.
47                  stop-run.
```

Figure 2.12 A COBOL compilation listing file.

SAMPLE   10-Jul-1990 17:02:23   VAX COBOL V3.2-42   Page 1
Cross Reference in Alphabetical Order 1-May-1990 15:00:03 [SCOOP.COBOL.TESTING]TEST.COB;1 (1)

10-OPEN	35#				
20-READ-FILE	39#	44			
30-CLOSE	45#	40			
INP-NUMBER	23#	41			
INP-TEXT	24#	42			
MULT-FACTOR	31#	38	41		
OUT-NUMBER	27#	41 *			
OUT-TEXT	28#	42 *			
SAMPLE	2#				
TEST-IN	17#	21#	36	40	46
TEST-IN-REC	22#				
TEST-OUT	18#	25#	36	46	
TEST-OUT-REC	26#	43			

SAMPLE   10-Jul-1990 17:02:23   VAX COBOL V3.2-42   Page 3
Compilation Summary   1-May-1990 15:00:03 [SCOOP.COBOL.TESTING]TEST.COB;1 (1)

PROGRAM SECTIONS

	Name	Bytes	Attributes								
0	$CODE	447	PIC	CON	REL	LCL	SHR	EXE	RD	NOWRT	Align(2)
1	$LOCAL	1172	PIC	CON	REL	LCL	NOSHR	NOEXE	RD	WRT	Align(2)
2	$PDATA	780	PIC	CON	REL	LCL	SHR	NOEXE	RD	NOWRT	Align(2)
3	COD$NAMES____2	24	PIC	CON	REL	LCL	SHR	NOEXE	RD	NOWRT	Align(2)
4	COB$NAMES____4	20	PIC	CON	REL	LCL	SHR	NOEXE	RD	NOWRT	Align(2)

DIAGNOSTICS

    Informational: 1 (suppressed by command qualifier)

COMMAND QUALIFIERS

    COBOL /LIS/CR TEST.COB

    /NOCOPY_LIST /NONMACHINE_CODE /CROSS_REFERENCE=ALPHABETICAL
    /NOANSI_FORMAT /NOSEQUENCE_CHECK /NOMAP
    /NOTRUNCATE /NOAUDIT /NOCONDITIONALS
    /CHECK=(NOPERFORM,NOBOUNDS) /DEBUG=(NOSYMBOLS,TRACEBACK)
    /WARNINGS=(NOSTANDARD,OTHER,NOINFORMATION)
    /STANDARD=(NOSYNTAX,NOPDP11) /NOFIPS

STATISTICS

    Run Time: 0.39 seconds
    Elapsed Time: 1.55 seconds
    Page Faults: 175
    Dynamic Memory: 414 pages

Figure 2.12 *(Continued).*

2.14   LINK

The LINK command is used to create executable images from object modules. The Linker automatically searches two system library files for unresolved symbol (and subroutine) references after all the files in the LINK command have been processed. These libraries are SYS$SYSTEM:IMAGELIB.OLB and SYS$SYSTEM:STARLET.OLB. The system services and *run-time library* (RTL) routines are in these files.

The LINK command has these commonly used qualifers:

/CROSS_REFERENCE Generates a cross reference of symbols and writes it in the linker listing file (file type is .MAP). The cross reference lists symbol references for separately compiled programs and also shows the position of the symbol in memory when the program is executed.

/DEBUG   Debugging code is inserted in the executable image. Normally, to use the debugger, this qualifier is used with the compilation and linking commands.

/MAP   Creates a memory allocation listing that shows symbols and program sections.

/LIBRARY   Placed after an object library file name. The library is searched for unresolved symbol references.

/OPTIONS   Used by some parameters that cannot be placed on the LINK command line, e.g., a shareable library. These parameters have to be put in an options file, and the file has to be specified on the link command line, followed by the /OPTIONS qualifier.

/SHAREABLE   Can be placed after the LINK command or after a file name in the /OPTIONS file. If placed after the LINK command, the output created is a shared image. If placed in the /OPTIONS file following a file name, the file is an input shared image.

+--------------------------+
! Object Module Synopsis !
+--------------------------+

Module Name	Ident	Bytes	File	Creation Date	Creator
SAMPLE	0	2443	TEST.OBJ;1	1-May-1990 15:01	VAX COBOL V3.2-42
COB$RMS_BLOCKS	X-1	100	SYS$COMMON:[SYSLIB]STARLET.OLB;1	8-Apr-1988 01:32	VAX-11 Bliss-32 V4.2-761
SYS$P1_VECTOR	X-1	0	SYS$COMMON:[SYSLIB]STARLET.OLB;1	8-APR-1988 04:20	VAX MACRO V5.0-8
COBRTL	V05-000	0	SYS$COMMON:[SYSLIB]COBRTL.EXE;1	8-APR-1988 04:58	VAX-11 Linker V04-92
LIBRTL2	V05-000	0	SYS$COMMON:[SYSLIB]LIBRTL2.EXE;1	8-APR-1988 04:54	VAX-11 Linker V04-92

+---------------------------+
! Program Section Synopsis !
+---------------------------+

Psect Name	Module Name	Base	End	Length	Align	Attributes
$PDATA		00000200	0000050B	0000030C (780.)	LONG 2	PIC,USR,CON,REL,LCL, SHR,NOEXE, RD,NOWRT,NOVEC
	SAMPLE	00000200	0000050B	0000030C (780.)	LONG 2	
COB$NAMES___2		0000050C	00000523	00000018 (24.)	LONG 2	PIC,USR,CON,REL,LCL, SHR,NOEXE, RD,NOWRT,NOVEC
	SAMPLE	0000050C	00000523	00000018 (24.)	LONG 2	
COB$NAMES___4		00000524	00000537	00000014 (20.)	LONG 2	PIC,USR,CON,REL,LCL, SHR,NOEXE, RD,NOWRT,NOVEC
	SAMPLE	00000524	00000537	00000014 (20.)	LONG 2	
$LOCAL		00000600	00000AF7	000004F8 (1272.)	LONG 2	PIC,USR,CON,REL,LCL,NOSHR,NOEXE, RD, WRT,NOVEC
	SAMPLE	00000600	00000A93	00000494 (1172.)	LONG 2	
	COB$RMS_BLOCKS	00000A94	00000AF7	00000064 (100.)	LONG 2	
$CODE		00000C00	00000DBE	000001BF (447.)	LONG 2	PIC,USR,CON,REL,LCL, SHR, EXE, RD,NOWRT,NOVEC
	SAMPLE	00000C00	00000DBE	000001BF (447.)	LONG 2	

+-------------------------+
! Symbol Cross Reference !
+-------------------------+

Symbol	Value	Defined By	Referenced By ...
COB$AB_NAM	00000A98-R	COB$RMS_BLOCKS	SAMPLE
COB$AC_SCR	00000E4C-RX	COBRTL	SAMPLE
COB$DISP_NO_ADV	00000E50-RX	COBRTL	SAMPLE
COB$HANDLER	00000E8-RX	COBRTL	SAMPLE
COB$IOEXCEPTION	00000E48-RX	COBRTL	SAMPLE
COB$POS_ACCEPT	00000E54-RX	LIBRTL2	SAMPLE
LIB$AB_CVTPT_U	00000E68-RX	LIBRTL2	SAMPLE
LIB$AB_CVTTP_U	00000E64-RX	LIBRTL2	SAMPLE
SAMPLE	00000C00-R	SAMPLE	
SYS$CLOSE	7FFEE1B8	SYS$P1_VECTOR	SAMPLE
SYS$CONNECT	7FFEE1C0	SYS$P1_VECTOR	SAMPLE
SYS$CREATE	7FFEE1C8	SYS$P1_VECTOR	SAMPLE
SYS$EXIT	7FFEDF40	SYS$P1_VECTOR	SAMPLE
SYS$GET	7FFEE180	SYS$P1_VECTOR	SAMPLE
SYS$IMGSTA	7FFEDF68	SYS$P1_VECTOR	
SYS$OPEN	7FFEE208	SYS$P1_VECTOR	SAMPLE
SYS$PUT	7FFEE188	SYS$P1_VECTOR	SAMPLE

Figure 2.13 A MAP file created by the LINK command.

```
SYS$SYSDEVICE:[SCOOP.COBOL.TESTING]TEST.EXE;1          1-MAY-1990 15:02      VAX-11 Linker V05-02      Page   2

Symbol           Value          Defined By                 Referenced By ...
------           -----          ----------                 ------------------


                 Key for special characters above:
                 +-------------------+
                 ! *  - Undefined    !
                 ! U  - Universal    !
                 ! R  - Relocatable  !
                 ! X  - External     !
                 ! WK - Weak         !
                 +-------------------+
```

Figure 2.12 (*Continued*)

```
                                            +-------------------+
                                            ! Image Synopsis !
                                            +-------------------+

Virtual memory allocated:              00000200 00000FFF 00000E00 (3584. bytes, 7. pages)
Stack size:                            20. pages
Image header virtual block limits:     1. (    1. (    1. block)
Image binary virtual block limits:     2. (    8. (    7. blocks)
Image name and identification:         TEST 0
Number of files:                       6.
Number of modules:                     6.
Number of program sections:            11.
Number of global symbols:              366.
Number of cross references:            32.
Number of image sections:              15.
User transfer address:                 00000C00
Debugger transfer address:             7FFEDF68
Number of code references to shareable images:     7.
Image type:                            EXECUTABLE.
Map format:                            DEFAULT WITH CROSS REFERENCE in file SYS$SYSDEVICE:[SCOOP.COBOL.TESTING]TEST
Estimated map length:                  42. blocks

                                            +------------------------+
                                            ! Link Run Statistics !
                                            +------------------------+

Performance Indicators                 Page Faults      CPU Time     Elapsed Time
----------------------                 -----------      --------     ------------
  Command processing:                      65           00:00:00.05   00:00:00.06
  Pass 1:                                 237           00:00:00.45   00:00:01.73
  Allocation/Relocation:                   22           00:00:00.03   00:00:00.21
  Pass 2:                                 202           00:00:00.26   00:00:01.01
  Map data after object module synopsis:   10           00:00:00.03   00:00:00.03
  Symbol table output:                      2           00:00:00.01   00:00:00.09
Total run values:                       538           00:00:00.83   00:00:03.13

Using a working set limited to 10000 pages and 82 pages of data storage (excluding image)

Total number object records read (both passes): 122
  of which 23 were in libraries and 3 were DEBUG data records containing 66 bytes
59 bytes of DEBUG data were written,starting at VBN 9 with 1 blocks allocated

Number of modules extracted explicitly       = 0
  with 2 extracted to resolve undefined symbols

0 library searches were for symbols not in the library searched

A total of 0 global symbol table records was written

LINK/CROS/MAP TEST
```

Figure 2.13 (*Continued*)

Here is an example of a MAP file created by the LINK command.
Figure 2.13 shows the MAP file created by the command:

```
$ LINK/MAP/CROSS_REFERENCE  TEST
```

To run the program, use:

```
$ RUN TEST
```

2.15 SUMMARY

Basic features of VAX/VMS were introduced in this chapter. A
beginner to VAX/VMS usually starts off by learning the digital
command language. DCL was introduced in this chapter. The VT
series terminals, which are ubiquitous in VAX environments, were
mentioned. User activity is within a process in the operating system, and the process was introduced. The EVE editor for creating
text files was discussed. Finally, program development was discussed by showing how to create, compile, link, and run a program.
The next chapter starts off a discussion on VAXclusters.

3

VAXclusters and Other High-Availability Systems

This chapter discusses VAXclusters in very general terms. Various types of cluster configurations are introduced. Terms like high availability and fault tolerance are discussed. The VAXcluster architecture is compared to other related architectures.

3.1 VAXcluster BASICS

As mentioned previously, a VAXcluster is a collection of VAXes with associated peripherals. VAXclusters offer a number of additional features over independent (stand-alone) VAX computers as is described briefly in this section and elaborated in later chapters. The words VAXcluster and cluster are used synonymously in this book.

Figure 3.1 shows a sample VAXcluster. The components of this cluster are:

1. *Three VAXes*. VAX 6000-440 has four VAX processors. VAX 9000-210 and VAX 6000-510 are single processor computers. Each VAX has an independent physical memory of 128 Mbytes each. VAX/VMS runs on each of the three VAXes. A separate set of processes is running within the VAXes.

2. *Computer Interconnect (CI) bus*. This bus is composed of a set of coaxial cables. The CI has a bandwidth of 70 Mbits/sec. It is

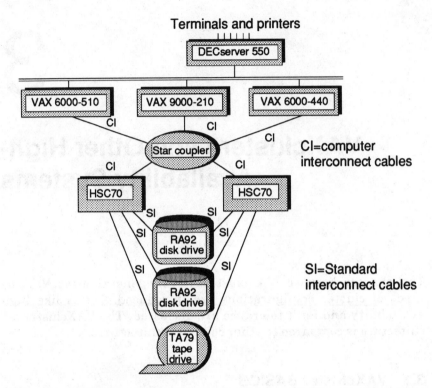

Notes: Dual HSC70s are used for redundancy. All CI connections have dual paths for redundancy.

Figure 3.1 A VAXcluster.

used for cluster communications. The CI bandwidth is used mostly for transferring disk and tape data between the physical memory of the VAXes and the drives connected to the HSC70. Other uses of the CI are mentioned later. Each CI connection has two paths for hardware redundancy.

3.   *A star coupler.* The star coupler is a junction box for interconnecting CI cables from the nodes on a cluster. The device does not have its own power supply.

4.   *Hierarchical storage controller (HSC70).* This is an intelligent node on the cluster that manages I/O to disk and tape drives.

5.   *Disk and tape drives.*

6.   *Ethernet.* In this configuration, the Ethernet is used for DECnet communications and allows terminals and the printer con-

nected to terminal servers on the Ethernet to communicate with the VAXes (by the local area transport protocol described later). Ethernet is not required to cluster VAXes. However, devices which can connect to Ethernet are ubiquitous in the VAX world; thus, most clusters have an Ethernet network.

7. *A Terminal server.* Terminals and printers are connected to the server. The printers can be shared by all the VAXes.

This VAXcluster configuration has a number of advantages over three independent VAX computers:

1. *Resource sharing.* The three VAXes in the cluster can share the tape and disk drives. In fact, the same disk file can be accessed by all the VAXes; although it would not make sense to have the VAXes simultaneously access the same record for updates. Also the task of maintaining backups is less tedious since only one system's disks, i.e., the cluster's, needs to be backed up.

2. *High availability.* If one VAX has a hardware failure, the users can use one of the other VAXes. In fact, as will be explained later, users can be automatically switched to the other VAXes in the event of a VAX failure (or, using industry parlance, crash). If an HSC70 fails, the other HSCs take over automatically. Later, we will see how disks can be shadowed so that if a disk fails, other disks will automatically handle further disk I/Os.

3. *High throughput.* This is achieved when, for example, a single on-line transaction processing application is running on all the VAXes on the cluster. The application can share the same set of disk files. In this case, the processing speed for the transaction is determined by the sum of the speeds of the VAX CPUs. Since such applications are usually highly integrated internally, the common application will be inefficient when it is run on three independent VAX computers.

4. *Convenient system management.* System management is more efficient on a cluster than on a set of independent systems. Common databases can be maintained for user profiles (accounts), network databases, and so on. A common operator console can be created. User activity can be monitored from one terminal. Most software products have to be installed only once for access by all the VAXes.

5. *Expandability*. If the aggregate processing power does not meet the user demand, more VAXes can be popped into the cluster. More HSCs and disk drives can also be easily added if I/O is a bottleneck.

VAXclusters have some disadvantages over independent VAX systems:

1. Normally, they are more *expensive* than independent VAX systems providing the same throughput. Also, software products for clusters cost more than for independent VAX systems. If the product is to be used by, for example, just two VAXes in a six-VAX cluster, the cluster license may be more expensive than the license for two independent VAX systems.

2. *More system management expertise* is required. For example, since clusters have more drives than a single VAX system, more restrictions may have to be enforced on users. Improper management of votes and quorums (described later) can cause disks to be corrupted. Security management is more complex on a cluster than on independent VAX systems. Also, since there are many options for implementing an application functional requirement, the system designer has to determine what the options are and judiciously select one.

3. Some sites use two separate VAX systems, each having a different power supply source. If the clusters use *two independent power sources*, more planning is required to safeguard against failure of power from the two sources than from a single source.

4. Some sites have *security audit requirements* that the software development and on-line production applications be physically independent and that production applications should not be available to the developers unless there is a critical software problem. A cluster does not meet these requirements. A solution could be to maintain separate clusters.

5. *Local Area VAXclusters* (LAVcs), which will be described later, use Ethernet instead of CI for cluster communications. This may cause *congestion* on the Ethernet.

6. Software bugs on one computer may cause the *whole cluster to crash*.

7. VAXes on a cluster take *more time to boot* than if they were independent.

8. On CI-based VAXclusters, the trade-off for the high-bandwidth (70 Mbits/sec) CI cluster communications path is that the cluster has to be *within a radius of about 45 meters*.

3.2 HOMOGENEOUS AND HETEROGENEOUS CLUSTERS

As mentioned before, individual member VAXes on the cluster run the VAX/VMS operating system. The operating system is loaded from disk when a computer is brought up (or booted, as it is called). All the VAXes can share a common set of operating system files, thus saving disk space and simplifying system management. Such a cluster is called a *homogeneous VAXcluster*. Not all the system files can be common. For example, many of the DECnet database files must be unique for each member VAX. These files contain node-specific information. The AUTHORIZE file, which contains profiles of each user, can be common to all the VAXes on the cluster or it can be separate for each VAX. Normally, the entire operating system resides on one common system disk. Paging and Swap files are different for each VAX on the homogeneous cluster, though all of them can be on the same common disk.

Failure of the system disk can cause the whole cluster to stop functioning on a homogenous VAXcluster. Disks can be shadowed to mitigate the effects of disk failures. Volume shadowing is described later in its own chapter.

A heterogeneous cluster is one that has VAXes loading the operating system from different disks. Such clusters are also known as multiple-environment clusters. Such clusters are more customizable and, as a corollary, require more system management effort. For example, VAXes on the cluster can run different versions of the operating system.

3.3 VAXcluster TYPES: CI-BASED, NI-BASED, AND MIXED-INTERCONNECT

A *CI-based cluster* uses the CI bus for cluster communications. The bus was previously described in this chapter. The CI has a high bandwidth of 70 Mbits/sec which only the larger VAXes can handle efficiently. The 6000 and the 9000 series VAXes can be members of a CI-based cluster; the MicroVAX 3000 series and 4000 series VAXes cannot be members.

A *local area VAXcluster* uses Ethernet for cluster communications. LAVcs are also called NI-based VAXclusters; NI is an acronym for *network interconnect*. The maximum theoretical Ethernet bandwidth is 10 Mbits/sec; in practice though, the bandwidth is about 3 Mbits/sec is used because of message collisions and wait states. Also, Ethernet is normally used for DECnet and other kinds of traffic. For these reasons, LAVcs have a lesser throughput than CI-based clusters. Any VAX, including ones from the MicroVAX 3000 or VAX 4000 series, can be members of a LAVc.

Typically, in a LAVc, one node on the Ethernet is a boot server. The boot server is a VAX that has the operating system on one of its local disks; the other VAXes on the LAVc boot with this copy of the operating system. VAXes that boot off the boot server are called *satellites*. Satellites access system files from the boot server's system disk, while page and swap files are usually located on local disks

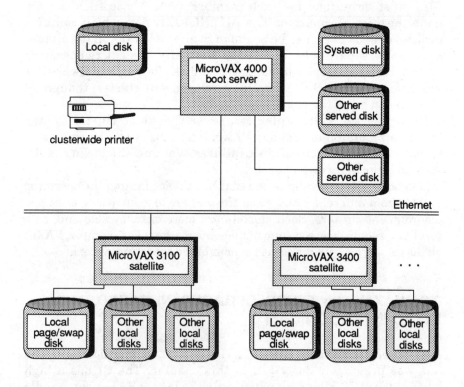

Figure 3.2 A local area VAXcluster.

on the satellite node. Satellites can also have other disks for local files that are normally not required by other nodes. Because the boot server is handling disk I/O on behalf of a number of satellites, the boot server is normally the VAX with the highest CPU speed on the LAVc. If a VAX is serving disks to the cluster and the disks are used intensively by other VAXes, all Ethernet traffic will slow down. The hardware configuration has to be carefully analyzed for potential disk I/O bottlenecks when planning for a LAVc with a number of cluster-wide disks. A LAVc can have multiple boot servers. Figure 3.2 shows a local area VAXcluster configuration.

A *mixed-interconnect VAXcluster* is a hybrid of both CI-based and local area VAXcluster so, Figure 3.3 shows a mixed-interconnect VAXcluster.

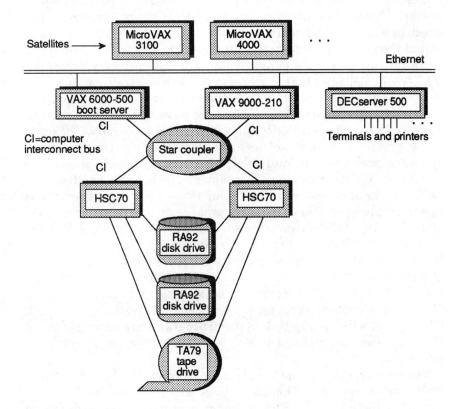

Notes: The VAX 6000-500 is the boot node for the LAVc and is also a member of the CI VAXcluster. The VAX serves the RA92s to the MicroVAXes.

Figure 3.3 A mixed-interconnect VAXcluster.

The discussions in this book are valid for all three VAXcluster types mentioned here (unless specified otherwise).

3.4   PARALLEL PROCESSING AND VECTOR PROCESSING

Some of the high-end VAXes have more than one VAX processor sharing the physical memory. The 6000 and 9000 series VAXes support such multiprocessing. For example, the VAX 6000-440 has four processors in the same cabinet enclosure. The VAX/VMS operating system, starting from version 5.0, has been designed to exploit the processing power of all the processors in the VAX. The operating system code and processes can be executed on any processor. This technique is called *symmetric multiprocessing*. The execution of some I/O-related low-level code on only one processor, called the primary processor, is an exception. This is because hardware interrupts can be generated on only the primary processor. VAX/VMS utilizes all the processors when scheduling user programs; however, normally this is transparent to the user. Individual member VAXes on a VAXcluster can have multiple processors.

A single program normally runs on one processor only. The operating system will run multiple programs (within the context of software processes) on multiple processors, but each program is run on only one processor. Programmers can write explicit code (with the help of system library routines) to have their programs use multiple processors for faster processing, i.e., shorter elapsed time. Usually, this is cumbersome. Some of the compilers, like the VAX FORTRAN and C language compiler, generate parallel code for some set of statements (typically, computational-intensive loop statements). It should be noted that multiprocessing has more overhead than single-processor processing for the same program. Hence on a system running a number of programs, the overall throughput will usually be less if the programs are parallel than if the programs are allowed to run with each program on only one processor.

Vector processing is optionally supported on the VAX 6000 and 9000 series systems. The basic VAX architecture has been extended to include about 63 new vector-processing instructions and a set of vector registers. Computational-intensive applications like scientific, engineering, and stock market analytics will run faster if the hardware vector processor is used. Vector processing and multiprocessing is supported within the same processor complex.

Individual member VAXes on a VAXcluster can have vector processors (and multiple ordinary processors).

3.5 DECnet AND ETHERNET

DECnet is DEC's architecture for communications between computers. It attempts to adhere to the OSI standard seven-layer scheme, though it does not comply completely. It also has support for communications with TCP/IP (ubiquitous in UNIX environments), X.25 (packet-switched networks like Tymnet and Telenet), and IBM's *system network architecture* (SNA).

This chapter discusses DECnet Phase IV, which is currently used at many sites. DECnet Phase V will be OSI compliant. Many of the services and protocols used currently will be gradually replaced by new ones. Figure 3.4 shows a small configuration of networked VAXes.

Computers on a network are known as nodes. DECnet interconnects VAX nodes using two main methodologies:

1. *Ethernet.* Ethernet is usually used when the VAXes are not far from each other, normally within a radius of a few thousand feet. Such a network is called a *local area network* (LAN).

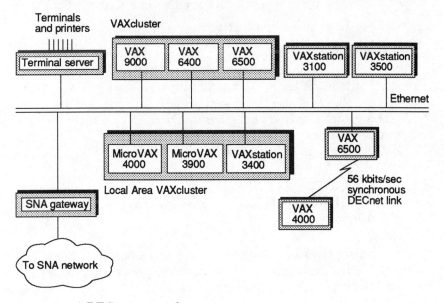

Figure 3.4 A DECnet network.

Actually, Ethernet LANbridges are available that extend the range of Ethernet from, for example, New York to London. Such networks are called wide area networks (WANs). So, the term local area network may be misleading.

2. *DDCMP* (Digital data communications protocol). This protocol is used when VAXes are using DECnet over communications lines. It is a point-to-point protocol. Two VAXes can be connected to each other by a synchronous or asynchronous line. Line speeds of 9.6 or 56 kbits/sec are typical. Any two VAXes on a network can communicate with each other provided there is a path between them, which can be either a direct line or through other VAXes.

Another point-to-point protocol, HDLC, will be supported in DECnet Phase V. In this section, multipoint and multidrop connections are treated as point-to-point connections. The network control program (NCP) is used to set up and maintain network-related information on each node.

Typical uses of a DECnet network are:

- Copying files

- Logging into other VAXes

- Sharing of resources like fast line-printers and software packages

- Running distributed applications

Terminal servers are nodes on an Ethernet network. They allow terminals, printers, and other serial and parallel devices to be connected to the Ethernet for communcations with VAXes and other nodes. However, terminal servers use Ethernet not DECnet; these servers use the *local area transport* (LAT) protocol for normal communications. Figure 3.5 shows an Ethernet network with some devices that can be connected to the network.

3.6 NETWORKS, PARALLEL COMPUTERS, AND VAXclusters

Single processor systems do not meet many of today's business, scientific, and engineering computational requirements for decentralized operations, fault tolerancy, ease of system operations and

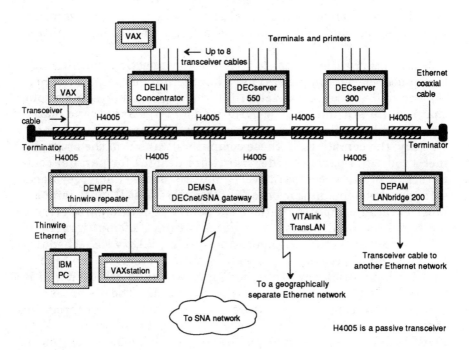

Figure 3.5 Ethernet devices.

expandability, and raw computing power. Networks, parallel computers, and VAXclusters attempt to fulfill these needs.

Networks are made up of loosely connected systems. In typical network topologies, point-to-point communication lines (like a 56 Kbits/sec synchronous line) or a local area network (like those that use Ethernet) are used for network communications. File transfer and message passing are the more common uses of these networks. Typically, computers on the network handling on-line applications operate independently with occasional interactions with other computers. Recently, distributed database architectures have been implemented for commercial applications. These database systems attempt to localize the database; the network is used only when it is imperative to access databases on other computers.

A *parallel computer* is a system with multiple processors sharing the physical main memory. The VAX 6000 and 9000 series computers support multiple processors. The VAX 6000-540 is one such computer. It has four VAX processors in its processor complex. Normally, parallel computers run one common operating system and the users perceive the parallel processors as one computer. These systems address the need for a large amount of computing power.

Massively parallel computers (like the connection machine and transputer-based computers) have a large number of parallel processors and are used for scientific and engineering applications that require arithmetic to be performed on large arrays and matrices of numbers. Hundreds of processors/CPU are not uncommon. Usually, the compilers on these computers transform the programmer's code into parallel code. Hardware designs for parallel computers are at a comparatively mature stage today; systems software development for parallel computers is still in its infancy. Most parallel computers cannot efficiently generate parallel code for business applications. A major advantage of multiprocessor VAX computers is that the operating system, VAX/VMS, schedules the running of programs (processes on the system) on the processors for high efficiency. Thus, multiprocessing is achieved and is transparent to the running of the programs. The technique is called symmetric multiprocessing. In cases where a single program requires the power of all the processors, a language (like VAX FORTRAN) whose compiler generates parallel code can be used. Alternatively, the programmer can analyze the program and use system library routines (PPL$ routines) to create parallelism within the code.

VAXclusters are *more tightly coupled than networks*. Member VAXes of the cluster can access the same disk and tape drives very much like local devices. On a CI-based VAXcluster, the cluster communications path between the nodes has a bandwidth of 70 Mbits/sec. Distributed application design is relatively simple. The distributed lock manager (described later), which is part of the systems software, facilitates synchronization between programs on different computers on the cluster.

VAXclusters are *not as tightly coupled as parallel computers*: VAXes in the cluster do not have a common main memory. It is not a simple task to make use of all the VAXes in a cluster to efficiently run a parallel program on multiple cluster VAXes. Even if the code is made parallel, the communications path among the nodes is usually too slow for most such programs. On a parallel computer, it takes a few nanoseconds to move data from a register in one processor to a register in another processor. Even faster transfer rates are on the horizon! On a VAXcluster, it takes a few hundred microsec to move data from one processor's register to those of another on a different VAX.

3.7 HIGH-AVAILABILITY SYSTEMS VERSUS FAULT-TOLERANT SYSTEMS

Fault tolerance is defined as the ability of a complete system to withstand failures of computers and subsystems. By this definition, VAXclusters are fault tolerant. In a properly planned cluster configuration with correspondingly planned software applications, no single hardware failure can cause the application to abort (though performance may degrade and users may have to reestablish sessions). In fact, multiple hardware failures, depending on the types of components that are failing, are usually tolerated by VAXclusters.

For example, disk volumes can be shadowed (mirrored) on a VAXcluster with the HSC hardware for controlling disk and tape drives. (Using VMS version 5.4, HSCs are not required for volume shadowing.) In a three volume shadow set, the same information is written to all three disks. Users on the system will not be affected in any way if one or even two of these drives fail. Similarly, suppose there are three VAXes in a VAXcluster and the application is designed so that users can log in and use it from any of these VAXes. Usually, this does not require a major programming effort if the application designers understand the VAXcluster architecture. In such a VAXcluster, if any two VAXes fail, the application will still be available from the third VAX. Users who logged in on the VAXes that failed will have to reestablish a session on the remaining VAX. Of course, for the cluster to handle the potential failing of any two VAXes, each VAX must have the processing power to handle all the users.

However, the common perception in the computer industry is that fault-tolerant systems are those that will withstand hardware failures without the end users noticing the failure. Actually, such systems are *transparently fault tolerant.* In the scenario mentioned in the previous paragraph where two out of three VAXes in a VAXcluster have failed, the users on the failing VAXes do notice the failures since they have to log into the remaining VAX and possibly redo some of the work they already did on the failed VAXes. In this sense, VAXclusters are not completely fault tolerant. Moreover, for most commercial fault tolerant systems (like the Tandem and Stratus computers), fault tolerancy is achieved without the software designers having to explicitly take care of potential failures in their programs. For example, on a Stratus system, failure of a processor is not noticed by end users and software developers can assume that the databases on disk needed for their program are accessed by one processor when, actually, another processor will access the databases if the primary processor fails. On a VAXcluster, the member VAXes may access the same databases, however, the burden of ensuring synchronized access is on the application software. For these reasons, DEC uses the term *high availability* for VAXclusters. The VAXft systems described below are transparently fault tolerant.

Note that even for highly fault-tolerant systems, if the user's terminal fails, access to the system is noticed by the user. In that sense, no system is completely fault tolerant. Also, tape drive failures are not adequately handled by most current implementations of transparently fault-tolerant systems.

Fault tolerance, as conceptualized in the industry, and high availability have their advantages and disadvantages. Fault-tolerant hardware and systems software is expensive. Power blackouts can cause complete system failures. Processor failures are adequately handled by standby processors and associated hardware. VAXclusters, which are high-availability systems, can tolerate multiple failures. The level of fault tolerance can be planned for in a VAXcluster. Disk drive failures, which are one of the most common hardware failures, are handled in a completely fault-tolerant way. If there are no hardware failures, the processing power of all the VAXes in the cluster can be exploited. In the event of a VAX failure, some of the lower priority applications may have to be stopped so that the remaining VAXes can provide adequate processing power for critical applications. VAX failures are generally not transparent to the end users; they will have to reestablish sessions on other VAXes. However, for many applications, this may be just a minor inconvenience. It should be emphasized that applications have to be properly designed to exploit the fault-tolerant features of VAXcluster.

3.8   THE FAULT-TOLERANT VAXft SYSTEM

In 1990, DEC announced a fault-tolerant series of VAX systems called the VAX*ft* 3000. These systems are truly fault tolerant in the sense that all critical hardware is completely duplicated and no special software coding is required; VAX/VMS and standard applications on the non-fault-tolerant VAXes can be run on VAXfts without any code modifications.

An example is the VAX*ft* Model 310. The computer is rated at 3.8 *VAX units of processing* (VUPs), which means that the CPU speed is 3.8 times that of a VAX 11/780. Each VAX*ft* computer includes two sets of components called *zones*. Typically, a zone contains a VAX CPU, memory, and controllers. Each zone is in a separate cabinet. The zones are interconnected by high-speed cables that allow the two computers, one in each zone, to run in lock-step. The CPU in the two zones run synchronously, executing the same instruction at the same time. Failure of a single hardware component in a zone cannot affect an application because the other zone will continue to operate. In fact, a complete zone can fail and still the users will not be affected. Each zone also has an *uninterruptible power supply* (UPS) that allows the zone to operate for up to 15 minutes in a 24-hour period without any external power supply.

Figure 3.6 shows a VAXft system. Each zone has its own VAX CPU and memory. The disks are shadowed (mirrored) so a logical disk consists of multiple physical disks with the same data on them. Failure of a disk does not affect the running of applications as data is then accessed through the other shadow member or members. One Ethernet port in each zone is connected to the Ethernet network. That way terminals and other Ethernet devices are redundantly connected to the computer. Two separate Ethernet segments can be set up, in which case two Ethernet ports from each zone can be connected to the segments. Such a configuration will tolerate failure of a Ethernet segment. The tape drive subsystem is not fault tolerant.

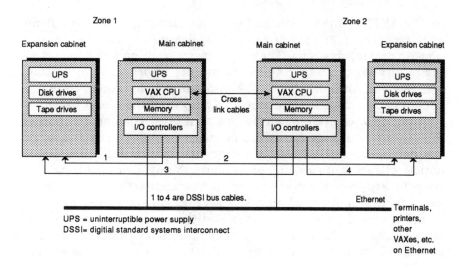

Figure 3.6 Fault-tolerant VAXft Model 310.

The VAXft systems can be part of a network of VAXes. They can also participate in local area or mixed-interconnect VAXclusters (but not in CI-based VAXclusters).

A few comments on the VAXft systems:

- The systems are relatively expensive because of the hardware redundancy.

- The two CPUs run synchronously (in lockstep). On the Model 310, each CPU is rated at a speed of 3.8 VUPs and the aggregate throughput is also the same. In the Tandem computers, described in the next section, two CPUs run different tasks while each monitors the other CPU. A higher throughput is achieved using such a design.

- Because the two CPUs run synchronously, a timing-related software bug can cause the CPUs in both zones to crash together.

- The redundancy scheme cannot handle multiple hardware failures of the same type. For example, the computer cannot be configured to accommodate two CPU failures. More than two zones cannot be interconnected to create an even more reliable system.

3.9 TANDEM Non-Stop COMPUTERS

In the 1970s banks, airlines, stock exchanges, and other firms were rapidly replacing many batch applications by on-line transaction-processing systems. These systems were highly dependent on computers for providing up-to-the-minute information to customers. Some of these systems like *automatic teller machine* (ATM) networks can literally lose money if they malfunction. A batch job running on a computer can be run at a later time or on another computer if there are hardware failures. Customers, by and large, are not affected. However, if an on-line system fails, customers notice within minutes, if not seconds. Many firms address this issue by keeping two systems for on-line applications, one system running the application and the second system acting as a hot standby. One disadvantage is the additional cost. The main drawback is that if the primary system fails, some amount of time, typically 5 to 40 minutes, elapses before the second system picks up. Moreover, some of the transactions being entered or just entered when the primary system fails may have to be redone.

The solution is to design systems so that failure of hardware components has no effect on the application. Tandem Computers Incorporated was founded in 1974 to design and market such continuously available systems. Currently, Tandem manufactures a wide variety of systems with a primary focus on the fault-tolerant series of computers, generically called NonStop systems.

The *NonStop architecture* is currently supported by three series of Tandem computers: CLX, VLX, and Cyclone. The operating system on these computers is called *Guardian*. Individual computers in a system are housed in separate enclosures. The computers are interconnected by interprocessor communication paths called DYNABUS. I/O among the processors is through a separate path. The NonStop systems can be classified as *loosely coupled systems*.

The Guardian operating system is designed as a set of processes using the message-passing mechanism for communication. A system can consist of multiple computers. For every process on a computer, there is a backup process on another computer. The process pairs work in close coordination. A primary process sends checkpointing messages to the backup process. The messages describe changes to the state of the primary process. The backup process incorporates these changes in its environment. In case the primary computer fails, the backup computer becomes the primary computer and the processes continue operation from the last checkpoint.

Figure 3.7 shows a Tandem NonStop Cyclone configuration. The fault tolerant features are:

1. Failure of a processor causes the backup processor to become the primary processor as explained above.

2. Memory failures are handled as processor failures.

3. Disk drives are mirrored. In case a drive fails, the remaining drive is used for I/O.

4. The interprocessor communications network DYNABUS has dual paths for redundancy.

5. Each I/O controller has dual ports so it can be connected to two processors. Effectively, all peripheral devices are accessible from at least two processors.

6. Each disk drive can be connected to two controllers. This way a controller failure will not affect running applications.

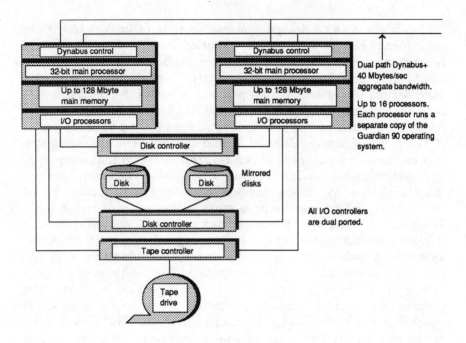

Figure 3.7 A Tandem NonStop Cyclone system.

7. Two separate power sources allow redundant components to be separated from the primary components.

For software development, Tandem offers NonStop SQL, a distributed relational database management system. It implements ANSI standard SQL and supports transaction processing. The product fully exploits the NonStop hardware architecture for fault tolerance. Programmers can use SQL without any special coding requirements to facilitate the failover of hardware components in case of failures. SQL statements can be embedded in COBOL, C, and Pascal programs.

The Tandem *transaction monitoring facility* (TMF) is a key system software for transaction processing. It maintains database consistency and integrity even for distributed databases. The NonStop SQL system software makes use of TMF. SQL calls can be issued from high-level language programs. Programs written in standard high-level languages have to be coded appropriately to support fault tolerancy.

PATHWAY is a *distributed transaction processing* software. It supports fault tolerancy. It can be used from high-level language programs. PATHWAY uses TMF internally. Programs can also issue calls directly to the TMF for database operations.

A few comments on the Tandem NonStop systems:

- The systems support distributed transaction processing. Because they support fault tolerancy, distributed fault-tolerant applications can be easily designed.

- Unlike the VAXft systems, the backup computer does not run in lockstep with the primary computer. The advantage of Tandem systems is that the primary and backup computers' processing power can be utilized by an application for a higher aggregate throughput. Moreover, a timing-related software bug can cause the VAXft system to crash. However, since the primary and backup processors on Tandem systems are not running completely in synchronization, the probability of both processors crashing is very low.

- To support fault tolerancy, programs have to be written accordingly on Tandem systems. This is not the case with VAXft, which can run any VAX program with hardware fault tolerancy without code changes.

- The hardware configuration of a VAXcluster can support fault tolerancy just like the Tandem systems. However, VAXcluster runs the VMS operating system, which was not designed for fault tolerancy. Programmers have to write complex code to make a cluster hardware fault tolerant.

- The system does not support multiple failures of the same type. For example, failure of the primary and secondary processors is not fault tolerant— the application will fail.

- A VAXcluster can support a range of VAX processors, small and larger. The Tandem NonStop systems have a limited set of processor types.

- NonStop SQL allows the system to run industry standard SQL with fault tolerancy and transaction-processing support. This allows fast development of mission-critical on-line applications.

Tandem also offers UNIX-based fault-tolerant systems called Integrity S2. These systems, based on RISC technology, run the NonStop-UX operating system, which is based on UNIX system V, Release 3.

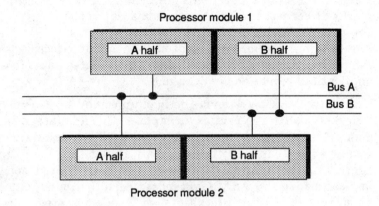

Figure 3.8 Stratus pair-and-spare architecture.

3.10   STRATUS COMPUTERS

The CPU on Stratus computers is designed around the Motorola 68000 and later series microprocessors. The first Stratus computer FT200 was announced in 1981. The current series of computers are called XA2000. These systems are hardware fault tolerant. The basic fault-tolerant architecture has remained the same for all the systems.

Fault tolerance is achieved by the Stratus *pair-and-spare archi-tecture*. Consider how the CPU fault tolerance is achieved. There are two processor boards as shown in Figure 3.8. The two proces-sors duplicate each other.

Each processor board has two halves, A and B. These halves are (nearly) duplicates of each other. The processor board contains logic circuitry that continuously compares the output of the two halves. If there is a mismatch; one of the two halves on the board is not functioning properly. In this case the complete board is dis-abled. The other board continues operating so the system is not affected.

The I/O buses are also duplicated. As seen in the figure, Bus A is driven by the output of the A halves of all the boards. The bus signal is the logical OR (wired OR) of the board outputs of the A halves. Bus B is similarly driven by the B halves. The backplane bus in the system is called *StrataBus*. Modules (like the processor

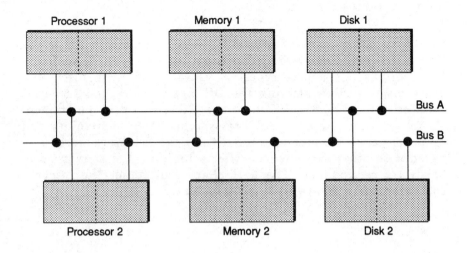

Figure 3.9 A Stratus configuration.

and memory boards) are interconnected by a message-passing Stratus intermodule bus.

An example STRATUS system is the XA2000 Model 2860, which has 48 duplexed processors and 1 Gbyte of duplexed main memory. It is considered to be competitive with VAX 9000s. The operating system is VOS, which is proprietary to Stratus. Some of the Stratus systems support FTX (which is UNIX system V compatible) and Pick (an open architecture operating environment).

Figure 3.9 shows a simple Stratus configuration. A few comments on the Stratus systems:

- The systems are hardware fault tolerant (like the VAXft). No special programming considerations for fault tolerancy are required.

- Failed boards can be replaced while the system continues to operate.

- The system uses a single system clock.

- Four processor halves are used for fault tolerance (two processor boards each with half A and half B). Each half has a processor, real throughput is equivalent to one half (i.e., one processor).

3.11 SUMMARY

VAXclusters are made of individual VAX computers running the
VAX/VMS operating system. This chapter shows how VAXclusters
are configured. Various types of VAXclusters were discussed.
Since most clusters also use the DECnet network and Ethernet
connectivity products, DECnet and Ethernet were mentioned.
VAXclusters are high-availability systems. High availability and
fault tolerance were compared. Finally, VAXclusters were compared with other systems that offer a high level of software and
hardware redundancy. The next chapter discusses the internal
software and hardware of the VAXcluster.

4

VAXcluster Components and Terminology

As explained in the previous chapter, there are three types of VAXclusters: CI-based VAXclusters that use the CI bus, local area VAXclusters that use Ethernet, and mixed-interconnect VAXclusters that use both the CI bus and Ethernet for clustering. Local area VAXclusters are also known as NI-based VAXclusters, where NI is an acronym for network interconnect. Some of the hardware used to form a cluster was introduced in the last chapter. In this chapter we explore further the software and hardware components. Refer to the VAXcluster figures shown in the previous chapter when reading this chapter.

4.1 THE SYSTEM COMMUNICATION ARCHITECTURE

The *system communication architecture* (SCA) defines the cluster communications protocol. It is comparable to *digital network architecture* (DNA) that is the basis for DECnet communications. For efficient communications, SCA is partially implemented in the hardware controllers connected to the nodes on the CI bus. Figure 4.1 shows the various layers of SCA.

An instance of SCA runs on each node of the VAXcluster. Every node on the cluster periodically *polls* other nodes and maintains a list of active cluster members. The SCA software uses this list to maintain a *virtual circuit* between each pair of nodes.

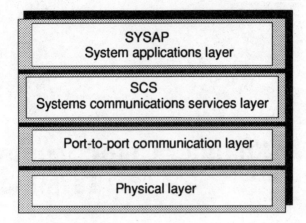

Figure 4.1 The layers of SCA.

Originally, SCA was designed for communications over the CI bus, but now the architecture has been extended to support Ethernet. The functions performed by the CI port (controller) are performed by port-emulation software in an Ethernet-based VAXcluster node.

The basic functions of SCA are:

1. Cluster configuration management

2. Buffer management

3. Connection management

4. Directory services

5. Datagram and sequenced-message services

6. Named-buffer transfer services

System communication services (SCS) is part of SCA. SCS is the software on each cluster node that implements communications in the cluster. SCS handles communications for the six functions mentioned above. SCS makes use of the VAXport drivers described later in this chapter.

4.1.1 Datagrams, Sequenced Messages, and Data Blocks

When the SCA software communicates with its counterpart on another node, one of three types of information packets are transmitted over the communications link: datagrams, messages, or data blocks.

A *datagram* has a size of 576 bytes. A node sending out a datagram does not wait for an acknowledgment from the node that is supposed to receive it. Delivery of datagrams is not guaranteed. Noncritical status messages are transmitted using datagrams.

A *sequenced message* has a size of 112 bytes. Delivery of messages is guaranteed. As mentioned before, a virtual circuit is maintained between the sending and receiving node. Sequence numbers of sent and received messages are also maintained as part of the virtual circuit information. Messages are properly sequenced so that the receiving node can discard duplicate messages (if there are any). Examples of messages are disk read or write requests from a host VAX to a HSC.

A *data block* can be of any size. Delivery of data blocks is guaranteed. Normally the data is a block of memory locations in a process's virtual address space. The CI port hardware can directly access such a block of data and move it to another node on the CI bus. The technique is called *direct memory access* (DMA). It is an efficient way of copying a large amount of data from one node to another. On Ethernet, the data is moved by the cluster port emulator software hence, the process is comparatively more time consuming. Examples of data block moves are disk data reads and

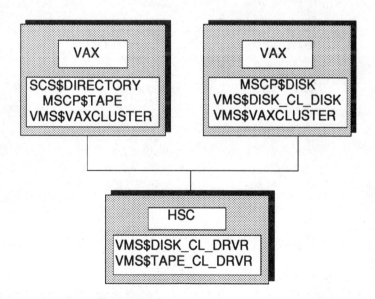

Figure 4.2 Some common SYSAPs.

writes. Data block transfers are also known as named-buffer transfers.

4.1.2 SYSTEM APPLICATIONS

System applications (SYSAPs) are software components within the operating system and the firmware within the CI controllers. SYSAPs on a node communicate with their counterparts on other nodes in the cluster to implement functions like low-level disk I/O from a VAX to a HSC. The information tranfer is performed by SCS, which communicates with the SYSAPs. Figure 4.2 illustrates this.

Examples of SYSAP functions are disk class drivers and VAXcluster connection manager. Each SYSAP on a node has a name, e.g., VMS$VAXCLUSTER, which is the VAXcluster connection manager. The LOC_PROC_NAME option of the SHOW CLUSTER command displays a list of SYSAPs running each node:

```
$ SHOW CLUSTER/CONTINUOUS
command> ADD LOC_PROC_NAME
```

The output is shown in Figure 4.3

```
View of Cluster from system ID 1036  node: SCOOP2        13-AUG-1990 12:30:02

    +-------------------------------------+ --------------- +
    |         SYSTEMS         |          CONNECTIONS         |
    +------------------ + ------------------------------------+
    |        NODE        |          LOC_PROC_NAME           |
    +------------------ + ------------------------------------+
    |       SCOOP2       |          SCS$DIRECTORY           |
    |                    |          MSCP$TAPE               |
    |                    |          VMS$VAXcluster          |
    |                    |          MSCP$DISK               |
    |       HSC002       |          VMS$TAPE_CL_DRVR        |
    |                    |          VMS$DISK_CL_DRVR        |
    |       SCOOP1       |          MSCP$DISK               |
    |                    |          VMS$DISK_CL_DRVR        |
    |                    |          VMS$VAXcluster          |
    |       HSC003       |          VMS$DISK_CL_DRVR        |
    |                    |          VMS$TAPE_CL_DRVR        |
    +------------------ + ------------------ +--------------- +
```

Figure 4.3 SYSAPs on each node of a VAXcluster.

4.1.3   Cluster Configuration Management

To handle the communications among the nodes in the cluster, each node must build a topology of the interconnections. This topology is maintained by SCA software.

When a node joins the cluster, the node *polls* the CI (or NI) bus asking for every node on the cluster to identify itself. This information is used to make a list of cluster members. Each node periodically polls the bus to maintain an up-to-date list of cluster members within its SCA database.

Once the list of cluster members is known, the node opens a *port-to-port virtual circuit* with each of the other cluster members. This is achieved by a series of handshake messages between the node and each of the other cluster members. The information on a virtual circuit between the node and a remote node is stored in a data structure within SCA called a system block.

A node can have multiple CI ports (controllers). In this case a port-to-port virtual circuit is created between each port and each remote node. Information specific to a particular virtual circuit is stored in a path block. Path blocks for virtual circuits between the node and a remote node are chained to the system block for the two nodes. This is illustrated in Figure 4.4.

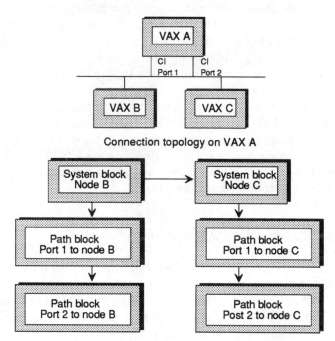

Figure 4.4 Three VAXes and their associated topology data structures.

4.1.4 Buffer Management

VAXcluster communications takes place at a very high speed so buffers for data sent or received over the cluster must be efficiently managed. For a node, sending messages to another node does not pose much of problem provided the receiving node has adequate buffers available. However, if the receiving node does not have adequate receiving buffers and unsolicited data is sent by other nodes, buffers will have to be dynamically created. There is a possibility that not enough buffer space is available, requiring retransmissions by the sending nodes. This problem is addressed by preallocating receiving buffers. A node is allowed to send a message to a receiving node only if the receiving node has at least one buffer (called *credit*) free for the sending node. SCA manages two kinds of buffers: SCA control messages and SYSAP data messages.

Control messages consist of a command and response pair. A response is expected for each sent command. To avoid delays, when a buffer is allocated, it is large enough to accommodate both a command and a response. Each SCA path has two buffers; one for sending a command and receiving its response, and one for receiving a command and sending its response.

SYSAP messages are not simple command and response pairs. The buffer requirements depend on the application. In this case, SCA does not create buffers for SYSAPs. Instead, SYSAPs allocate as many receiving buffers as are required for a connection to its counterpart on a remote node. The buffer information is conveyed to SCA which then manages the buffers. Each receiving buffer is a credit for the sending node. The number of credits a remote node's SYSAP has with another node's SYSAP is conveyed to the remote node. The remote node cannot send messages to the other node if the remote node does not have adequate credits. This scheme guarantees that there will be buffer space on a receiving node for any message sent to it by another node.

4.1.5 Connection Management

SYSAPs on a node is a layer of software residing above the SCS. SYSAPs communicate with their counterparts on other nodes via SCS. SYSAPs are identified by a name that is up to 16-characters long. Figure 4.2 shows the names of some SYSAPs. A SYSAP can request a connection with a SYSAP on another node by issuing a connect call to SCS specifying the remote node and the remote SYSAP name. SCS then communicates with its counterpart on the other node to establish the connection.

A node may have multiple SYSAPs communicating with their counterparts on other nodes. SCA maintains a connection between each pair of communicating SYSAPs. These connections communicate via the underlying virtual circuits between nodes.

4.1.6 Directory Services

When a node joins a cluster, SYSAPs on that node will want to form connections with SYSAPs on other nodes. To accomplish this, the SYSAP will need to know which nodes are running the SYSAPs it should connect with. Each node's SCA software maintains a list of cluster members. However, it would be inefficient for the cluster to maintain a list of SYSAPs on each node.

One node on the cluster maintains a list of SYSAPs on all the nodes and offers SYSAP directory services. SYSAPs on any node can query this node to find partner SYSAPs. This directory service is actually a SYSAP named SCS$DIRECTORY. The SYSAP periodically polls the cluster to maintain an up-to-date list of SYSAPs on all the nodes. Other SYSAPs on the cluster can query the directory service by requesting a SCA connection to SCS$DIREC-TORY.

4.1.7 Datagram and Sequenced Message Services

Datagrams and sequenced messages are used by SCS between connections over virtual circuits. A connection is the logical communications path between two SYSAPs. SYSAP pairs communicate with each other by datagrams and messages. Datagrams and sequenced messages are packets of information sent from one node to another over the cluster communications medium. Delivery of sequenced messages is guaranteed; delivery of datagrams is not.

When a datagram is sent from SYSAP A to SYSAP B, the SCS where SYSAP B resides checks the datagram-receive credit for SYSAP A. If the credit is inadequate, the datagram is discarded. Credits correspond to available buffers in a receiving SYSAP.

When a sequenced-message is sent from SYSAP A to SYSAP B, the SCS where SYSAP A resides checks the message credits it has for SYSAP B. If the credit is inadequate, SYSAP A waits until SYSAP B informs it that adequate credit is available.

In summary, datagrams are discarded at the receiving node if there is no buffer available, while sequenced messages are queued at the sending node if the receiver does not have adequate buffers. Datagrams are used for noncritical information.

4.1.8 Named-Buffer Transfer Services.

Named-buffer transfers, also known as data block transfers, are transfers of the contents of blocks of the host processor's memory to the memory of another node in the cluster. The transfer, unlike that of datagrams and sequenced messages, is performed by the CI controller without host CPU intervention. Block transfers on Ethernet-clustered VAXes require CPU intervention. Normally, the amount of data is on the order of hundreds or thousands of bytes. Typically, disk block I/O is performed using named buffers.

On an Ethernet-based VAXcluster, named-buffer transfers involve the CPUs of both the sending and receiving nodes; the Ethernet controllers are not designed for direct memory access of blocks of data. This is a major reason, as well as the lower Ethernet bandwidth, why Ethernet-based VAXclusters are slower than CI-based VAXclusters.

4.2 HARDWARE COMPONENTS

The CI VAXclusters use a set of hardware components that normally would not be used if the VAXes were not clustered. These components are described here. The NI (Ethernet) VAXclusters do not require any special hardware to cluster the VAXes on an Ethernet network; the cluster is formed and operates over the Ethernet.

Figure 4.5 shows the hardware components of a CI-based VAXcluster. Note that HSCs are not required for forming a CI-based VAXcluster. However, most configurations will have at least one of these controllers.

4.2.1 The Computer Interconnect Bus

Nodes on a CI-based VAXcluster connect to other nodes via the CI bus. Normally, the CI connection cables extend from the VAX to a central unit called the star coupler. The CI connection has four

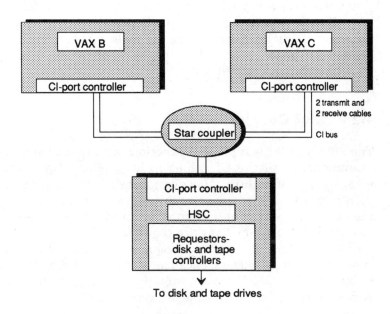

Figure 4.5 CI-based VAXcluster hardware components.

cables, two transmitting and two receiving cables. These are coaxial cables using *baseband signaling* with *Manchester encoding*. *Dual paths* are used so that if one path fails, the other will automatically handle the traffic. If the two paths are functioning, then both are used for better performance. Currently, the bus has a bandwidth of 70 Mbits/sec.

The CI ports (controllers) on the cluster are responsible for bus arbitration. The technique is *carrier sense multiple access* (CSMA). Note that Ethernet uses *carrier sense multiple access / collision detection* (CSMA/CD). On the CI, when data is to be transmitted from a node, the CI port on that node waits until the bus is quiet. It further waits for the bus to be quiet for a node-specific delay time. If the bus is still quiet, the port can transmit data. The delay times are different for different ports so there is never a simultaneous transfer from two nodes (collision). This arrangement favors a port with a short delay time. Therefore, under heavy loading, the ports alternately use two delay times, one short and one relatively long. Effectively, under heavy load the bus is shared in a round-robin method.

Acknowledgments are sent by a receiving node immediately after a data packet is received. This is possible because the shortest node-specific delay time (before the node can send out a packet) is designed to be longer than the time between receipt of a packet and its acknowledgment.

4.2.2 Star Coupler

The *star coupler* is a passive junction box. As its name implies, it interconnects all the CI cables in a "star" configuration. It is a single point of failure. However, because it does not have any power supply or electronic circuitry, the chances of it failing are remote. Each star coupler supports up to 32 nodes; multiple star couplers can be used if they are required.

Currently, the distance between a node and the star coupler cannot exceed *45 meters* because of electrical signal *attenuation* problems with the electrical signal. This means that the cluster nodes have to be within a sphere having a radius of 45 meters.

4.2.3 CI Controllers

Each node connects to the CI via a controller called a VAXcluster port or CI-port controller. These controllers are the interface between systems software and the CI bus. The CIBCA controller works with the VAXBI bus, and the CIBCD controller works with the XMI bus.

4.2.4 The Hierarchical Storage Controller

The *hierarchical storage controller* (HSC) controls RA (or SA) series disk drives and TA series tape drives. The HSC is connected to the CI bus and has floppy drives from which the systems software is loaded during a boot. Though an HSC is not required on a VAXcluster, nearly every CI-based cluster will have one.

Currently, two versions of the HSC are available: HSC40 and HSC70. The major difference between the two is the number of drives they support. The HSC40 supports up to 12 disk and tape drives, and the HSC70 supports up to 32 disk drives or a combination of some disk drives and up to 12 tape drives. The HSC40 can be upgraded to a HSC70; mainly, more boards are added.

The HSCs support disk-to-disk backups without any interaction with the host VAXes. The backup is a block-by-block copy of one disk to another; the VMS BACKUP utility is not used. The backup is fast, however, the files are not made more contiguous.

The HSCs also support volume shadowing where a write to a logical disk, initiated by a VAX, is actually performed on a number of disks that are part of the same shadow set. Reads are performed from any one disk in the shadow set; an optimizing algorithm within the HSC software chooses a disk. If a disk malfunctions, the HSC sends an appropriate message to the host VAXes and does not use the disk until the problem is rectified and appropriate restart commands are issued by the host VAX (or VAXes). Volume shadowing is described in a later chapter.

4.3 SOFTWARE COMPONENTS

Each VAX node on a cluster has logical layers of software that handle cluster communications. These software components are either part of the VAX/VMS operating system on each node or they work closely with the VAX/VMS operating system. The software does not have to be purchased separately; it is bundled with the operating system. The clustering software is mostly transparent to users. However, a knowledge of these components provides an insight into how the cluster operates. These software components are described here (Figure 4.6).

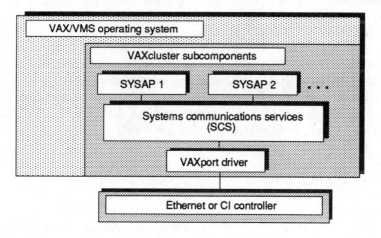

Figure 4.6 VAXcluster software components.

4.3.1 VAXport Drivers

VAXport drivers are software device drivers, similar to other device drivers on the nodes. There are two VAXport drivers: PADRIVER.EXE and PEDRIVER.EXE. PADRIVER.EXE is used by CI-based VAXes to communicate over the cluster hardware. PEDRIVER.EXE is used by Ethernet-based local area VAXclusters.

On the CI bus, the hardware controllers on the VAXes guarantee delivery of messages. The controllers also perform block data transfers from one node's memory to another node's memory without much intervention from the host CPUs. The hardware is optimized for efficient cluster communications. The controllers were designed specifically for the cluster. The PADRIVER software, which is the interface between the operating system and the CI bus controller, is designed accordingly.

CI-based clusters are relatively expensive in a small VAX data center. Moreover, the smaller Qbus-based MicroVAXes cannot handle the high-speed data transfers of a CI bus. Most VAX installations have an Ethernet network, so DEC decided to allow Ethernet-based VAXes to be clustered together using Ethernet as the cluster communications medium. The communications protocol on Ethernet and the CI bus are significantly different. The clustering software at the high level had to be compatible on both types of clusters. DEC designed a driver for Ethernet cluster communications that performed the functions of a PADRIVER and any additional functions required for clustering over Ethernet. This driver is called PEDRIVER. The driver emulates some of the hardware functionality of the CI controller. For example, the CI controllers support direct memory block data transfers from one VAX's memory to another's. The Ethernet controllers do not support such direct memory access. The PEDRIVER emulates such memory-to-memory transfers. The CPUs of both the sending and receiving nodes are involved in these transfers, which can cause significant performance degradation on the cluster. Figure 4.7 shows how the various components of a CI-based and an Ethernet-based (NI-based) VAXcluster fit together at the low level.

4.3.2 System Communications Services (SCS)

System communications services (SCS) is the software on each cluster node that implements communications in a cluster. It makes use of the VAXport drivers.

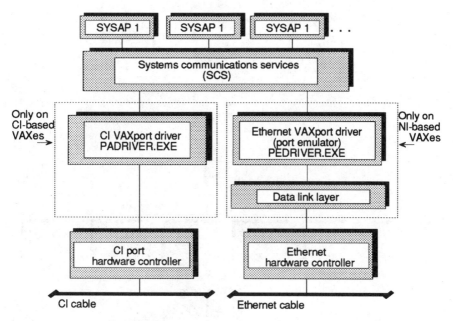

Figure 4.7 CI versus NI VAXcluster components.

4.3.3 Connection Manager

Connection manager is the software on each node that manages cluster connectivity. It is found in a layer above SCS and manages cluster integrity when nodes are added to or removed from the cluster. The connection manager uses the quorum and votes scheme described below to prevent a cluster from partitioning into more than one cluster.

4.3.4 Distributed File Services

Distributed file services is the cluster software on each node that manages disk and file sharing. It also controls record locking by users on the cluster. It is a form of distributed RMS for file access. RMS is an acronym for *record management services.*

Before VAXclusters were designed, a process called the *ancillary control program* (ACP) used to handle disk I/O for the single VAX. I/O requests from user programs (processes) went to the operating system which in turn directed them to the ACP. The ACP performed I/O on behalf of all the processes, one request at a time. This solved the problem of maintaining disk file integrity when

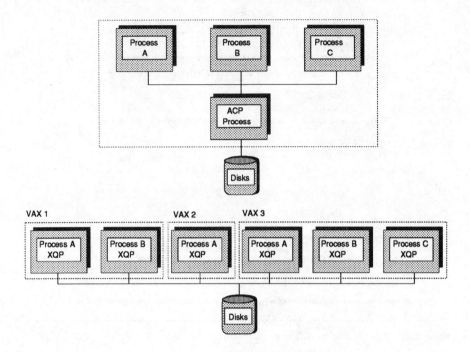

Figure 4.8 ACP-based and XQP-based file system.

multiple users were accessing the files concurrently. The technique cannot solve the problem of concurrent disk (and file) access by users on different nodes on a cluster. As a result, ACP was replaced by the *extended QIO processor* (XQP). XQP runs in the process context of each process on the cluster nodes. File access by the nodes is synchronized by the XQPs on the nodes. Figure 4.8 shows the traditional ACP-based and the VAXcluster XQP-based file systems.

The XQPs use the distributed lock manager for synchronization. The comments which follow here outline what is involved in maintaining file system integrity when multiple users on multiple computers access the same set of disks and files, possibly sharing the same file. Since the XQPs on each node maintain caches of disk blocks, a modification to a disk block must invalidate the corresponding cache block, if present, on all the nodes. A lock is associated with each block in the cache. A sequence number is maintained in the value block of the lock. When a block is updated, the sequence number in the lock is incremented and a copy is kept with the data block. If, subsequently, the block is to be accessed from the cache, the sequence number in the lock and the sequence number with the data block are compared. If they are different, then some other node modified the block and the block in the cache is invalid; thus, the block must be fetched from the disk.

4.3.5 Distributed Lock Manager

The *distributed lock manager* is the key component of the clustering architecture that synchronizes operations between nodes. It is used by other cluster software subproducts like the distributed file service and distributed job controller. Users can synchronize clustered applications by using $ENQ and $DEQ system calls. These calls are the same regardless of whether they are used on an independent VAX computer or on a VAXcluster. So, the distributed lock manager is an elegant extension of the standard lock manager.

The lock resources (locks) are maintained by various nodes on the cluster. A lock directory is maintained on some of the VAXes in the cluster. Logically, the directory is one entity. However, for performance reasons the lock directory may be distributed over a number of VAXes. The directory nodes maintain a list of all the lock resources used by all the nodes in the cluster. When a process on a node attempts to create a new lock resource, the local node sends the lock information to the directory node. The directory node notes the information and then allows one of the cluster nodes to manage the new lock resource. Normally, a request for a new lock resource from a process is managed by the VAX on which the process is running. This way, other processes on the same node accessing the lock do not incur any cluster overhead. When a process on a nonlocal node wants to access the lock, the node first queries the directory node to determine which node is actually managing the lock resource and then communicates with the resource manager node. Once the nonlocal node is using a lock resource on another node, further requests for the lock resource do not go through the directory node. Instead, the resource manager node is contacted directly.

If any node fails, the locks managed by it are released. Locking activity on the cluster is blocked temporarily, while the remaining nodes rebuild their lock tables and directory structure. Locking activity resumes after all the remaining nodes have synchronized their lock databases.

4.3.6 Distributed Job Controller

A *distributed job controller* manages clusterwide batch and print queues. For example, a printer attached to one VAX can be used by all the VAXes in the cluster with the DCL PRINT command. Batch queues can be set up to distribute jobs to VAXes that are least busy. The jobs can be submitted from any VAX.

The distributed job controller extensively uses DLM mentioned above for coordinating execution of jobs on the individual cluster members. The chapter on managing VAXclusters shows how to set up clusterwide queues.

4.3.7 Mass Storage Control Protocol Server

Disks that are local to a VAX are made available to other VAX nodes on the cluster by the *mass storage control protocol* (MSCP) server. Effectively the VAX acts as an intelligent disk controller for the other VAXes. The other VAXes access the disk as if the VAX was accessing locally connected disks. The MSCP server can serve disks over Ethernet, which makes the server particularly useful on local area VAXclusters that do not have HSCs. In fact, the common system disk on a LAVc is shared by other VAXes via the MSCP

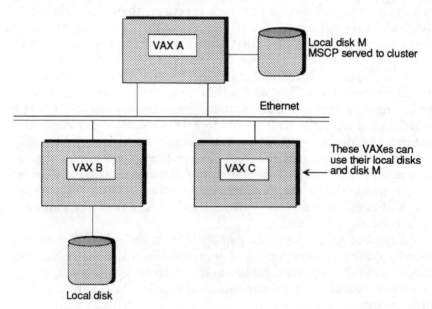

Figure 4.9 An MSCP-served disk.

server. Note that the VAX that is serving the disks must be powerful enough to handle disk I/O on behalf of all the VAXes it serves. Figure 4.9 shows how a disk is served.

4.4 QUORUMS AND VOTES

VAXes on a cluster share common resources like disks. If the cluster is not properly set up, the cluster may become partitioned into two or more logical clusters in certain situations, e.g., when VAXes leave or join the cluster. Such clusters use the same communications hardware and software. However, access to common resources is not coordinated among the multiple clusters. This can lead to *loss of system integrity*, and data on disks may be corrupted. (Personally, I believe that this is a flaw in the fundamental design of the cluster architecture. Why cannot shared resources be taken care of, irrespective of nodes entering or leaving the cluster, without the system manager having to take special precautions? But then I am just describing the design as it exists.)

The connection manager software is responsible for maintaining cluster integrity. The software on each node communicates with its counterpart on other nodes to ensure that all the nodes are part of only one cluster. To do this, it uses certain parameters set on each VAX. These are SYSGEN parameters that can be modified by the system manager. The key parameter is VOTES.

Each VAX on the cluster contributes a certain number of *votes* (given by the SYSGEN parameter VOTES). The connection manager uses this value from each VAX to determine a quorum for the cluster (as described below). If the cluster does not have a quorum, the cluster stops functioning (in industry parlance, the cluster hangs). The *quorum value*, calculated by the connection manager based on the votes of the member VAXes, is such that more than half the VAXes that are (or were) in the VAXcluster are still in the cluster. So if the VAXes that left the cluster try to form a cluster, the potentially new cluster will never have a quorum (since they are less than half the VAXes in the original cluster). If this is a bit confusing, complete reading this section and then read it again.

Here is how the scheme works. When a node boots, the connection manager reads a SYSGEN parameter called EXPECTED_VOTES. This parameter is an estimate of the sum of votes of all the VAXes on the cluster. The system manager has to create this estimated value. The parameter is used to estimate the cluster quorum, using the formula:

$$\text{Estimated quorum} = \frac{\text{expected\_votes}+ 2}{2}$$

The calculated quorum is calculated as follows:

$$\text{Calculated quorum} = \frac{(\text{sum of votes of cluster} + 2)}{2}$$

The quorum is assumed to be the maximum of the values of the current cluster quorum, estimated quorum, and calculated quorum. In addition, the quorum may increase but it can never decrease. Therefore, if a node drops out of the cluster, the quorum value remains the same. The cluster ceases to function if the sum of the votes of the cluster members fall below the quorum value.

Here is an example. Suppose there are 3 VAXes in a cluster each with 4 votes and an expected vote of 12 (predetermined SYSGEN parameters set by the system manager). Without the quorum scheme, the cluster can partition into two clusters; one with two VAXes in it and the other with one. We will see how this cannot happen.

Consider the events when the cluster is brought up one VAX at a time. With the quorum scheme, when the first VAX boots, the connection manager will determine that the estimated quorum = (12+2)/2 = 7. Since the number of votes on the cluster is 4, then the calculated quorum = (4+2)/2 = 3. Also, on a new cluster, the current cluster quorum = 0. The cluster will not operate since 7 (the maximum of 7, 3, and 0) is greater than the sum of votes, which is 4. The VAX just boots and displays a message at the console effectively saying that the VAX is waiting for a cluster state transition.

When the second VAX boots, the estimated quorum is (12+2)/2 = 7. The calculated quorum is (8+2)/2 = 5. The current cluster quorum is 0. The new quorum is 7 (which is the maximum of 7, 5, and 0). The sum of votes is 4+4 = 8. Since the sum of votes exceeds the quorum, the cluster will start operating with two VAXes. The current quorum becomes 7.

When the third VAX boots, the estimated quorum is again 7, the calculated quorum is (12+2)/2 = 7, and the current quorum is 7. The new quorum is 7 (which is the maximum of 7, 7, and 7). Again the sum of votes exceeds the quorum so the cluster now operates with three VAXes.

If a VAX fails, then the quorum is 7 and the sum of the votes of the remaining two VAXes is 8. Therefore, the two-VAX cluster will continue to operate. If a second VAX fails, then the quorum is 7, but now the sum of votes of the remaining VAXes (in this case one VAX only) is 4. The votes do not exceed the quorum so the single-VAX cluster will cease to function. This is fortunate because if the single-VAX cluster did operate, there is the danger of the other two VAXes coming up and forming their own cluster. The cluster can continue operating only if one more VAX joins the cluster.

4.5   QUORUM DISK

In a two-VAX cluster, using the quorum scheme outlined above, the cluster will cease to function if one VAX fails. To ensure that the remaining node continues to operate in case of a single VAX failure, a disk on the cluster is used as a quorum disk. The disk contributes votes to the cluster. So the quorum scheme now considers *two VAXes and a disk* as if they were three VAXes. A single VAX failure allows the cluster to operate, provided that the quorum disk is still part of the cluster. If the failed VAX boots, it cannot form a cluster with just itself as a cluster member since it does not have enough votes. Nor can the failed VAX use the quorum disk on its own since the disk is being used by the other VAX.

To specify that a quorum disk is being used, the SYSGEN parameter DISK_QUORUM is set to the name of the quorum disk. The votes contributed by the quorum disk is given by the SYSGEN parameter QDSKVOTES. The quorum disk cannot be shadowed or MSCP served.

4.6   ALLOCATION CLASS

Allocation classes allow the VAXcluster to automatically route disk and tape I/O traffic through other routes if one route fails. The disk and tape devices must have dual ports for connections to two nodes.

Consider the VAXcluster shown in Figure 4.10. The disk and tape drives are accessible via one of the two HSCs. One way to build redundancy would be to access the drives from HSC1 and check for I/O completion. If there is an error accessing the drives, the program can try the path to the drives through the other HSC. This is not convenient for programmers; if an HSC fails, the system should route disk and tape I/Os through the other HSC automatically. This is achieved through the use of allocation classes.

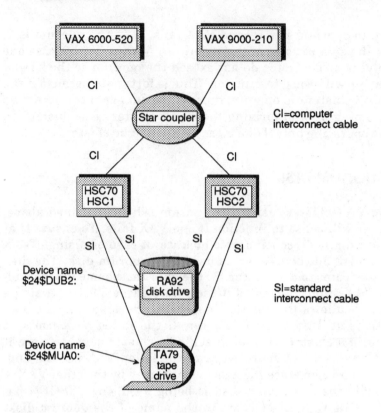

Figure 4.10 A VAXcluster with dual-ported disk and tape drives.

Suppose the two HSCs are called HSC1 and HSC2. Also suppose the disk drive is called DUB2:. If an allocation class is not used, the disk drive name on the VAXes would be HSC1$DUB2: and HSC2$DUB2:, depending on the HSC selected for I/O. To allow the system to choose a path automatically, both HSCs should be given the same allocation class, for example, 31. This can be done by the following command given at the HSC console:

```
HSC> SET ALLOCATE DISK 31
```

Now the disk drive will have one name on the VAXes, 31DUB2:. When the disk is accessed from a VAX, the VAX will send a request to one HSC to perform the I/O. If the HSC fails, the VAX will send the request to the second HSC.

Allocation classes can be from 0 through 255. 0 indicates no allocation class. They can also be used for MSCP-served disks that are dual ported from two VAXes. Consider Figure 4.11 where a

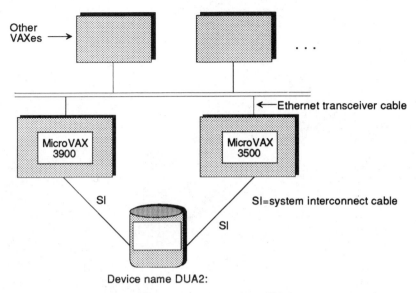

Figure 4.11 Dual-porting disks without using a HSC.

RA70 is "local" to two VAXes. The two VAXes have the SYSGEN parameter ALLOCLASS set to 39. The disk names must be the same from the two VAXes, e.g., DUA2:. The disk must be MSCP served to other VAXes by both VAXes. Other VAXes can access the drive by the name 39DUA2:. The actual path will be through VAX1 or VAX2, which is transparent to the user of the drive.

4.7 SUMMARY

VAXes within a cluster communicate cluster-related information to each other somewhat like VAXes communicating over a DECnet network. The cluster communications methodology is called system communication architecture. SCA runs on every node that is a cluster member. The chapter discussed the layers and functions of SCA. The CI-based and mixed-interconnect VAXclusters use unique hardware components for cluster communications. This hardware includes the CI cables, HSC, CI port controllers, and the star coupler. These components which are normally not used in nonclustered computers, were discussed. The QUORUM and VOTES technique for maintaining cluster integrity was discussed. The next chapter discusses issues of concern when installing a new VAXcluster.

5

Creating a VAXcluster

In this chapter we discuss how to install the operating system VAX/VMS for the VAXes in a VAXcluster. VAX/VMS has to be installed once for a homogeneous VAXcluster configuration. A *homogeneous cluster* is one that has a common system disk for all the VAXes in the cluster. For heterogeneous VAXclusters, the operating system has to be installed on each disk that will be used as a system disk by the VAXes on the cluster. We will emphasize homogeneous VAXclusters; the reader can extrapolate the discussions to heterogeneous clusters.

When VAX/VMS is first installed on a VAX, the operating system will run on the VAX on which it is installed (on a local system disk). To run the operating system on other VAXes in the cluster, the command file SYS$MANAGER:CLUSTER_CONFIG.COM is used to create entries on the system disk for each VAX that will be a cluster member. The command file can also be executed to make changes to the cluster configuration after a cluster environment is created.

5.1 VAXcluster HARDWARE SELECTION

The exact hardware requirements for setting up a VAXcluster environment depends on a number of factors like the nature of the applications, anticipated computing requirements, company policy, and budgetary constraints. Here we offer some comments that can aid in planning a VAXcluster configuration.

A local area VAXcluster (LAVc) uses Ethernet for cluster communications. VAXes can serve disks to other VAXes in the cluster. When the other VAXes access such served disks, the I/O instructions and data are communicated between the VAXes via Ethernet. In the case of CI-based VAXclusters, the cluster communications path is the *cluster interconnect* (CI) bus. The CI bus has a speed of 70 Mbits/sec; Ethernet has a theoretical speed of 10 Mbits/sec. Normally, CI-based VAXclusters have a much higher disk I/O throughput than local area VAXclusters. This is one of the key reasons for Ethernet-based VAXclusters being slow and requiring more careful planning.

The performance of CI-based VAXcluster consisting of two VAX 9000-210 computers, *hierarchical storage controllers* (HSCs) and an appropriate configuration of disks, tapes, printers and terminals is equivalent to that of most small mainframe computers with a mix of batch and on-line applications.

In general, the 3000 series VAXes are slower than the 6000 or 9000 series VAXes. The 3000 series VAXes can be part of a local area VAXcluster (or a mixed-interconnect VAXcluster). However, they cannot be part of a CI-based VAXcluster. The main reason is that the 3000 series VAXes are not powerful enough to handle the fast traffic on the CI bus. The 6000 and 9000 series VAXes can be part of any cluster. Moreover, the 6000 and 9000 series VAXes have faster I/O buses than the 3000 series VAXes. To complicate the issue, the VAX 4000 has a CPU as fast as that of a VAX 6410. However, the VAX 4000 has a Qbus and cannot be part of a CI-based VAXcluster. Normally, a CI-based cluster will provide a higher application throughput than a local area VAXcluster with the same number of VAXes.

Hierarchical storage controllers offload some of the disk and tape I/O burden from the host VAXes. HSCs can be connected to the CI bus but cannot be used on the Ethernet-based local area VAXclusters. I/O to HSC-connected disks from a VAX is direct, i.e., it does not go through another VAX. In a local area VAXcluster, a common disk is served by a VAX on the cluster, so all I/O to the disk, initiated by any VAX, must be processed by this VAX serving the disk.

A local area VAXcluster is suitable where a number of departments in a company have their own separate applications and the company wishes to "loosely" integrate these applications by offering a powerful central computer (or computers) and a central "disk farm" for occasionally used files and data archives. A mixed-interconnect VAXcluster can be used if the common computers and databases are to be heavily used.

Local area VAXclusters also make sense in a department where each user has many local files and requires a large amount of local computational power. In this case, common disks on the cluster, including the common system disk, can be attached to a powerful VAX like the MicroVAX 4000 while smaller VAXes like the MicroVAX 3100 (VAXstation) can be given to each user or maybe shared by two to three users. All the VAXes will be interconnected by Ethernet and each VAX will have some local disks so that access to the common disks is minimized. Such a configuration may be useful in a brokerage firm's trading floor where each stock trader has a VAX with local databases accessed for relatively static data. The local area VAXcluster will have a set of common VAXes that receive and process data from on-line data feeds and provide "interpreted" data to the traders.

5.2   A LOCAL AREA NETWORK VERSUS A LOCAL AREA VAXcluster

Ethernet is used to interconnect VAXes in a DECnet network. Ethernet is also used to form a local area VAXcluster. However, there are a few significant differences between the two types of logical interconnections:

1. A VAX on the LAVc can serve a disk that is local to the cluster. All the VAXes in the cluster can "see" the disk as a local disk. Of course, all I/O will be going through the VAX serving the disk. There is no mechanism in DECnet to form such common disks.

2. A common system disk can be used by all the VAXes in a LAVc. The disk can be connected to a VAX that serves the disk to the other VAXes in the cluster. Alternatively, the disk can have an integrated intelligent controller (like the RF71 ISE disks used with the DSSI bus), in which case the cluster VAXes can directly boot off the disk without going through another VAX. In contrast, VAXes on a DECnet network must have separate system disks.

3. Because LAVcs can have common disks, an integrated application, which can run off multiple VAXes in a cluster is easy to write. Such applications can be designed to tolerate failures of

VAXes and other hardware without having a major impact on the users. However, integrated applications running on multiple VAXes using DECnet require complex DECnet programming.

4. Satellite VAXes on a LAVc need not have any local disk storage, i.e., they can boot off a VAX serving its system disk. In contrast, at least one disk, the system disk, is required for every VAX on a DECnet network.

5. LAVcs have a greater communications overhead than VAXes interconnected by DECnet. Moreover, in a LAVc, disk I/O traffic to and from a cluster-common disk travels over the Ethernet. This can seriously degrade internode communications performance, even for VAXes not part of the LAVc that use the Ethernet for DECnet communications. Other protocol traffic (like LAT and TCP/IP) over the Ethernet will also be affected.

5.3 INSTALLING THE OPERATING SYSTEM VAX/VMS

As mentioned in previous chapters, each VAX on a cluster runs VAX/VMS. In a homogeneous cluster (which has a common system disk), the operating system is installed once on one of the disks. This disk must be available to other VAXes on the cluster. The disk is available to other VAXes on the cluster if it is on an HSC and all the VAXes can access the HSC. This is usually the case on a CI-based cluster. On local area VAXclusters, where Ethernet is the cluster communications medium, the system disk is usually local to a VAX. The operating system is installed from this VAX. The VAX, after booting, must serve the disk to the other VAXes so that all the VAXes can boot off this disk. This VAX is called the boot server. The next section describes how to serve local disks to other VAXes. On mixed-interconnect VAXclusters, the system disk is usually on an HSC. The VAXes that can directly access the HSC can boot off this disk. However, at least one of these VAXes must serve the system disk to the cluster so that the remaining VAXes can boot off the system disk (via one of the VAXes serving the disk).

Once a disk has been designated to be the system disk, VAX/VMS must be installed from a VAX that has this disk as a local disk. The installation procedure is the same as that which is used when installing the operating system on an independent VAX (nonclustered) computer. The first step of the installation is to load the core set of system files on the system disk from the distribution medium using the stand-alone BACKUP utility. Typically the distribution medium is standard nine-track ½ -inch spool tapes, TK50 cartridge tapes, or a CD-ROM. BACKUP can be loaded into memory by booting off the distribution medium. Though the boot procedure is simple, it varies for the different VAXes and distribution media.

Once the core VMS files are on disk, the VAX must be rebooted from the system disk. A set of questions will be asked. The relevant ones are shown here. Not all the questions may be asked; this depends on your response to previous questions.

- Will this node be a cluster member (Y/N)? The response should be "Y."

- What is the node's DECnet node name? Each node on the system will have a unique name. Here, the question is asking for the name of the VAX. An example is MAYUR.

- What is the node's DECnet node address? Each node on the system will have a unique address. Here, the question is asking for the address of the VAX. An example address is 4.121.

- Will the Ethernet be used for cluster communications (Y/N)? If this cluster will be a local area VAXcluster or a mixed-interconnect VAXcluster, the response should be "Y," otherwise it is "N."

- Enter this cluster's group number: This question is asked if Ethernet will be used for cluster communications. Multiple independent clusters can coexist on the same Ethernet network. The group number must be unique to each cluster so that the clusters do not affect each other. An example group number is 3.

- Enter this cluster's password: This question is asked if Ethernet will be used for cluster communications. The cluster password is used to authenticate VAXes attempting to join the cluster. An example password is TTCON.

- Will xxxxxx be a disk server (Y/N)? "xxxxxx" is the DECnet node name entered above. An example is MAYUR. If this VAX is going to serve local disks to other VAXes on the Ethernet, the response must be "Y." Disk serving is described in the next section.

- Will xxxxxx serve HSC disks (Y/N)? An HSC disk is local all to the VAXes connected to the CI bus. However, one of these VAXes may serve some of these disks to VAXes on the Ethernet but not on the CI bus. If this VAX is going to serve HSC disks, the response should be "Y."

- Enter a value for xxxxxx's ALLOCATION parameter: Allocation classes are described in the chapter on VAXcluster components and terminology. An example value is 4.

- Does this cluster contain a quorum disk? Quorum disks were described in the chapter on VAXcluster components and terminology. Typically, a quorum disk is used if the cluster consists of 2 VAXes. If your response is "Y," then the name of the quorum disk will also have to be entered.

This completes the installation procedure. The VAX will have to be rebooted from the system disk. The VAX is now configured as a cluster member. The next step will be to run the CLUSTER_CONFIG.COM procedure to set up the system disk for use by other VAXes in the cluster. This step is described later in this chapter.

5.4 SERVING LOCAL DISKS TO THE CLUSTER

When Ethernet is used for cluster communications, all VAXes in the cluster can access a VAX's local disks if the VAX serves this disk. Usually, MSCP (*mass storage control protocol*) is the protocol used to communicate between a VAX and a locally connected disk. Disks can be served to other VAXes if the local VAX is using MSCP for disk access; that is why served disks are also called MSCP-served disks.

Two SYSGEN parameters determine whether a local disk can be served by a VAX: MSCP_LOAD and MSCP_SERVE_ALL. If MSCP_LOAD is set to 1, then the MSCP server software is loaded when the VAX boots. If MSCP_SERVE_ALL is set to 1, then the VAX can serve its disks to the cluster. These parameters are set to the appropriate values when you answer the questions that are asked during the VAX/VMS installation or during a CLUSTER_CONFIG session.

The disk to be served must be mounted with the /CLUSTER qualifier. For example, suppose a VAX with DECnet name GARUDA has a local disk DUA3:, and the disk volume label is TESTDISK. The disk can be served to the cluster by:

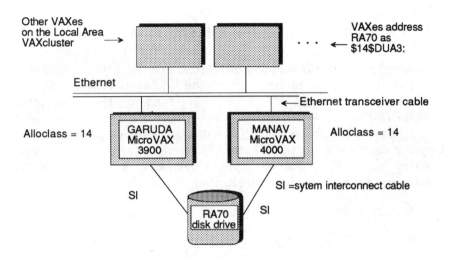

Figure 5.1 Dual-ported MSCP disk.

```
$ MOUNT /CLUSTER DUA3:  TESTDISK
```

All the VAXes can access the disk by the device name:

```
$GARUDA$DUA3:
```

Disk drives can be dual ported for redundancy. Consider the configuration shown in Figure 5.1. Here, DUA3: is dual ported from the VAXes GARUDA and MANAV. Both the VAXes must have the same value, e.g., 14, for the ALLOCLASS parameter in their SYSGEN parameter lists. No other VAXes on the cluster can have the same allocation class value. Also, the disk hardware must be set up so that each of the two VAXes access the disk by the same device name DUA3:. The following commands must be issued from each VAX:

```
$ SET DEVICE/DUAL_PORTED DUA3:
$ MOUNT /CLUSTER  DUA3:  TESTDISK
```

All the VAXes in the cluster can access the disk by using the device name:

```
$14$DUA3:
```

Failure of either GARUDA or MANAV will still allow all users to access the disk by the same name (14DUA3:).

5.5 LAYOUT OF THE COMMON SYSTEM DISK

Most system files, such as the operating system, drivers, compilers, and utilities, are common for all the VAXes in a homogeneous VAXcluster. The system disk will contain the directory [VMS$COMMON], which contains subdirectories for all these common system files. The system disk will also have one private directory for each node on the cluster. These directories have names starting with "SYS." For example, a system disk for a two-VAX cluster can have these three directories:

```
[VMS$COMMON]
[SYS0]
[SYS1]
```

where [SYS0] will be used by one VAX, [SYS1] will be used by the other VAX, and [VMS$COMMON] will be used by both the VAXes.

Figure 5.2 shows the layout of the common system disk for a two-VAX cluster. Refer to it when reading this section.

Logical names are normally used when referring to system directories. Two logical names (of interest here) are set up by the operating system when it is booted from each VAX: SYS$SPECIFIC and SYS$COMMON. These logical names point to the appropriate system directories for that VAX. Consider SYS$SPECIFIC. This logical name points to the VAX's private system directory. For one of the VAXes in the two-VAX cluster, SYS$SPECIFIC will be defined as:

```
SYS$SPECIFIC = DUA0:[SYS0.]
```

where DUA0: is the system disk. The other VAX will have the logical name defined as:

```
SYS$SPECIFIC = DUA0:[SYS1.]
```

So two users, one on each VAX, refering to files under SYS$SPECIFIC are actually referring to a separate set of files.

The SYS$COMMON logical name is used when referring to files on the system disk that are common to all the VAXes. SYS$COMMON is defined as:

```
SYS$COMMON = DUA0:[SYS0.SYSCOMMON.]    ! For one of the VAXes
```

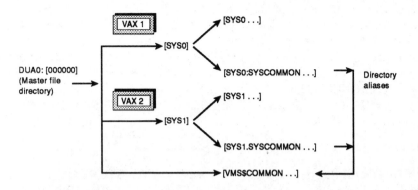

Figure 5.2 Directory structure on a common system disk for a two-VAX cluster.

```
SYS$COMMON = DUA0:[SYS1.SYSCOMMON.]    ! For the other VAX
```

As can be seen, SYS$COMMON is actually a subdirectory under SYS$SPECIFIC. The system disk is set up in such a way that the directories SYSCOMMON.DIR under each VAX's SYS$SPECIFIC are actually all pointing to VMS$COMMON.DIR. The [VMS$COMMON] directory is an alias for all of the VAX's SYS$COMMON directories. (Aliases can be created by the "$ SET FILE/ENTER" command.) Effectively, when a user on any VAX accesses a file using the logical device SYS$COMMON:, the user is accessing the common directory [VMS$COMMON]. The operating system could have been designed so that the logical name SYS$COMMON points directly to [VMS$COMMON], however, this technique is not used for reasons that will not be discussed here.

In summary, files under SYS$SPECIFIC are either private to the VAX or, if they refer to the subdirectory [SYSx.SYSCOMMON], are common to all the VAXes in the cluster. Files under SYS$COMMON are common to all the VAXes on the cluster.

Typically, users on a VAX like to refer to files in their private system directories, if they are present there. If the files are not present in the users' directories, they would like to access the equivalent files in the common system directories. To make this process convenient, the operating system defines a logical name called SYS$SYSROOT.

SYS$SYSROOT is a search list that points to SYS$SPECIFIC and SYS$COMMON:

```
SYS$SYSROOT = SYS$SPECIFIC,SYS$COMMON
```

When a file under the (logical) directory SYS$SYSROOT is accessed, VAX/VMS first searches for the file under SYS$SPECIFIC (for that particular VAX). If the file is not found, the system continues the search under SYS$COMMON. This is the basis for system file customizations on a homogeneous VAXcluster. Files for software products that can be run from any VAX on a cluster are installed under SYS$COMMON. The files are installed under SYS$SPECIFIC for a particular VAX only if the products are to be run from that VAX. A similar technique is used for files that cannot be common to the cluster.

For example, consider the file SYSUAF.DAT, which contains user profiles. (Actually, RIGHTSLIST.DAT and NETPROXY.DAT are also part of the user profile database. However, we will ignore these files in this discussion.) When a user attempts to log in, the operating system reads this file from the logical name (device) SYS$SYSTEM: to authenticate the user login. This logical name is actually a search list—SYS$SYSROOT:[SYSEXE],SYS$COMMON:[SYSEXE]. Here the directories SYS$SPECIFIC:[SYSEXE] and SYS$COMMON:[SYSEXE] are scanned in that order. The file SYSUAF.DAT can be common to the cluster, so the same login information can be used by a user when logging into the system from any VAX in a cluster. On the other hand, the system manager may wish to customize the cluster so that a certain set of users can log in from only one VAX on the cluster. To keep a common cluster file, the file should be present in SYS$COMMON:[SYSEXE] and not be present in SYS$SPECIFIC:[SYSEXE]. If each VAX is to have an independent user login profile, the file must be present in each of the VAXes SYS$SPECIFIC:[SYSEXE] directory. Note that if the file is present in SYS$SPECIFIC:[SYSEXE] for some of VAXes and also in the common directory SYS$COMMON:[SYSEXE], the operating system will use the one in SYS$SPECIFIC:[SYSEXE] for those VAXes that have the file there; for the other VAXes, the common file is used.

5.6   ADDING VAXES TO THE CLUSTER

Once the operating system is installed from a VAX on one of its local disks, the VAX can boot and be a cluster member. To allow other VAXes to boot from this disk and be cluster members, the CLUSTER_CONFIG.COM command procedure will have to be used to make entries for each of the other VAXes on the system disk. The command procedure is menu driven and resides in the SYS$MANAGER: directory. The ADD option should be selected to add a VAX to the cluster. A set of questions will be asked. The relevant one's are shown here. Not all of the questions may be asked; this depends on your response to the previous questions. Many of the questions are the same as those that are asked when installing the operating system as described above.

- What is the name of the new system root [SYS6]? The system root corresponds to SYS$SPECIFIC for the new VAX that is being added to the cluster. It should be unique to each cluster member. This command procedure will enter a number of files in the VAX's private directories. The default that is specified is usually an acceptable value.

- What is the VAX's hardware address? This question is asked if the new VAX is going to use Ethernet (rather than the CI bus) to boot from this VAX's local disk. The hardware address is required to be in this VAX's DECnet database. The address can be determined by entering the following command at the new VAX's console prompt:

```
>>> SHOW ETHERNET
```

The address is used when the new VAX asks for a boot. It consists of 12 hex digits (48 bits), e.g., 08-00-2B-2F-C9-B6.

Once the questions have been answered, the new VAX can be booted into the cluster. For a MicroVAX 3000 series booting over Ethernet the following command can be entered at the console prompt:

```
>>> BOOT XQA0        !Boot over Ethernet
```

Note that the SYSGEN parameters, VOTES, EXPECTED_VOTES, and QDSKVOTES may have to be changed on each VAX to reflect the entry of a new VAX in the cluster. See the chapter on VAXcluster components and terminology for a description of these parameters.

In summary, when a VAX is added to the cluster, a private directory is created for the VAX on the system disk and a set of node-specific files are entered in the private directory and subdirectories. When the new VAX asks for a boot, the VAX specifies its private system root directory in register R3. A core part of the operating system is loaded from the common bootstrap area, which then loads the complete operating system by reading the node-specific files from the private root directory (and its subdirectories) and other files from the common system directories.

5.7 CLUSTER_CONFIG.COM

This command procedure was mentioned in the previous section. It is used to configure or change the configuration of a cluster. Its options are:

ADD

Add a new node's root directory on the common cluster disk and perform some other operations so that a new node can be booted into the cluster.

REMOVE

Deletes a node's root directory and the files within it.

CHANGE

Change some cluster options on the local node. Examples of options are ALLOCATION class value and enabling the local VAX as an MSCP disk server.

CREATE

Duplicate the system disk and remove all system roots from the new disk.

5.8 SATELLITE NODES

On a local area VAXcluster, one powerful VAX can have a common system disk that is accessed by a number of cluster member VAXes for booting over Ethernet. These VAXes are called satellites. Satellites do not require any local disk. The CLUSTER_CONFIG procedure can be used to define the satellites on the common disk of the VAX serving the common disk. The satellite VAX is booted by a command like

```
>>> BOOT XQA0        !Boot over Ethernet
```

entered on the console terminal of the satellite.

A local area VAXcluster with most VAXes having little or no local disk storage (diskless workstations) can be cost effective in environments where the CPUs are heavily used while disk I/O is minimally used. Such VAXclusters could be used in stock market analysis, computer-aided design, and engineering applications where computers are used for string manipulations and number crunching.

5.9 VAXcluster PASSWORD

Security is a special concern on local area VAXclusters. Ethernet is the cluster communications medium on a local area VAXclusters. The same Ethernet can be used by nonclustered VAXes. A user owning, for example, a VAXstation (on the Ethernet) which is not supposed to be part of the cluster, can attempt to join the cluster by configuring the VAXstation to masquerade as a cluster member. Security on the cluster may be compromised if arbitrary VAXes join the cluster. For example, a user of an illegal cluster member that has all of the privileges can modify files on a disk served to all cluster members. There must be a mechanism to prevent VAXes that are not supposed to be cluster members from joining the cluster.

The VAXcluster password is such a mechanism. The password is asked for during CLUSTER_CONFIG.COM execution. An encrypted form of the password is stored in SYS$SYSTEM:CLUSTER_AUTHORIZE.DAT. When a VAX which will have a separate system disk is being set up to be a cluster member by CLUSTER_CONFIG.COM, the same password must be specified. When a VAX attempts to join an already formed cluster, the cluster password from the VAX's CLUSTER_AUTHORIZE.DAT file is compared with that of the cluster. If there is a mismatch, the VAX is not allowed to join the cluster. Of course, if a VAX boots off the common system disk, the VAX must have been declared on the disk by CLUSTER_CONFIG.COM, so it cannot be considered an intruder.

If a VAX has a local system disk and is being set up to join the cluster, the proper cluster password must be specified during execution of CLUSTER_CONFIG.COM so that the SYS$SYSTEM:CLUSTER_AUTHORIZE.DAT file on the local system disk contains a valid encrypted cluster password.

5.10 SUMMARY

This chapter mentioned the parameters to be specified when installing VAX/VMS on a VAX that will be a cluster member and discussed how disks local to a VAX can be served to other VAXes on the cluster. The layout of the system disk was described. The CLUSTER_CONFIG.COM procedure for adding, removing, and changing cluster configurations was discussed. The next chapter discusses issues of concern to a VAXcluster system manager.

6

Managing a VAXcluster

Setting up a VAXcluster for daily operations requires more planning than setting up independent (nonclustered) VAX/VMS systems because there are more ways to customize clustered systems than nonclustered systems. This chapter discusses various VAXcluster management issues that are of interest to system managers.

6.1 CREATING USER PROFILES (THE AUTHORIZE DATABASE)

Each user has a profile on the VAXcluster. The profile contains information about the user such as user name, password, and resource quotas. These profiles are maintained by the AUTHORIZE utility. The profile database consists of three files:

SYSUAF.DAT   !contains user names, resource quotas, etc.

NETPROXY.DAT   !contains DECnet login information for users
                    !logging over the network.

RIGHTSLIST.DAT   !contains rights identifiers and related
                    !information.

These files are normally in SYS$SYSTEM:. Since SYS$SYSTEM is a search list that searches for files first in a VAX's node-specific directory SYS$SPECIFIC:[SYSEXE] and then in the common directory SYS$COMMON:[SYSEXE], the set of files can be placed in the common directory if the user can access the cluster from any VAX. If a separate profile is to be maintained for a particular VAX in the cluster, the three files mentioned above must be stored in that VAX's SYS$SPECIFIC:[SYSEXE] directory.

Note that the AUTHORIZE utility by default searches SYS$SYSTEM for the profile files. However, this can be changed by using system-level logical names as in:

```
$ DEFINE/SYSTEM SYSUAF    "DUA0:[SPECIAL]SYSUAF.DAT"
$ DEFINE/SYSTEM NETPROXY  "DUA0:[SPECIAL]NETPROXY.DAT"
$ DEFINE/SYSTEM RIGHTSLIST "DUA0:[SPECIAL]RIGHTSLIST.DAT"
```

Because logical names are specific to a VAX, the logical names can be different for the VAXes on the cluster, effectively allowing a separate profile to be maintained for each VAX.

6.2 CREATING BATCH AND PRINT JOB QUEUES

A set of commands which make up a job can be run from a terminal. Batch queues are created on a system to allow users to submit jobs for execution in background when no intervention is required during execution. Print queues control output to printers when multiple users access common printers. On a VAXcluster, the queues are managed by the software component called *distributed job controller*.

Each VAX on a VAXcluster can have its own (batch and print job) queues. Jobs can be submitted to these queues from the VAX on which the queues are defined. A VAXcluster can have clusterwide queues called *generic queues*. The main use of such queues is resource sharing and load balancing.

Consider Figure 6.1, which shows a three-VAX cluster with two printers. VAX A can print jobs on any of the three printers. VAX B and VAX C can print on either of the two LP29 printers. The advantages of this setup are:

- *Load balancing.* The two LP29s can belong to a generic queue. If a job is submitted to the queue, it will be printed on one of the two LP29s, depending on which one is available.

- *Resource sharing.* VAX C does not have any printer, yet it can print jobs on printers attached to other VAXes.

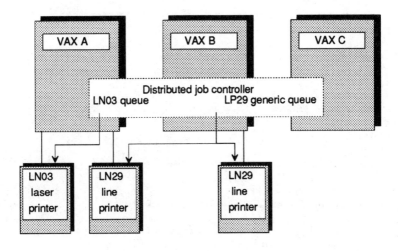

Figure 6.1 Clusterwide print queues.

Figure 6.2 shows a command file that can be run from all the VAXes to set up a generic queue for the two LP29 printers. The device names are assumed to be LP29:. Note that the queue file JBCSYSQUE.BAT must be a common file for all the VAXes.

Actually, there is no difference between the usage of a local queue and usage of a clusterwide queue. Users on any VAX on the cluster can use even local queues on other VAXes.

Batch queues can be created for clusterwide access. Again, a batch queue is defined on each VAX on the cluster that will run clusterwide batch jobs. A generic queue is then defined that points to the individual batch queues. Jobs submitted to the generic queue are run on a VAX that has a clusterwide batch queue and the smallest load. The load is the ratio of executing jobs to job_limit for the batch queue. Figure 6.3 shows how a clusterwide generic batch queue can be created on a three-VAX cluster. Only VAX B and VAX C will run batch jobs.

Note that all batch jobs perform an implicit login. If a job is submitted by a user on VAX A for execution on the batch queue on VAX B (or VAX C), the user must have a valid account on VAX B (or VAX C). If a clusterwide-common AUTHORIZATION file (SYSUAF.DAT) is being used, this should not pose any problem. Also note that the job running on VAX B will be using system logical names, disk names, etc. as defined on VAX B (or VAX C) and not on VAX A.

```
$! This command file
$! 1. creates a queue, VAXA_QUEUE_LP29 on node VAXA
$! 2. creates a queue, VAXB_QUEUE_LP29 on node VAXB
$! 3. creates a clusterwide generic queue,
$!    CLUSTER_QUEUE_LP29
$!
$! A user on VAX on the cluster can print a job
$! by a command like:
$! PRINT/QUEUE=CLUSTER_QUEUE_LP29  myjob.cob
$!
$! The output will be sent to either one of the two LP29s.
$!
$! Start the queue manager
$ start/queue/manager sys$common:jbcsysque.dat
$!
$! Find out what node this command file is executing on.
$ node = F$getsyi("nodename")
$!
$! Create and start the two printer queues on their
$! own nodes only.
$ if node .eqs. "VAXA" then -
    initialize/queue/start/on=VAXA::LP29:  VAXA_QUEUE_LP29
$ if node .eqs. "VAXB" then -
    initialize/queue/start/on=VAXB::LP29:  VAXB_QUEUE_LP29
$!
$! Define a clusterwide generic queue for the two printers
$ start/queue/generic=(VAXA_QUEUE_LP29,VAXB_QUEUE_LP29) -
    CLUSTER_QUEUE_LP29
```

Figure 6.2 A queue startup command files for the two LP29 printers.

6.3   VAXcluster ALIAS FOR DECnet COMMUNICATIONS

A VAXcluster can be part of a DECnet network consisting of independent systems and multiple VAXclusters. Each VAX node on the network, including each one of the VAXcluster members, has a DECnet node name and address. A user on any node who performs a DECnet operation on a VAXcluster node specifies the node's DECnet name (or address) when establishing a connection with the node. For example, a user can copy a file from his or her VAX node onto a common disk on the VAXcluster by specifying one of the nodes in the VAXcluster in the output file specification:

```
$ COPY MYFILE.DAT  CNODE1::DISK$CLUS:[TEST]MYFILE.DAT
```

Here, CNODE1 is the DECnet name of one of the VAXes in the cluster. The node name of any VAX in the cluster could have been

```
$! This command file
$! 1. creates a queue, VAXB_BATCH on node VAXB
$! 2. creates a queue, VAXC_BATCH on node VAXC
$! 3. creates a clusterwide generic queue,
$!    CLUSTER_BATCH
$!
$! The batch queue on VAXB can run three jobs
$! simultaneously; the queue on VAXC can run one
$! job at a time. This was set up that way because
$! VAXC is a slower computer than VAXB.
$!
$! A user on the VAX on the cluster can run a
$! batch job by:
$! SUBMIT/QUEUE=CLUSTER_BATCH  my_job.com
$!
$! The job will execute on either VAXB or VAXC
$! (even if the job is submitted from VAXA).
$!
$! Start the queue manager
$ start/queue/manager sys$common:jbcsysque.dat
$!
$! Find out what node this command file is executing on
$ node = F$getsyi("nodename")
$!
$! Create and start the two batch queues on their
$! own nodes only.
$ if node .eqs. "VAXB" then -
    initialize/queue/batch/start/job_limit=3 -
    /on=VAXB::  VAXB_BATCH
$ if node .eqs. "VAXC" then -
    initialize/queue/batch/start/job_limit=1 -
    /on=VAXC::  VAXC_BATCH
$!
$! Define a clusterwide generic batch queue.
$ start/queue/batch/generic=(VAXA_BATCH,VAXB_BATCH) -
    CLUSTER_BATCH
```

Figure 6.3 A batch queue startup command file.

specified. From DECnet's perspective, each node in the cluster is treated like any other node on the cluster, although in many other ways the cluster operates as one homogeneous system.

A more elegant and fault-tolerant approach is to define a common DECnet name for each of the nodes in the VAXcluster. (This name is in addition to the individual node names.) This way the VAXcluster appears more homogeneous on the DECnet network. Users need not know the individual node names when establishing

DECnet links with a VAX on the cluster; the link will be established with one node on the cluster as determined by DECnet. Also, users do not need to know if some nodes in the cluster are not operational; a DECnet connection will be established with one of the operating VAXcluster nodes. Such a common DECnet node name is called an *alias node name*. An alias node address is a common DECnet address for the nodes in a VAXcluster. An alias node identifier is either the alias node name or the alias node address for a VAXcluster.

NCP is the *network control program* for setting network parameters. To establish a common node name for a VAXcluster, the common node name and a corresponding node address must be declared in the DECnet NCP database of each of the nodes:

```
NCP> DEFINE NODE 3.14 NAME CLUS1
```

After that, the node name is declared to be the cluster alias by issuing in each of the node's DECnet NCP database a command like the one which follows:

```
NCP> DEFINE EXECUTOR ALIAS NODE CLUS1
```

Note that each VAX will then have an individual node name and a common VAXcluster node name. A user on any VAX on the DECnet network can now copy the file to a common VAXcluster disk by writing:

```
$ COPY MYFILE.DAT  CLUS1::DISK$CLUS:[TEST]MYFILE.DAT
```

Some comments on the VAXcluster alias node identifier:

- If a user needs to establish a DECnet link with a specific VAX in the VAXcluster, the VAX's DECnet node name (or node address) not the alias identifier must be used. For example, a VAX on the cluster may have a local disk not directly accessible to the other VAXes in the cluster. A user on the network can access files on this disk by specifying the VAX's node name; specifying the VAXcluster node name may cause a DECnet link to be established with another VAX in the cluster that does not have access to the disk.

- While a VAXcluster can have one alias node identifier, individual VAXes need not have this alias defined in their NCP database. This way, the cluster can be customized so that certain VAXes do not accept DECnet connection requests when it is for the alias node.

■ When establishing a DECnet link with the alias node, no as-
sumption should be made as to which specific VAXcluster node
the connection will be established with. If multiple DECnet
links are to be established with one node on the cluster, the
cluster alias cannot be used.

6.4 CLUSTER-COMMON LAT SERVICE

A typical VAXcluster is accessed from terminals connected to
terminal servers on a Ethernet network. The LAT (*local area
transport)* protocol is used for communications between a VAX and
the terminal server. Users connect to a service offered by the
VAXes on the network. Normally, each VAX offers a service with
the same name as its DECnet node name. For example, a VAX in a
cluster with DECnet address NODE1 can offer a LAT service
called NODE1:

```
$ MCR LATCP CREATE SERVICE NODE1
```

Multiple services can be offered a VAX. Users can connect to the
VAX by using any one service name. Users can connect to other
VAXes by using their correponding service names. Each VAX in a
cluster can offer the same service. In this case, users connecting to
the service will be connected to one of the VAXes in the cluster.
This technique has two advantages:

1. A user connecting to a common service is connected to the least
   busy VAX in the service. This way the VAXes in the cluster are
   load balanced. The LAT software determines the load on a VAX by
   using various parameters such as CPU speed, number of users and
   processes on the computer, and the static service rating of the
   node.

2. Users identify the cluster by one common service name. They
   need not be aware of individual VAXes in the cluster. Moreover, if some of the cluster VAXes are temporarily inoperational, the user is connected to one of the other nodes without
   being aware of the fact that some VAXes are not operational.

6.5 THE VAXcluster CONSOLE SYSTEM

Many VAXcluster sites have one operator console per VAX. The
VAXcluster console system (VCS) allows a cluster to be monitored

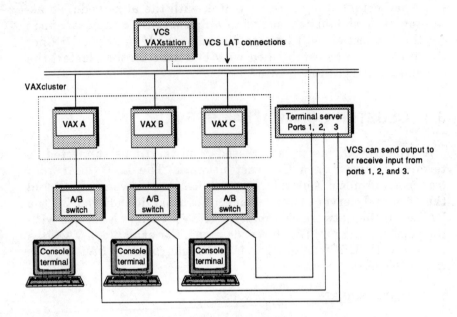

Figure 6.4 A VAX console system (VCS) configuration.

and controlled from a single terminal. In fact, VCS can act as a console for independent VAX computers also. The VCS software can run on any VAX computer. However, a dedicated VAXstation is usually used as the central console.

Figure 6.4 shows how VCS could be set up for a three-VAX cluster. Basically, all I/O to and from the normal computer consoles is handled by the VAXstation console. The two-way switch on each computer console connection allows console I/O traffic from the system to be directed either to the local console or to the VAXstation. Each window on the VAXstation can display messages from one VAX. The advantages of using VCS are:

1. VCS provides a central point of control for the VAXcluster.

2. The VCS software logs console messages on disk.

3. The VCS software provides a pictorial view of the cluster. Messages from the nodes can be associated with icons on the screen. If excessive hardware errors are being generated by a

particular component, the color of the corresponding icon changes to reflect the problem.

4. Multiple windows on a VAXstation can allow simultaneous display of console messages from a number of VAXes.

VCS can also be used to control VAXes that are not in a cluster. The VCS software manual describes how to set up and customize the console subsystem.

One disadvantage of VCS is that a failure of the VCS VAX can lead to loss of critical console messages from all the nodes of the VAXcluster. It should be noted that the messages to the console are logged in the file SYS$MANAGER:OPERATOR.LOG on each VAX but not messages to OPA0: which are printed on the console terminal.

6.6 CUSTOMIZING SYSTARTUP_V5.COM

In a homogeneous VAXcluster, the same system start-up command file is executed by each node when the node boots. Normally, this file is SYS$MANAGER:SYSTARTUP_V5.COM. In many cases, different start-up commands have to be executed for different VAXes in the cluster. The F$GETSYI DCL lexical function can be used within the start-up file to determine on what node the file is being executed and what command or commands should be correspondingly executed. Here is DCL code for a system start-up file that will mount a local disk on each of two nodes in a VAXcluster.

```
$ this_node = F$GETSYI("NODENAME")
$ if this_node .eqs. "NODE1"
$ then MOUNT/SYSTEM DUA4: DISK$USERS1
$ else if this_node .eqs. "NODE2"
$     then MOUNT/SYSTEM DUA4: DISK$USERS2
$     else write sys$output -
       "System booting from unknown node"
$     endif
$ endif
```

6.7 THE HIERARCHICAL STORAGE CONTROLLER

The *hierarchical storage controller* (HSC) is an intelligent disk and tape I/O controller ("hierarchical" is a misnomer). It is a computer by itself, which boots off a local floppy disk drive and has its own console. Tape and disk devices are connected to controller cards within the HSC. These controllers are called requestors. There are separate requestor cards for tape and disk drives. A single requestor card can control multiple devices. When shadowed disks are being used, each member disk should be on a separate requestor card so that a card failure cannot halt logical disk I/O.

When a CTRL/Y is entered on the console, the HSC displays the prompt:

```
HSC>
```

Various commands can be entered to monitor and control the HSC's operation. The following commands will display the tape and disk drives connected to the HSC:

```
HSC> SHOW DISKS
HSC> SHOW TAPES
HSC> SHOW REQUESTORS
```

Figures 6.5, 6.6, and 6.7 show sample outputs of these commands. The SHOW DISK display indicates:

- There are five disk drives connected to the HSC.

- There are two shadow sets, units 0 and 20. Shadow set 0 has two physical drives—units 0 and 1. Shadow set 20 has two physical drives—units 20 and 23.

- The requestor card and port number to which each drive is connected. Typically, a requestor has ports for four drives.

The SHOW TAPES display indicates:

- There are three tape drives connected to the HSC.

- Drive unit 0 is available for use. Units 2 and 3 are being used by a VAX on the VAXcluster.

- All three drives are connected to requestor card 2.

The SHOW REQUESTOR display indicates:

- The HSC has seven requestor cards with slots for two more if more devices need to be connected to the HSC.

- The "k.sti" requestor is used for controlling tape drives. Up to four drives can be connected to the requestor.

```
HSC>  SHOW  DISK
 Unit      Req      Port      Type          Status              Version
   0        3        0    RA90      On-line, HostAccess MC - 10,   HV - 17
                          Member of Shadow Unit 0
   1        4        0    RA90      On-line, HostAccess MC - 10,   HV - 17
                          Member of Shadow Unit 0
   2        3        2    RA70      On-line, HostAccess MC - 78,   HV - 7
  20        6        3    RA90      On-line, HostAccess MC - 13,   HV - 17
                          Member of Shadow Unit 20
  23        7        3    RA90      On-line, HostAccess MC - 13,   HV - 17
                          Member of Shadow Unit 20
   0     (virtual)        RA90      On-line, HostAccess Member Count:   2
  20     (virtual)        RA90      On-line, HostAccess Member Count:   2
The Disk NOHOST_ACCESS Table is empty.
SETSHO-I Program Exit
```

Figure 6.5 Displaying disk drives on a HSC.

- The "k.sdi" requestors are used for controlling disk drives. Up to four drives can be connected to each of the requestors.

- Requestors 0 and 1 handle I/O to and from VAXes on the CI bus.

Dual HSCs can be used for hardware redundancy as explained elsewhere in this book. These HSCs must have the same allocation class value, which can be set by commands like the following that must be issued on both HSCs:

```
HSC>  SHOW  TAPE
 Unit      Req      Port      Type          Status              Version
   0        2        0    TA79      Available, HostAccess   DMC - 0, DHV - 0
                          Density: GCR 6250     FMC - 5, FHV - 255
   2        2        3    TA81      On-line, HostAccess DMC - 0, DHV - 0
                          Density: PE 1600      FMC - 84, FHV - 11
   3        2        3    TA81      On-line, HostAccess DMC - 0, DHV - 0
                          Density: PE 1600      FMC - 84, FHV - 11
The Tape NOHOST_ACCESS Table is empty.
SETSHO-I Program Exit
```

Figure 6.6 Displaying tape drives on a HSC.

```
HSC> SHOW REQUESTOR
      Req         Status         Type          Version      Next Microcode
                                                                 Load
0 Enabled    P.ioj
1 Enabled    K.ci       MC- 54 DS- 2    Pila-65 K.pli-5
2 Enabled    K.sti      MC- 27 DS- 2
3 Enabled    K.sdi      MC- 42 DS- 3
4 Enabled    K.sdi      MC- 42 DS- 3
5 Enabled    K.sdi      MC- 42 DS- 3
6 Enabled    K.sdi      MC-  7 DS- 4
7 Enabled    K.sdi      MC-  7 DS- 4
8 Enabled    Empty
9 Enabled    Empty
```

Figure 6.7 Displaying the controller cards on a HSC.

```
HSC> RUN SETSHO
SETSHO> SET ALLOCATION DISK 21
SETSHO> SET ALLOCATION TAPE 21
```

The HSC can also be used to back up disks to other disks or tape. This is a local backup, which does not require host intervention. The backup utility is invoked by a command like:

```
HSC> RUN LB:BACKUP
```

where LB: is a floppy drive on the HSC.

Backup is performed sequentially, starting at physical block 0 and continuing until the last block is copied over. The backup is different from the usual system backup, which is a logical backup of files based on the Files-11 on-disk file structure. The main advantages of a HSC backup are:

- The HSC backup backs up every block, so it always takes about the same time for a backup. The time it takes for a standard VMS BACKUP depends on the number of files on the disk. If the disk is nearly full of files, the HSC backup is faster than the standard VMS backup.

- The backup does not require the use of any VAXes.

The disadvantages are:

■   If there are not many files on the disk, the VMS backup is
    faster than the HSC backup since the VMS backup performs a
    file backup while the HSC backup performs a block-by-block
    backup of the complete disk.

■   Files cannot be selectively restored from a HSC backup; only
    complete disks can be restored.

■   The VAXcluster has separate consoles for the VAXes and the
    HSC; therefore, the operator will have to use the HSC console
    for the backup.

Also, disk logs cannot be created when performing HSC backups.

6.7.1   Accessing the HSC from a VAX

The commands described in the previous section were issued on
the HSC console. The commands can be issued from a VAX on the
cluster by loading the FYDRIVER and issuing SET HOST for the
HSC. Here is a sample session:

```
$ MCR SYSGEN
SYSGEN> CONNECT FYA0: /DRIVER=SYS$LOADABLE_IMAGES:FYDRIVER.EXE /NOADAPTER
$ SET HOST /HSC HSCTOP
%HSCPAD-I-LOCPROGEXE, Local program executing - type ^\ to exit, ^Y for prompt
HSC> SHOW DISKS
    .
    .
    .
HSC > <Control and \>
%HSCPAD-S-END, Control returned to node GANESH
$
```

6.8   THE DCL SHOW CLUSTER COMMAND

The SHOW CLUSTER command can be used to display or log
information from the clustering software's internal databases. The
information is particularly useful to system managers for studying
cluster activity. The command is discussed in detail in the SHOW
CLUSTER manual, which is part of the *system management* series
of manuals.

```
View of Cluster from system ID 1036  node: GARUDA        31-JUN-1990 13:40:08

    +---------------------------------------+---------------+
    |                 SYSTEMS               |    MEMBERS    |
    +-----------------+---------------------+---------------+
    |      NODE       |       SOFTWARE      |     STATUS    |
    +-----------------+---------------------+---------------+
    |     GARUDA      |       VMS V5.2      |     MEMBER    |
    |     HSC00A      |       HSC V395      |               |
    |     GANESH      |       VMS V5.2      |     MEMBER    |
    |     HSC00B      |       HSC V395      |               |
    +-----------------+---------------------+---------------+
```

Figure 6.8 Output of the basic $ SHOW CLUSTER command.

6.8.1   Using the Command

The basic form of the command is:

```
$ SHOW CLUSTER
```

The output in Figure 6.8 shows that the cluster has two VAXes, GARUDA and GANESH, running VAX/VMS version 5.2. The cluster has two HSCs running the HSC software version 3.95. This output is derived from the *systems communications services* (SCS) databases within the cluster-internal databases on the different nodes.

The SHOW CLUSTER/CONTINUOUS command displays the same information, but the command also refreshes the display every 15 sec with the latest information. When this form of the command is used, various subcommands can be entered. When the first character of the subcommand is entered, the following prompt is displayed:

```
Command>
```

Example subcommands are:

```
Command> ADD CLUSTER
Command> REMOVE LAST_TRANSITION
```

The screen would look as in Figure 6.9 after these two subcommands are issued.

```
View of Cluster from system ID 1036  node: GANESH      1-JUL-1990 15:02:21

     +---------------------------------------+ --------------- +
     |                   SYSTEMS             |     MEMBERS     |
     +----------------- + -----------------+--------------- +
     |       NODE       |     SOFTWARE     |     STATUS      |
     +----------------- + -----------------+--------------- +
     |      GARUDA      |     VMS V5.2     |     MEMBER      |
     |      HSC00A      |     HSC V395     |                 |
     |      GANESH      |     VMS V5.2     |     MEMBER      |
     |      HSC00B      |     HSC V395     |                 |
     +----------------- + ----------------- +--------------- +


  +------------------------------------------------------------------- +
  |                              CLUSTER                               |
  +--------- +---------- +--------- +-------- +--------- +---------- +
  | CL_EXP   CL_QUORUM  CL_VOTES   QF_VOTE  CL_MEMBERS   FORMED      |
  +--------- +---------- +--------- +-------- +--------- +---------- +
  |   12         7         12        YES         2      28-JUN-90 11:36|
  +--------- +---------- +--------- +-------- +--------- +---------- +
```

Figure 6.9 Another SHOW CLUSTER output.

The CLUSTER display shows general information on the cluster. The fields are EXPECTED_VOTES, QUORUM, whether a quorum disk is in use, MEMBERS, and cluster formation date and time. The cluster actually has two VAXes and a quorum disk, each having a VOTE of 4.

6.8.2 Output of the SHOW CLUSTER Command

Each entity of data displayed by the SHOW CLUSTER command is called a field. Related fields are displayed together as a class. Related classes of data are displayed in one window. There are three types of windows:

- System communications services window
- CLUSTER window
- LOCAL_PORTS window

The classes in each window are shown in Figure 6.10

Window	Class	Type of Information
SCS	CIRCUITS	Virtual circuits between the nodes. An example field is NUM_CON, which shows the number of connections from a node to other nodes.
	CONNECTIONS	The logical connections between the computers over the virtual circuits. An example field is the process on the node that has established the connection.
	COUNTERS	Cumulative totals of traffic over the connections. An example field is DGS_SENT, which shows the number of datagrams sent by applications over the connection.
	CREDITS	Send and receive credit counts for each node.
	MEMBERS	Node specific cluster parameters. An example field is VOTES, which shows the number of votes contributed by each node to the cluster
	SYSTEMS	Nodes in the cluster. An example field is node name.
CLUSTER	CLUSTER	Overall cluster parameters. An example field is LAST_TRANSITION which show the last time a node left or joined the cluster.
LOCAL_PORTS	ERRORS	Number of errors on each port. An example field is NUM_ERRORS, which shows the number of errors on the port since the computer was booted.
	LOCAL_PORTS	Data on each of the cluster ports on the node from which this command is being executed. An example field is CMDS, which shows the total number of datagrams, messages, and port commands queued for transmission.

Figure 6.10 Classes of output from the SHOW CLUSTER command.

When the SHOW CLUSTER/CONTINUOUS command is used, all the fields in a class can be displayed by using a subcommand like:

```
Command> ADD CONNECTIONS/ALL
```

Fields within a class can be selectively displayed by a command like:

```
Command> ADD FORMED
```

If a particular form of the display is required whenever the SHOW CLUSTER command is used, an initialization file can be created. The file must be pointed to by the logical SHOW_CLUSTER$INIT, as done in the following command:

```
$ DEFINE SHOW_CLUSTER$INIT my_cluster_initialization.com
```

The file should contain all the subcommands required. Then, whenever the SHOW CLUSTER command is used, the subcommands in the initialization file are executed before the first screen is displayed.

6.8.3 Sending the SHOW CLUSTER Output to a File

The SHOW CLUSTER command can be used to collect output in a file for later analysis, for example, by a program. An example command is:

```
$ SHOW CLUSTER/CONTINUOUS /BEGINNING=21-JUL-1990:09:30 -
    /ENDING=21-JUL-1990:17:00/OUTPUT=CLUS.LOG
```

Here, the output will be from 9:30 a.m. to 5:00 p.m. on July 21, 1990. The initialization file, if the SHOW_CLUSTER$INIT logical name is defined, will be executed before data collection begins.

6.9 THE MONITOR UTILITY

The MONITOR utility is a tool for collecting and displaying system performance statistics. It contains some options for displaying cluster-oriented information.

The MONITOR CLUSTER command output is shown in Figure 6.11. The output shows clusterwide CPU, memory, disk, and locking information. All the rates are per second. The output shows that VAX GARUDA has a CPU utilization of 16 percent, has used 13 percent of the available main memory and has a lock ENQing, DEQing, and conversion rate of 95/sec. A more detailed output can be created by using $ MONITOR CLUSTER /ALL.

The MONITOR SCS output is shown in Figure 6.12. The output shows the rate at which memory is mapped for block transfer. Block transfers are used for copying blocks of disk data from one node to another, and the display shows the rate of this activity. A

```
Statistic: Current        VAX/VMS Monitor Utility        2-JUN-1990 16:15:46
                            CLUSTER STATISTICS
                 CPU                    |              MEMORY
CPU Busy        0   25  50  75  100 |%Memory In Use    0   25  50  75  100
                +----+---+---+---+   |                  +----+---+---+---+
GANESH        50|* * * * * * * *     | GARUDA         13|* *
GARUDA        16|* * *               | GANESH          5|*
                |                     |                  |
                |                     |                  |
                |                     |                  |
                |                     |                  |
                |                     |                  |
-------------------------------------+-------------------------------------
                 DISK                  |              LOCK
                                       |
I/O Oper Rate   0   25  50  75  100 |Tot ENQ/DEQ Rate  0   25  50  75  100
                +----+---+---+---+   |                  +----+---+---+---+
$1$DUS1:      18|* * *               | GARUDA         95|* * *
$1$DUS3:      14|* *                 | GANESH         57|* *
$1$DUS21:     14|* *                 |                  |
$1$DUS3:       2|                    |                  |
$1$DUA5:       1|                    |                  |
                |                     |                  |
```

Figure 6.11 The $MONITOR CLUSTER command output.

```
                        VAX/VMS Monitor Utility
                            SCS STATISTICS
                           on node GANESH
                        2-JUN-1990 17:09:59


   Kbytes Map Rate           CUR         AVE         MIN         MAX

   GANESH                    0.00        0.00        0.00        0.00

   HSC002                   42.85      291.98       23.41      667.48

   GARUDA                    0.00        0.00        0.00        0.00

   HSC003                    0.00        0.00        0.00        0.00
```

Figure 6.12 The $MONITOR SCS command output.

```
                         VAX/VMS Monitor Utility
                  DISTRIBUTED LOCK MANAGEMENT STATISTICS
                             on node GANESH
                          2-JUN-1990 17:17:56

                                  CUR       AVE       MIN       MAX
New ENQ Rate          (Local)     2.12      2.10      1.33      2.33
                   (Incoming)     0.00      0.00      0.00      0.00
                   (Outgoing)     2.00      2.00      2.00      2.00
Converted ENQ Rate    (Local)     0.00      0.00      0.00      0.00
                   (Incoming)     1.11      8.44      1.10      9.67
                   (Outgoing)     0.00      0.00      0.00      0.00
DEQ Rate              (Local)     2.33      2.33      2.33      2.33
                   (Incoming)     0.00      0.00      0.00      0.00
                   (Outgoing)     2.00      2.00      2.00      2.00
Blocking AST Rate     (Local)     0.00      0.00      0.00      0.00
                   (Incoming)     0.00      0.00      0.00      0.00
                   (Outgoing)     0.00      0.00      0.00      0.00
Dir Functn Rate    (Incoming)     7.66      7.66      7.66      7.66
                   (Outgoing)     2.66      2.66      2.66      2.66
Deadlock Message Rate             0.00      0.00      0.00      0.00
```

Figure 6.13 The $MONITOR DLOCK command output.

more detailed output can be created by using $ MONITOR SCS /ALL.

The MONITOR DLOCK command output is shown in Figure 6.13. The statistics are on the distributed lock manager's activity. For monitoring cluster locking activity, the "incoming" and "outgoing" fields rather than the "local" fields should be analyzed.

6.10   VAX PERFORMANCE ANALYZER

VPA (*VAX performance analyzer*) is a layered product that has to be purchased separately from DEC. VPA collects and logs system parameters that can be used to generate reports on system behavior. VPA will give suggestions on what to do to gain better performance from the system. The latter feature is based on *artificial intelligence* techniques. VPA is an expert system with a rule database. The collected data is checked against the rules, and if the rules are being violated, VPA displays suggestions stored with the rules. VPA does not provide continuous displays of system usage. On a VAXcluster, VPA generates a report consisting of subreports for each node in the cluster followed by a subreport on the cluster.

There are two phases to using VPA for generating reports and graphs. The first phase is data collection. The command to start data collection is:

```
$ @SYS$STARTUP:VPA$STARTUP.COM
```

This command file creates a process, VPA_DC, which records various system parameters and resource usage metrics.

A report can be generated by a command like:

```
$ ADVISE/REPORT=(PERFORMANCE_EVALUATION, ANALYZE)
```

The time interval covered is the start of day or start of data collection until the present time. The report gives a summary of CPU and MEMORY and I/O utilization, and, perhaps most importantly, the report also includes suggestions on what can be done to improve performance. Figure 6.14 shows a sample report. The output has been edited to reduce the number of pages printed.

Some interesting features of VPA are:

- When generating reports, the ANALYSIS option invokes a rule database that is used by VPA to make suggestions on how to improve performance. For example, there may be excessive page faulting because some users require more memory than their *working set extent* allows. VPA will give the names of users whose WSEXTENT parameter in the authorization file should be increased.

- The rule database can be customized to report potential combination of events, depending on the site requirements.

- The report displays hotfiles. These files are accessed the most and can be made contiguous or placed on separate disks to improve peformance.

- VPA can be used to generate reports on a group of users called a workload. So, for example, if four users are working on a particular application, VPA could be set up to produce reports on system usage by the application.

- VPA can be used for capacity planning and modeling. For example, suppose a system has four applications divided into four workloads for VPA. Suppose the number of users of an application is

```
VPA V2.0 Analysis                    CLUSTER                      PAGE 30
        Report                Friday 1JUN90  09:00 to 17:00
```

CONCLUSION 6.

Queues existed on disks which have a low I/O operation rate and a low throughput. This suggests a delay caused by either path contention, shadow set rebuilding, or partial hardware failure.

Suggested Remedies:

1.   Shadowset members are being copied, the delay is normal.

2.   If you have an HSC, make sure that the device ports (K.sdi channels) on the HSCs are evenly loaded and free from contention.

3.   Check for path delays caused by contention for shared resources such as controllers and channels.

4.   Excessive head seeks (possibly aggravated by file fragmentation) may also slow the response time. So, refresh the disk if fragmentation is apparent.

5.   Use $SHOW ERROR to make sure device errors are not generated on the noted volumes and their ports, controllers, and channels.

Volume name(s)	Number of Samples
APPDISK	2

CONDITIONS

1. CW_DISK_IO_RATE .LT. DISK_IO_RATE_THRESHOLD

2. CW_DISK_THRUPUT_RATE .LT. DISK_THRUPUT_RATE_THRESHOLD

3. DISK_QUEUE_AT_SERVER .GE. 1.50 .OR. (MAXIMUM_DISK_QUEUE .GE. 1.50 .AND. DISK_IS_SERVED .EQ. 0.00)

4. CW_DISK_CHANNEL_RATIO .GE. 75.00 .OR. CW_DISK_CHANNEL_IO .LT. DISK_IO_RATE_THRESHOLD

5. OCCURRENCES .GE. 1

EVIDENCE

```
VPA V2.0 Analysis                    CLUSTER                      PAGE 31
            Report              Friday 1JUN90  09:00 to 17:00
```

Disk Volume	Avg I/O per sec	Avg Que	IO Sz Pages	Src Node	Serv Node	Shadw Rbld Flag	Time of Occurr	Hottest File
APPDISK	21.85	1.54	32.8	GARUDA	HSC002		1-JUN 11:16:00	TRANSACTION . DAT
APPDISK	22.12	2.57	53.0	GARUDA	HSC002		1-JUN 16:02:00	SYSLOG .OLB;1

Figure 6.14 An edited VPA report on a two-VAX cluster.

```
VPA V2.0 Analysis                  CLUSTER                    PAGE 32
       Report           Friday 1JUN90  09:00 to 17:00

CONCLUSION 7.
```

The LOCK MANAGER has detected deadlocks occurring. Deadlocks are
caused by applications that use the LOCK MANAGER and incorrectly handle their locking activity. Deadlocks can cause cluster-wide performance degradation because deadlock searches are initiated at
high priority and are not necessarily restricted to any one node.

Try to isolate the application(s) that cause the deadlocks and redesign the locking algorithms.

Total number of samples supporting this conclusion: 2

CONDITIONS

1. DEADLOCK_FIND_RATE .GT. 0.00

2. OCCURRENCES .GE. 1

EVIDENCE

Node on which deadlock was found	Number of deadlocks per second	Time oc occurrence
GARUDA	0.02	1-JUN 10:32:39
GARUDA	0.05	1-JUN 10:34:00

```
VPA V2.0 Analysis                  CLUSTER                    PAGE 33
       Report           Friday 1JUN90  09:00 to 17:00

CONCLUSION 8.
```

The LOCK MANAGER has detected deadlock searches occurring with no
deadlock finds. It is likely that applications are holding restrictive locks for too much time (thereby triggering a deadlock search).
Deadlock searches can cause cluster-wide performance degradation.
Deadlock searches are initiated at high priority and are not necessarily restricted to any one node.

Try to isolate the application(s) which cause the deadlock searches
and redesign the locking algorithms to hold restrictive locks for as
short a time as possible.

In addition, consider increasing the SYSGEN parameter PIXSCAN on
cluster nodes where processes executing below DEFPRI may be acquiring locks on critical resources and cannot release them until a priority boost is provided. Also note that increasing PIXSCAN too much
may also increase the interrupt stack CPU mode (system overhead).

Figure 6.14 (*Continued*)

To increase it, include an ADD_PIXSCAN entry to MODPARAMS.DAT and run AUTOGEN.

Total number of samples supporting this conclusion: 44

CONDITIONS

1. DEADLOCK_FIND_RATE .EQ. 0.00
2. DEADLOCK_SEARCH_RATE .GT. 0.10
3. SYSGEN_DEADLOCK_WAIT .GT. 5.00
4. OCCURRENCES .GE. 1

EVIDENCE

Node on which deadlock was found	Number of deadlocks per second	DEADLOCK-WAIT	Time oc occurrence
GANESH	0.12	20	1-JUN 09:04:00
GANESH	0.13	20	1-JUN 09:46:00

```
+-----------------------------------------------------------------+
| The following table gives a summary of the average amount of lock |
| traffic per second in the cluster                               |
+-----------------------------------------------------------------+
```

Node	Local ENQ/CVT/DEQ	Incoming ENQ/CVT/DEQ	Outgoing ENQ/CVT/DEQ	Waiting locks	LOCK-DIRWT	Deadlk find	Deadlock search
GARUDA	9/12/ 9	3/ 1/ 3	2/ 1/ 2	0	0	0	0
GANESH	15/29/15	2/ 1/ 2	2/ 1/ 2	1	0	0	0
Total	23/41/23	4/ 2/ 4	4/ 2/ 4	1		0	0

VPA V2.0 Analysis Report   CLUSTER   PAGE 35
          Friday 1JUN90 09:00 to 17:00

```
+-----------------------------------------------------------------+
| CI, NI, and Adapter Statistics   (values are rates/sec )        |
+-----------------------------------------------------------------+
```

Circuit	Node	Component	Datagrams	Messages	Disk Operation	Disk KB Thruput	Block Transfers KB Thruput
PAA0		**total**	0.0	83.3	28.0	385.1	379.2
PEA0		**total**	0.0	0.0	0.0	0.0	0.0
PAA0	GARUDA	CIBCA-B	0.0	53.3	13.3	131.8	126.3
PEA0	GARUDA	NI	0.0	0.0	0.0	0.0	0.0
PAA0	GANESH	CIBCA-B	0.0	56.1	14.6	253.3	253.0
PEA0	GANESH	NI	0.0	0.0	0.0	0.0	0.0
PAA0	HSC002		0.0	56.9	28.0	385.1	378.7
PAA0	HSC003		0.0	0.2	0.0	0.0	0.4

Figure 6.14 (*Continued*)

```
+----------------------------------------------------------------------+
| The following table gives a summary of all disk activity as seen     |
| by the indicated node. An "*" for service node indicates that more   |
| than one was detected                                                |
+----------------------------------------------------------------------+
```

Disk Volume	Avg IO per sec	Avg Que	Avg Kb/s	IOsz in pgs	Source Node	Service Node	% Busy	% IO Read	% IO Split	Type	# of Samples
APPDISK	(1DUS10)										
	8.36	0.42	106.5	25.5		HSC002		70	17	RA90	
	8.91	0.45	113.6	25.5	GARUDA		27.42	70	17		225
	0.01	0.00	0.0	3.8	GANESH		0.03	86	20		240
DISKDB	(1DUS5)										
	10.42	0.53	239.6	46.0		HSC002		82	0	RA90	
	0.00	0.00	0.0	0.0	GARUDA		0.00	0	0		225
	10.42	0.53	239.6	46.0	GANESH		51.52	82	0 0		240

VPA V2.0 Analysis   CLUSTER   PAGE 37
    Report   Friday 1JUN90 09:00 to 17:00

```
+----------------------------------------------------------------------+
| The following table gives the summary of all tape activity as seen   |
|    by the indicated node.                                            |
+----------------------------------------------------------------------+
```

				Metrics during active records		
Cluster Node	Tape Controller	Unit	Percent of records with activity	I/Os /sec	Errors/sec	Device Type
GARUDA	MUA	0	0.00	0.00	0.00	TA79
	MUA	6	0.00	0.00	0.00	TK70
GANESH	MUA	0	99.17	0.07	0.00	TA79
	MUA	6	0.00	0.00	0.00	TK70

```
+----------------------------------------------------------------------+
| The following table gives a summary of the top 10 hottest files      |
| as collected for disks with a queue higher than the /HOT_QUEUE value.|
+----------------------------------------------------------------------+
```

	IO Rate		%	%	Peak		
Dev	Totl	Peak	Ops Rds	Ops Spl	Time DD-HH:MM	Rec Cnt	File spec
1DUS10							
	8.21	8.21	0	50	1-14:08	1	[USER1.DAT]TRANSACTION.DAT;3
	7.54	15.40	1	7	1-13:06	6	[USER1.LIB]SYSLOG.OLB;1
	6.04	9.16	1	0	1-11:20	13	[APPL.LOG]MAIN_TREE.EXE;31
1DUS5							
	12.40	17.40	84	0	1-12:58	167	[MAINT.LOG]ERR.LOG;2
	0.04	0.09	100	0	1-09:52	7	[MATH.TREE]LOGARITHMS.DAT;2

Figure 6.14 (*Continued*)

```
+------------------------------------------------------------------+
| The following table gives a summary of the average CPU and MEMORY |
| utilization, and average number of jobs by type for each node.    |
+------------------------------------------------------------------+
```

```
                                    -----Average number of jobs-----
                  CPU     MEM      --------------------------------
  Node    Type   % Util  %Util   Interactive   Batch    Network    System
  ------  -----  ------- ------- ------------  --------  ---------  --------
GARUDA   6420    19.3    21.0       25.68       0.00      0.38      16.00
GANESH   6420    11.8    39.5       51.79       0.29      0.06      14.00
```

VPA V2.0 Analysis   CLUSTER   PAGE 37
     Report   Friday 1JUN90 09:00 to 17:00

```
+------------------------------------------------------------------+
|The following chart presents the status of each node in the cluster |
| over the report time period.                                       |
| Legend:                                                            |
| "." Node up with data                                              |
| "n" Node up (no data wanted)                                       |
| "N" Node up (no data found)                                        |
| "d" Node down                                                      |
| "u" unknown (and no data)                                          |
+------------------------------------------------------------------+
```

```
GARUDA |............dddn...........................................
GANESH |...........................................................
       |---------10------11-------12------13------14------15-----16--
```

       Each Column represents approximately 7 minutes starting from
          1-JUN 09:00:00 to   1-JUN 17:00:00

VPA V2.0 Analysis   CLUSTER   PAGE 37
     Report   Friday 1JUN90 09:00 to 17:00

```
*------------------------------------------------------*
|                    Legend:                           |
|    a = GARUDA                  b = GANESH             |
|    o = Cluster Utilization                            |
|        (Scaled by CPU speed)                          |
*------------------------------------------------------*
```

Figure 6.14 (*Continued*)

```
                    COMBINED CPU USAGE CHART
                    --------------------------
% utilized
 100    !
  95    !
  90    !
  85    !
  80    !
  75    !
  70    !
  65    !
  60    !
  55    !
  50    !
  45    !
  40    !
  35    !                  aa                    aaaa
  30    !              a..aaa             aa    ....a
  25    !             a......aa       aaa..aaa..000a        aaa a
  20    !            a..00000..a      aaa.0.0....00..b000000a...a.aaaa
  15    !b     bbb0000bb0000b..bb000a  a00000b0.0000.bbb      bb00000000000aaaaaa
  10    !0000000000    00   b bb  bbb00000      bbbbbbb         bbbb   000000
   5    !aaa      aa
   0    !
        !------10------11------12------13------14------15------16---
        Each Column represents approximately 7 minutes starting from
        1-JUN 09:00:00 to  1-JUN 17:00:00.   An "N" indicates NO DATA.


User Command: ADVISE/REPORT=(PERFORMANCE,ANALYSIS) -
              /BEG=1-JUN-1990 09:00:00.0/END=1-JUN-1990 17:00:00.00
```

Figure 6.14 (*Continued*)

likely to go up by 75 percent. VPA can be used to generate a
report on the likely system performance when there are more
users for a particular application. VPA can be used to model
system performance to see the likely effect of, for example, a
new disk and more memory added to the system.

6.10.1 Data Collector

The collector is started by the command:

```
@SYS$STARTUP:VPA$STARTUP.COM.
```

The collector stores the data in the directory VPA$DATABASE: with a file name like VPA$GARUDA_1990JAN14.CPD where GARUDA is the node name of the VAX. A new file is created for each new day. A file, VPA$SCHEDULE.DAT, also exists in VPA$DATABASE. This file determines when, during the week, data should be recorded and on what nodes (if the VAX is part of a cluster). The schedule file contents can be listed by:

```
$ ADVISE/COLLECT/INQUIRE=SCHEDULE
```

```
SCHEDULE FILE     _____ |   |_____
                  |   Node names       |   |Weekly Schedule for ALL nodes
Beginning         |   ---------------- |   |-----------------------------
   19-JAN-1990    |   GARUDA           |   | Sunday      0-24
Ending            |   GANESH           |   | Monday      0-24
   1-JAN-2010     |                    |   | Tuesday     0-24
Hot Files         |                    |   | Wednesday   0-24
   0.33           |                    |   | Thursday    0-24
Delete after      |                    |   | Friday      0-24
   60 Days        |                    |   | Saturday    0-24
```

The schedule file shows that data is collected for 24 hours a day, 7 days a week. Data is collected on two nodes of the cluster: GARUDA and GANESH. The schedule can be modified by commands like:

```
$ADVISE/COLLECT/SCHEDULE=(MONDAY=(9-17), NOSUNDAY)
$ADVISE/COLLECT/SCHEDULE/NODE_NAME=MAYUR
```

There is no need to stop the collection process explicitly since reports can be generated up to the current moment in time without having to stop the collector process (which is VPA_DC). The command to stop the collector is:

```
$ ADVISE/COLLECT/STOP
```

6.10.2 Generating VPA Reports

A typical command to generate a report is:

```
$ ADVISE/REPORT=(PERFORMANCE_EVALUATION, ANALYSIS) -
     /BEGINNING=29-JUL-1990:09:00 /ENDING=29-JUL-1990:17:00
```

The ANALYSIS option causes VPA to analyze the performance data and suggests what could be done to improve performance.

An example performance report was shown previously. Some examples of qualifiers are:

/BEGINNING=29-SEP-1989:09:00	Shows report start date and time
/ENDING=29-SEP-1989:17:00	Shows report end date and time
/IMAGE=applman	Generates image residency time histogram for the specified image.
/OUTPUT=vpa.report	Creates an output file rather than displays the report on the terminal.

The performance reports include statistics on CI, NI, adaptors, disks, tapes, hotfiles, locks, CPU modes, memory pool, processes, and SCS usage on clusters. The report output is quite self-documented.

6.10.3 Advice from VPA and the Knowledge Database

VPA is a rule-based expert system. It has a set of built-in rules that can be augmented by user-defined rules. Each rule has a five-character rule name. A rule file is also called a knowledge database. The file VPA$EXAMPLES:VPA$KB.VPR shows most elements of a rule file. Here is an example rule:

```
Rule R0030 Domain Summary
     Average_IRPs_InUse - SYSGEN_IRPCOUNT .ge. SYSGEN_IRPCOUNT *
             td_pool_expansion_ratio;
     Evidence =
          SYSGEN_IRPCOUNT
          SYSGEN_IRPCOUNTV
          Average_IRPs_InUse
          Maximum_IRPs_InUse;
```

Conclusion

> The average number of IRPs in use during the report period ex-
> ceeded the number of preallocated IRPs by at least 40%. This
> means that there was unnecessary VMS overhead to build addi-
> tional IRPs from available physical memory. If more IRPs were
> preallocated at boot time, less overhead would have been in-
> curred. However, be careful (in scarce memory situations) not
> to use more memory than is necessary.

> Use the AUTOGEN feedback mechanism to automatically increase
> the SYSGEN parameter IRPCOUNT. After successive uses of AUTO-
> GEN, the AUTOGEN feedback mechanism provides the system with
> ample IRPs.

Endrule

When generating a report with the ANALYSIS option, as in the sample command,

```
$ ADVISE/REPORT=(ANALYSIS, PERFORMANCE_EVALUATION)
```

VPA analyses the collected data against the built-in knowledge database (and the user-specified database, if one is specified). Rules meeting specified conditions get fired and the analysis is written out. Here is a typical page from the analysis report. The output is based on the rule shown above:

VPA V2.0 Analysis   GANESH (VAX 6420)   PAGE 4
        Report   Friday 29SEP89 00:00 to 12:50
CONCLUSION 3.   {R0030}

> The average number of IRPs in use during the report period ex-
> ceeded the number of preallocated IRPs by at least 40%. This
> means that there was unnecessary VMS overhead to build addi-
> tional IRPs from available physical memory. If more IRPs were
> preallocated at boot time, less overhead would have been in-
> curred. However, be careful (in scarce memory situations) not
> to use more memory than is necessary.

> Use the AUTOGEN feedback mechanism to automatically increase
> the SYSGEN parameter IRPCOUNT. After successive uses of AUTO-
> GEN, the AUTOGEN feedback mechanism provides the system with
> ample IRPs.

CONDITIONS

   1. AVERAGE_IRPS_INUSE - SYSGEN_IRPCOUNT .GE.   SYSGEN_IRPCOUNT * 0.40
EVIDENCE

```
Current IRPCOUNT.......1607
Current IRPCOUNTV......4821
Avg IRPs in use........2841
Max IRPs in use.......2973
```

To create your own knowledge database, use the file **VPA$EX-AMPLES:VPA$KB.VPR** as a template, creating, for example, **NEWRULES.VPR** in your directory. The rule file must be built by VPA:

```
$ ADVISE/BUILD  NEWRULES.VPR
```

The output will be a compiled knowledge base, **NEWRULES.KB.** This file can be specified for analysis by:

```
$ ADVISE/REPORT=ANALYSIS/RULES=NEWRULES.KB
```

VPA will first scan the factory rules database and then this rules database during the analysis phase.

6.10.4 Workloads: System Usage Reports Based on User Groups

The VPA reports discussed up to now are based on the three types of images on the system: interactive, batch, and network. When a number of independent applications are running on the system, reports based on resource utilization by individual applications may be more insightful. To do this, it is necessary to create workloads of users or program images. For example, a system may be running two major applications, word processing and an on-line banking application. The ADVISE/EDIT command can be used to create two user workloads:

```
$ ADVISE/EDIT
VPA-EDIT> ADD /WORKLOAD WORD_PROCESSING /USERNAMES=(ZITTO,PAUL,BROWN)
VPA-EDIT> ADD /WORKLOAD  BANKING        /USERNAMES=(BLY,SHAH)
```

The commands modifies a parameter file **VPA$DATA-BASE:VPA$PARAMS.DAT.** Workloads have to be grouped into families for reporting purposes. The two workloads created can be placed in a family called **MY_VAX_USERS** as shown here:

```
VPA-EDIT > ADD/FAMILY MY_VAX_USERS /WORKLOAD=(WORD_PROCESSING,BANKING)
```

Now, a report can be created that contains subreports on the two workloads:

```
$ ADVISE/REPORT=PERFORMANCE_EVALUATION/CLASSIFY_BY=US-
ERGROUPS=MY_VAX_USERS
```

There are two types of workload families: user group and transaction. The user group would normally contain workloads with groups of users in each workload, while the transaction workloads contain related set of images, such as all of the compiler images. Reporting is similar for the two types of families; the major difference is that the transaction family report also contains an implicit workload, Z-Frequency, which consists of all images that were not terminated during the reporting period. Here are some predefined families and workloads.

```
VPA-EDIT> SHOW/FAMILY *

     Workload Family                    Workload Member(s)
-------------------   -----------------------------------------------

MODEL_USERGROUPS      SYSTEM_USER, OPERATOR, DECnet
MODEL_TRANSACTIONS    SYSMAN, UTILITIES, EDITORS, COMPILES, NETWORK
EACH_USER             EACH_USER

VPA-EDIT> SHOW/WORKLOAD *

        Workload                       Selection Criteria
-------------------   -----------------------------------------------

SYSTEM_USER           Match is based on EITHER username or imagename.
          Usernames: SYSTEM
OPERATOR              Match is based on EITHER username or imagename.
          Usernames: OPERATOR
DECnet                Match is based on EITHER username or imagename.
          Usernames: DECnet
SYSMAN                Match is based on EITHER username or imagename.
         Imagenames: APLIC, ARRAY, BACKUP, BUTTON, CALC$MAIN,
                     CALNOTICE, CDU, CLEAR, CLR, CMS, CONFIGURE, CSP,
                     DBMMON, DIRFMT, DQS$SMB, DTM$FILTER, DVI2LN3,
                     EPC$REGIS, ERRFMT, EVL, HISTORY, HOSTCHECK,
                     INSTALL, JOBCTL, MONITOR, NOTICE, OPCOM, PAVN,
                     PLOT, PROCNAM, PROTS, QUEMAN, SCHED, SETRIGHTS,
                     START-UP, SYSGEN, VAXSIM, VPA$ADVISOR, VPA$BLDKB,
                     VPA$DC_V5, VPA$GRAPH, VPA$VME, VPA$EDIT, WHAT,
                     WHYBOOT
```

COMPILES	Match is based on EITHER username or imagename.
Imagenames:	BASIC, BLISS32, LINK, MACRO32, VAXC
UTILITIES	Match is based on EITHER username or imagename.
Imagenames:	COPY, CREATE, CREATEFDL, DELETE, DIFF, DIRECTORY, DTM, ENOTES, LNGSPLCOR, LOGINOUT, LPS$SMB, MAIL, NOTES$MAIN, NOTES$SERVER, PHONE, QUOTE_V0, RECOLOR, RENAME, REPLY, RUNOFF, SEARCH, SET, SETP0, SHOW, SHWCLSTR, SORTMERGE, SSU, SUBMIT, TYPE, VMSHELP, VTXPAD
EDITORS	Match is based on EITHER username or imagename.
Imagenames:	EDT, EMACS, EMACSSHR, LSEDIT, SED, TECO32, TEX, TPU
NETWORK	Match is based on EITHER username or imagename.
Imagenames:	ELF, FAL, FILESERV, LATCP, LATSYM, NCP, NETACP, NETSERVER, NM$DAEMON, NM$QUEMAN, NML, REMACP, RTPAD
EACH_USER	Unique Workload for each Username

6.10.5 Capacity Planning and Modeling

Capacity planning is the process of planning for future growth in system usage. Modeling allows you to study system performance on a hypothetical system. Typically, the current system is used as a basis and then VPA is asked to generate performance reports, assuming that the workload has increased by, for example, 50 percent or a new disk drive has been added.

The two steps for modeling are:

1. Create a model file that contains a description of the current hardware, workload, and performance parameters:

```
$ ADVISE/MODEL/BUILD  ENVIRON.MDL
/BEG=9:00/END=17:00
```

2. The command has qualifiers similar to that used with the /REPORT qualifier. The model file will have performance information based on the specified time interval.

3. Use the model file to generate a prediction report. This report will show system performance assuming workloads 25, 50, 75, and 100 percent of current workload:

```
$ ADVISE/MODEL/REPORT=PREDICTION  ENVIRON.MDL
```

Here is a prediction report:

```
VPA V2.0 Modeling              Model: ENVIRON              PAGE 1
  Prediction Report
                                  load increase (%)
                                  ----------------
                       0%      25%      50%      75%      100%     1928%
                    (baseline)                                   (critical)
-----------------------------------------------------------------------
Most Utilized Components

System     Name
Component  or Id.
-------    --------
   CPU     GANESH     4.4%     5.5%     6.7%     7.8%     8.9%     90.0%
   DISK    VMSRL5     1.7%     2.2%     2.6%     3.0%     3.5%     35.1%
   DISK    USER1DISK  0.7%     0.9%     1.1%     1.3%     1.5%     15.1%
   DISK    BANK2PRIM  0.5%     0.6%     0.8%     0.9%     1.0%     10.4%

CPU Utilizations

Type       Name or Id.
--------   --------
  6400     GANESH     4.4%     5.5%     6.7%     7.8%     8.9%     90.0%

Workload Throughputs

(transactions/sec)
----------------
   Z-FREQUENCY:    0.008    0.010    0.012    0.015    0.017    0.168
       SYSMAN:     0.001    0.001    0.002    0.002    0.002    0.020
    UTILITIES:     0.019    0.024    0.029    0.033    0.038    0.385
      EDITORS:     0.003    0.004    0.004    0.005    0.006    0.059
     COMPILES:     0.001    0.001    0.001    0.001    0.002    0.016
      NETWORK:     0.000    0.000    0.000    0.000    0.000    0.004
        Other:     0.003    0.003    0.004    0.005    0.006    0.057

Workload Response Times

(seconds)
----------------------
   Z-FREQUENCY:    1.44     1.53     1.61     1.69     1.77     7.17
       SYSMAN:    28.49    29.36    30.22    31.05    31.87    87.82
    UTILITIES:     1.54     1.62     1.69     1.76     1.83     6.42
      EDITORS:     3.73     3.97     4.21     4.43     4.66    19.55
     COMPILES:    21.02    21.99    22.94    23.86    24.76    85.57
      NETWORK:     2.59     2.75     2.92     3.07     3.23    13.44
        Other:     9.23     9.61     9.99    10.36    10.72    35.09
```

```
NOTE: "Critical" load is the load at which the utilization of one or more
components in the system exceeds 90%
ADVISE/MODEL/REPORT=PREDICTION ENVIRON.MDL
```

The report shows that if the current use is increased by 1928 percent, one component, the CPU in this case, will exceed 90 percent utilization. Clearly, the system is not heavily utilized, and no hardware upgrade is required in the near future. A more detailed report can be printed by using the qualifier /REPORT=ALL.

The model file can be modified to create hypothetical hardware environments (say, adding two new disks) or workload characteristics. The file can then be used to generate modeling reports. Another method to generate "what if " reports is to use the /PROMPT qualifier:

```
$ ADVISE/MODEL/PROMPT ENVIRON.MDL
```

The potential workload can be entered from the terminal as a percentage change from the current workload. The report will reflect the specified workload.

6.11   THE SYSMAN UTILITY

The SYSMAN utility allows the system manager to issue commands on the current node for execution on any node on a DECnet network or VAXcluster. The utility is convenient for managing a number of computers without explicitly logging into them.

To run SYSMAN, the commands are:

```
$ SYSMAN:==$SYSMAN
$ SYSMAN
SYSMAN>
```

DCL commands can be preceded by the word DO:

```
SYSMAN> DO DIR [SHAH]
```

SYSMAN communicates with the process SMISERVER on other VAXes when executing DCL commands. To execute commands on another node, e.g., GANGES, use:

```
SYSMAN> SET ENVIRONMENT/NODE=GANGES
Remote Password:
```

```
%SYSMAN-I-ENV, current command environment:
       Individual nodes: GANGES
       At least one node is not in local cluster
       Username SHAH       will be used on nonlocal nodes

SYSMAN> DO SHOW SYSTEM

%SYSMAN-I-OUTPUT, command execution on node GANGES
VAX/VMS V5.2 on node GANGES 29-JUL-1990 18:53:12.46 Uptime 1 03:47:59
```

Pid	Process Name	State	Pri	I/O	CPU	Page flts	Ph. Mem
00000081	SWAPPER	HIB	16	0	0 00:00:05.82	0	0
00000084	ERRFMT	HIB	8	1191	0 00:00:18.36	76	101
00000085	OPCOM	HIB	9	3867	0 00:02:12.02	647	166
00000086	JOB_CONTROL	HIB	9	207	0 00:00:03.03	132	357
00000087	NETACP	HIB	10	6447	0 00:02:40.34	189	367
00000088	EVL	HIB	6	90	0 00:00:19.92	26577	51_N
00000089	REMACP	HIB	8	8	0 00:00:00.29	68	36
000000A5	SMISERVER	LEF	8	231	0 00:00:03.88	377	514

On a cluster, a command can be executed on all the nodes by setting the environment to cluster. Here is an example where the SHOW LOGICAL command is issued once on the current node but executed by SYSMAN on each of the three VAXes in the cluster.

```
SYSMAN> SET ENVIRONMENT/CLUSTER

%SYSMAN-I-ENV, current command environment:

       Clusterwide on local cluster
       Username SHAH       will be used on nonlocal nodes

   SYSMAN> DO SHOW LOGICAL SYS$NODE

%SYSMAN-I-OUTPUT, command execution on node GARUDA

   "SYS$NODE" = "GARUDA::" (LNM$SYSTEM_TABLE)

%SYSMAN-I-OUTPUT, command execution on node GANESH

   "SYS$NODE" = "GANESH::" (LNM$SYSTEM_TABLE)

%SYSMAN-I-OUTPUT, command execution on node GANGES

   "SYS$NODE" = "GANGES::" (LNM$SYSTEM_TABLE)
```

The SYSMAN CONFIGURATION SET TIME command is useful to set the same time on all the nodes in a cluster. The command to change the time (shown below) is send by SYSMAN to all the nodes. However, because of delays in communications and differing CPU speeds and activities, the time on each of the nodes may differ slightly. This difference is usually a few hundredth of a second.

Here is how the cluster time is set:

```
SYSMAN> SET ENVIRONMENT/CLUSTER

%SYSMAN-I-ENV, current command environment:

      Clusterwide on local cluster
      Username SHAH      will be used on nonlocal nodes

SYSMAN> CONFIGURATION SET TIME 28-JUL-1990:13:23:00 SYSMAN>
```

SYSMAN can be used for other purposes. Each computer contains two start-up databases: SYS$STARTUP:VMS$LAYERED.DAT and SYS$STARTUP:VMS$VMS.DAT. These databases contain commands that are executed when the computer boots. The database VMS$VMS.DAT contains the operating system's start-up commands for starting OPCOM, security auditing, and other such functions. This file should not be modified. The VMS$LAYERED.DAT database can be modified to include start-up commands for software products installed on the nodes. The databases are maintained by SYSMAN start-up set of commands. The SYSMAN manual, which is part of the series of system management manuals, can be consulted for details.

Disk quotas can be managed by the SYSMAN DISKQUOTA set of commands. Quotas can be imposed on users on any disk on the nodes. The quotas are based on user names or UICs (*user identifier code*). The SYSMAN manual should be consulted for details.

6.12 SECURITY AUDITS

Setting up a secure environment is a complex issue. The key focus of security is on:

- Controlled access to the system, which is controlled by the AUTHORIZE database files

- Controlled access to devices and files, which is controlled by the UIC and ACL (*access control lists*) based file protection schemes.

These two issues are not discussed elsewhere in this book; this section describes how to enable logging of security-related messages and how to read these messages when performing an audit.

Logging of security information for future audit is independent on each node of a VAXcluster. A common log file is used so that when performing a clusterwide audit, only one file needs to be scanned. Security-related information is processed and logged by the process AUDIT_SERVER on each node on the cluster.

Previously, the events were logged in the operator log file SYS$MANAGER:OPERATOR.LOG. However, since the release of VMS V5.2, the events are logged in SYS$MANAGER:SECURITY_AUDIT.AUDIT$JOURNAL and optionally logged in the operator log file. Prior to V5.2, the SECAUDIT.COM file was used to display security events; this is replaced by the ANALYZE/AUDIT command in V5.2. The discussion here is on VMS V5.2 and later versions.

The command to enable logging of security messages is:

```
$ SET AUDIT /ALARM/ENABLE=alarm-types
```

where the alarm-types are:

ACL	Display objects that are accessed and have an ACL alarm set.
ALL	Report all types of alarms.
AUDIT	Display any SET AUDIT command executed.
AUTHORIZATION	Display fields modified in the systemauthorization files, i.e., SYS$SYSTEM:SYSUAF.DAT, RIGHTSLIST.DAT, and NETPROXY.DAT.
BREAKIN=ALL	Login break-ins.
FILE_ACCESS=ALL	Display file access by use of special privileges and unsuccessful file access attempts.
INSTALL	Install images.
LOGFAILURE=ALL	
LOGIN=ALL	
LOGOUT=ALL	
MOUNT	Display use of any MOUNT or DISMOUNT command for volumes.

Keywords other than "=ALL" are also possible; the HELP command or the manuals should be used to see all the options.

When the computer boots, a default set of alarms are set by the computer, effectively using the command:

```
$ SET AUDIT /ALARM/ENABLE=(AUDIT,AUTHORIZA-
TION,BREAKIN=ALL)
```

To display a summary of logging status, including what events are being logged, the command is:

```
$ SHOW AUDIT/ALL
```

```
List of audit journals:

    Journal name:          SECURITY
    Journal owner:         (system audit journal)
    Destination:           SYS$COMMON:[SYSMGR]SECURITY_AUDIT.AUDIT$JOURNAL
    Monitoring:            free disk space
    Warning threshold:     1000 blocks
    Action threshold:      250 blocks
    Resume threshold:      750 blocks


Security auditing server characteristics:

    Final resource action:  crash system

Security archiving information:

    Archiving events:       none
    Archive destination:

Security alarm failure mode is set to:

    WAIT       Processes will wait for resource

Security alarms currently enabled for:

    AUTHORIZATION
    BREAKIN:    (DIALUP,LOCAL,REMOTE,NETWORK,DETACHED)
```

Security related messages are stored in an internal binary format in the log file. The ANALYZE/AUDIT command can be used to display these messages in various forms. Here are some examples:

```
$ ANALYZE/AUDIT/SUMMARY
```

Total records read:	1272	Records selected:	1272
Record buffer size:	512	Format buffer size:	256
Server messages:	0	Customer messages:	0
Digital CSS messages:	0	Layered prod messages:	0
Audit changes:	14	Installed db changes:	145
Login failures:	99	Breakin attempts:	12
Successful logins:	368	Successful logouts:	229
System UAF changes:	249	Network UAF changes:	0
Rights db changes:	70	Object accesses:	0
Volume (dis)mounts:	86		

```
$ ANALYZE/AUDIT/BRIEF
```

Date / Time	Type	Subtype	Node	Username	ID Term
17-FEB-1990 18:29:58.06	LOGOUT	REMOTE	GANGES SHAH4	21A00A55 _RTA1:	
17-FEB-1990 18:31:15.31	BREAKIN	REMOTE	GARUDA SHAH4	217BB8BE _RTA2:	
17-FEB-1990 18:31:30.98	SYSUAF	SYSUAF_MODIFY	GANGES SHAH4	21A00A43	
17-FEB-1990 18:33:21.92	LOGOUT	LOCAL	GANGES SHAH4	21A008C8 _LTA429:	
				(SRVR/PORT_5)	
17-FEB-1990 18:59:36.25	LOGOUT	BATCH	GANGES MIXERFUN1	21A00A58	
17-FEB-1990 18:59:47.51	LOGIN	LOCAL	GANGES 0207	21A00A59 _OPA0:	
17-FEB-1990 18:59:54.72	LOGOUT	LOCAL	GANGES MIXERFUN1	21A00A56 _LTA471:	
				(LAT_08002B10E799/PORT_7)	
17-FEB-1990 19:00:27.86	MOUNT	VOL_MOUNT	GANGES 0207	21A00A59	
17-FEB-1990 19:56:33.38	LOGOUT	DETACHED	GANGES TEST1	21A00A5E	
17-FEB-1990 20:03:15.60	LOGIN	SUBPROCESS	GANGES TEST1	21A00A5F	

```
$ ANALYZE/AUDIT/FULL/SINCE:TODAY
%AUDSRV-I-NEW_FILE, now analyzing file
SYS$COMMON:[SYSMGR]SECURITY_AUDIT.AUDIT$JOURNAL;3
```

```
Security alarm (SECURITY) and security audit (SECURITY) on GANGES, system id: 1035
Auditable event:        Remote interactive login
Event time:             17-FEB-1990 18:29:55.95
PID:                    21A00A55
Username:               SHAH4
Terminal name:          _RTA1:
Remote nodename:        GANGES          Remote node id:  1035
Remote username:        SHAH4


Security alarm (SECURITY) and security audit (SECURITY) on GANGES, system id: 1035
Auditable event:        Remote interactive logout
Event time:             17-FEB-1990 18:29:58.06
PID:                    21A00A55
Username:               SHAH4
Terminal name:          _RTA1:
Remote nodename:        GANGES          Remote node id:  1035
Remote username:        SHAH4


Security alarm (SECURITY) and security audit (SECURITY) on GARUDA, system id: 1036
Auditable event:        Remote interactive breakin detection
Event time:             17-FEB-1990 18:31:15.31
PID:                    217BB8BE
Username:               SHAH4
Password:               SDF
Terminal name:          _RTA2:
Remote nodename:        GANGES          Remote node id:  1035
Remote username:        SHAH4
```

```
Security alarm (SECURITY) and security audit (SECURITY) on GANGES, system id: 1035
Auditable event:        System UAF record modification
Event time:             17-FEB-1990 18:31:30.98
PID:                    21A00A43
Username:               SHAH4
Image name:             $1$DUS0:[SYS0.SYSCOMMON.][SYSEXE]AUTHORIZE.EXE
Object name:            SYS$COMMON:[SYSEXE]SYSUAF.DAT;1
Object type:            file
User record modified:   SHAH4
Fields modified:        FLAGS

Security alarm (SECURITY) and security audit (SECURITY) on GANGES, system id: 1035
Auditable event:        Local interactive logout
Event time:             17-FEB-1990 18:33:21.92
PID:                    21A008C8
Username:               SHAH4
Terminal name:          _LTA429:  (SRVR4/PORT_5)


Security alarm (SECURITY) and security audit (SECURITY) on GANGES, system id: 1035
Auditable event:        Batch process login
Event time:             17-FEB-1990 18:59:23.06
PID:                    21A00A58
Username:               MIXERFUN1


Security alarm (SECURITY) and security audit (SECURITY) on GANGES, system id: 1035
Auditable event:        Volume Mount
Event time:             17-FEB-1990 19:00:41.96
PID:                    21A00A59
Username:               0207
Image name:             $1$DUS0:[SYS0.SYSCOMMON.][SYSEXE]BACKUP.EXE;2
Object name:            _$1$MUA0:
Object type:            device
Object owner:           [ OPER,0207 ]
Object protection:      SYSTEM:RWEDC, OWNER:RWEDC, GROUP:C, WORLD:C
Logical name:           TAPE$PAGESW
Volume name:            PAGESW
Mount flags:            /FOREIGN/NOASSIST/MESSAGE/NOCACHE/NOJOURNAL
```

```
$ ANALYZE/AUDIT/FULL/EVENT_TYPE=LOGFAIL
%AUDSRV-I-NEW_FILE, now analyzing file
SYS$COMMON:[SYSMGR]SECURITY_AUDIT.AUDIT$JOURNAL;3
```

```
Security alarm (SECURITY) and security audit (SECURITY) on GANGES, system id: 1035
Auditable event:        Local interactive login failure
Event time:             17-FEB-1990 18:43:50.70
PID:                    21A00A57
Username:               <login>
```

```
Password:              SDF
Terminal name:         _OPA0:
Status:                %LOGIN-F-CMDINPUT, error reading command input

Security alarm (SECURITY) and security audit (SECURITY) on GANGES, system id: 1035
Auditable event:       Local interactive login failure
Event time:            17-FEB-1990 19:16:19.94
PID:                   21A00A5A
Username:              MIXERCAT1
Terminal name:         _LTA472: (LAT_08002B10E799/PORT_7)
Status:                %LOGIN-F-INVPWD, invalid password
```

On a VAXcluster, security-related information from all the nodes is recorded in the common file SYS$MANAGER:SECURITY_AUDIT.AUDIT$JOURNAL (specifically, SYS$COMMON:[SYSMGR]SECURITY_AUDIT.AUDIT$JOURNAL). The file can be different for different nodes if that is required.

6.13 SUMMARY

One of the concerns of a VAXcluster system manager is whether to have a clusterwide common user profile database or have a separate database for each cluster member. The alternatives were discussed. Clusterwide batch and queue setup issues as well as commands to monitor cluster activity were discussed. The HSC was described. The next chapter presents programming features of VAXclusters.

7

VAXcluster Programming

This chapter discusses issues that are of concern to programmers developing applications for VAXclusters. Applications developed for independent VAX computers can be moved without modifications to run on an individual member of a VAXcluster. Running the application on several VAXes of a VAXcluster will usually require modifications.

General programming concepts are not discussed here. The topics that are discussed are useful when developing complex applications that use features specific to VAX/VMS and VAXclusters. Many of the discussed programming issues are applicable to single VAX computers and to cluster members but not necessarily to the cluster as a whole. For example, disk files can be shared by all the VAXes in a cluster. However, global sections cannot be shared. A proper understanding of VAX/VMS programming capabilities and limitations is required when designing clustered applications.

The chapter discusses:

- Mailboxes
- Shared logical names
- Global sections
- Event flags
- Locks for shared resources
- Object libraries
- Shared images

- Asynchronous system traps (ASTs)

- Exit handlers

- Task-to-task communications across the DECnet network

- Electronic disks

- The disk-striping driver

- Automatic failovers on a VAXcluster

- Generic print and batch queues

- Fiber optics technology

Files on VAXclusters are described in the chapter on *record management services* (RMS).

Since many of the programming topics are interrelated, it may be necessary to read this chapter more than once to understand the sample programs. The programs are in COBOL or C, which should be easy if you know a language. Many COBOL programmers are intimidated by system services since they are not like conventional language constructs. I hope the demonstration programs shown here demystify COBOL system calls.

7.1 INTERPROGRAM COMMUNICATIONS

There are three main methods for transferring data among processes on a VAX:

1. *Mailboxes*. These are used to send streams of data from one process to another. Normally, one or more processes would send data to a mailbox and one process would process the data.

2. *Logical names*. These are used to send small amounts of data such as status and counts from one process to another. They can be thought of as common "registers."

3. *Global sections*. These are common areas of memory for use by all or some processes.

The words "processes" and "programs" are used interchangeably since a program, when run, is an image in a process. Most of the examples used in this section show communications between two processes; however, the techniques can be extended for communications among more processes. Also, processes are assumed to be running from terminals so that output can be displayed. However, the techniques also apply to processes that do not have attached terminals (such as detached or batch processes).

Mailboxes, logical names, and global sections are (VAX) node specific, even if the nodes are part of a VAXcluster. DECnet and the *distributed lock manager* (DLM) can be used for communications between programs running on different nodes of the cluster.

7.2 MAILBOXES

Mailbox can be used for sending a stream of data from one process to another without resorting to disks as intermediate devices. Mailboxes are software devices. The device driver is SYS$SYSTEM:MBDRIVER.EXE and the generic device name is MB:. A sample mailbox device is MBA12:. One process would normally create a mailbox, and other processes would assign channels from their process to the mailbox. Processes can then use QIO (queued input/output) functions (system services) to read from or write to the mailbox. Mailboxes are not available clusterwide. DECnet task-to-task communications or locks can be used for internode traffic.

Figures 7.1 and 7.2 show two programs MAILBOX_WRITE.C and MAILBOX_READ.C. The first program creates the mailbox, writes to the mailbox, and waits for the data to be read by the second program. The second program reads the mailbox for data put in there by the first program, and sends the data to its terminal.

```
/* MAILBOX_WRITE.C          Jay Shah   15-DEC-1990
 * This mailbox demonstration program works in conjunction with
 * MAILBOX_READ.C.
 *
 * The program
 *  . creates a mailbox
 *  . writes a message to it
 *  . and waits for the message to be read by MAILBOX_READ.C.
 */
#include stdio
#include descrip
#include iodef
#include ssdef
```

Figure 7.1 Mailbox demonstration: the writing program.

```
main ()
{
int status;

/* variables used for creating mailbox */
char permanent_mbx = 1;      /* temporary mailbox */
short mbx_chan;              /* i/o channel to mailbox,
                        * returned by the $CREMBX call */
int  max_message_size = 0;   /* use VMS default */
int  max_buf_size = 0;       /* system dynamic memory for buffering
                        messages to mailbox. Use default */
int  protection_mask = 0;    /* access for all users */
int  access_mode = 0;        /* most privileged access mode */

$DESCRIPTOR(mbx_logical_name,"MAILBOX_DEMO");
char tmp[100];

/* variables for QIO output to mailbox */
struct
   {short cond_value; short count; int info;}
      io_status_block;
char *message = "Test message to mailbox";
int tmp1;
/* system service call to create mailbox and assign
 * it a logical name
 */
status= sys$crembx(
        permanent_mbx,
        &mbx_chan,
        max_message_size,
        max_buf_size,
        protection_mask,
        access_mode,
        &mbx_logical_name
        );
if (status != SS$_NORMAL) lib$stop(status);
                /* create mailbox error? */

/* send a message to the mailbox, wait until it is read */
tmp1 = strlen(message);
status = sys$qiow(
        0,                     /* event_flag */
        mbx_chan,
        IO$_WRITEVBLK | IO$M_NOW,
        &io_status_block,
        0,                     /* ast_address */
```

Figure 7.1 (*Continued*)

```
        0,                    /* ast_parameter */
        message,              /* parameter P1 */
        (int) strlen(message), /* length, parameter P2 */
        0,0,0,0               /* P3, P4, P5, P6 */
        );
if (status != SS$_NORMAL) lib$stop(status);    /* error? */
gets(tmp);
}
```

Figure 7.1 (*Continued*)

```
/* MAILBOX_READ.C          Jay Shah   16-DEC-1990
 * This program demonstrates use of mailboxes. It works in
 * conjunction with MAILBOX_WRITE.C.
 *
 * The program
 * . opens an existing mailbox (created by MAILBOX_WRITE.C)
 * . reads from it
 * . and displays the data read onto the terminal.
 *
 * The mailbox is created by the program MAILBOX_WRITE.C
 * which also writes to the mailbox. The mailbox is defined
 * by the logical name MAILBOX_DEMO.
 */

#include stdio
#include descrip
#include iodef
#include ssdef
main()
{
int status;
short mbx_chan;    /* i/o channel to mailbox */
$DESCRIPTOR(mbx_logical_name, "MAILBOX_DEMO");

/* variables for QIO input from mailbox */
struct
   {short cond_value; short count; int info;}
      io_status_block;
char message[256];
int message_len = 255;

/* system service call to assign a channel to the mailbox */
```

Figure 7.2 Mailbox demonstration: the reading program.

```
status = sys$assign(
        &mbx_logical_name,
        &mbx_chan,
        0,              /* access mode. Full access */
        0               /* associated mailbox name.
                         * Not used */
        );
if (status != SS$_NORMAL) lib$stop(status);    /* error? */

/* read a message from the mailbox */
status = sys$qiow(
        0,              /* event_flag number 0*/
        mbx_chan,
        IO$_READVBLK,
        &io_status_block,
        0,              /* ast_address  */
        0,              /* ast_parameter */
        message,         /* parameter P1 */
        message_len,     /* buffer size,
                         * parameter P2  */
        0,0,0,0          /* P3, P4, P5, P6
                         * ignored     */
        );
if (status != SS$_NORMAL) lib$stop(status);  /* error? */

printf ("%s",message);
}
```

Figure 7.2 (*Continued*)

Some notes on mailboxes:

- Mailboxes are either temporary or permanent. A temporary mailbox is deleted by VMS if no processes are accessing it. A permanent mailbox will remain in the computer until a reboot is performed or until the mailbox is explicitly deleted by the $DELMBX system service.

- Mailboxes can be written to and read from by multiple processes.

- Mailboxes are VMS devices, so device operations such as setting access protections can be performed on them. To see mailboxes on the VAX, use $ SHOW DEVICE MB or $ SHOW DEVICE/FULL MB.

7.3 LOGICAL NAMES

Logical names were described in the chapter on the operating system. Logical names created at the group or system level can be shared by other users. Group logical names can be read by members of the same group, while system logical names can be accessed by all processes. Figure 7.3 shows a COBOL program LOGI-CAL_NAMES_DEMO.COB that modifies or displays a group logical name called COMMON_LOGICAL_NAME. The program can be run by two users in the same UIC (*user identification code*) group from different terminals. Any modification made to the logical name by one user can be displayed by the other user. The users will require the GRPNAM privilege to modify group-level logical names.

```
Identification Division.
  Program-id.  Logical-names_demo.
  Author.    Jay Shah.
  Installation. VAX/VMS V5.2.

* This is program LOGICAL_NAMES.COB.

* This program demonstrates how small amounts of
* data can be transferred from one process to another;
* effectively performing task-to-task communications.
* The program creates a group-level logical name,
* COMMON_LOGICAL_NAME, if it does not exist. This
* requires the privilege GRPNAM. The program then loops
* indefinitely to allow the user to display the equivalent
* name or enter a new equivalent name for the logical
* name. The program can be run by different users in the
* group. Modifications made to the logical name by one
* user will be displayed by the other users on their
* terminals.

* To run the program, the set of commands are:
*    $cobol logical_names_demo
*    $link logical_names_demo
*    $run logical_names_demo

Environment Division.
Configuration Section.
```

Figure 7.3 Interprocess communication with logical names.

```
Special-names.
     symbolic user-mode is 4.

Data Division.
Working-storage Section.

  01 lognam-attributes  pic 9(9)  comp value 0.
  01 lognam-table       pic x(9)  value is "LNM$GROUP".
  01 lognam             pic x(20) value is "COMMON_LOGICAL_NAME".
* access mode is user (not super, exec or kernel).
  01 access-mode        pic x     value user-mode.
  01 itemlist.
     03 eqv-len         pic 9(4)  comp value 10.
*     lnm$_string has a value of 2.
*     This is used for equivalent name.
     03 item-code       pic 9(4)  comp value 2.
     03 eqv-addr        usage is  pointer value is reference eqv-nam.
     03 ret-len-addr    usage is  pointer value is reference ret-len.
     03 terminator      pic 9(9)  comp value 0.
  01 eqv-nam            pic x(10).
  01 ret-len            pic 9(4)  comp.
  01 call-status        pic s9(9) comp.

* A value SS$_NOLOGNAM is returned when attempting
* to use a logical name that is not defined.
* SS$_NOLOGNAM is declared in the system object
* library file, STARLET.OLB. Its value is 444 in
* VMS version 5.2. Since its value can change when
* the operating system is upgraded, the value is
* looked up by the linker from the object library,
* STARLET.OLB, when the "value external" clause is
* used as shown here.

  01 no-lognam          pic s9(9) comp value external SS$_NOLOGNAM.
  01 response           pic x.


Procedure Division.
10-start.
* If the logical name (COMMON_LOGICAL_NAME) is not
* created, create it.

* Get value of logical name.
  call "sys$trnlnm" using
                    by reference   lognam-attributes,
                    by descriptor  lognam-table,
```

Figure 7.3 (*Continued*)

```
                    by descriptor  lognam,
                    by reference   access-mode,
                    by reference   itemlist,
                    giving         call-status.

* If no such logical name, create it.
  if call-status = no-lognam
        move "       " to eqv-nam
        call "sys$crelnm" using
                    by reference   lognam-attributes,
                    by descriptor  lognam-table,
                    by descriptor  lognam,
                    by reference   access-mode,
                    by reference   itemlist,
                    giving         call-status
  end-if.
  if call-status is failure then call "sys$exit" using
                    by value call-status.

20-menu.
* loop to display the logical name or change the
* value of the logical name.

   display " ".
   display "Group logical name COMMON_LOGICAL_NAME has a value of: ",
                                        eqv-nam.
   display " ".
   display "Enter 1 to modify the value, 2 to see current value: "
                            with no advancing.
   accept response.
   if response = "1" then
        display "Enter new value for COMMON_LOGICAL_NAME: "
                            with no advancing
        accept eqv-nam

* Change value of the logical name.
        call "sys$crelnm" using
                    by reference   lognam-attributes,
                    by descriptor  lognam-table,
                    by descriptor  lognam,
                    by reference   access-mode,
                    by reference   itemlist,
                    giving         call-status
        if call-status is failure then call "sys$exit" using
                    by value call-status end-if
        end-if.
```

Figure 7.3 (*Continued*)

```
* Get value of logical name.
  call "sys$trnlnm" using
                      by reference    lognam-attributes,
                      by descriptor   lognam-table,
                      by descriptor   lognam,
                      by reference    access-mode,
                      by reference    itemlist,
                      giving          call-status.
  if call-status is failure then call "sys$exit" using
                      by value call-status.
  go to 20-menu.
```

Figure 7.3 (*Continued*)

Logical names can be manipulated using system calls or DCL commands as shown in the following table:

Operation	How to perform the operation	
	From a program	From DCL
Create a name	System call $CRELNM	Define command
Translate a name	System call $TRNLNM	F$TRNLM lexical function
Delete a name	System call $DELLNM	DEASSIGN command

The logical name value can also be displayed by users in the same group at other terminals by using:

```
$ SHOW LOGICAL/GROUP *
```

or

```
$ SHOW LOGICAL/GROUP COMMON_LOGICAL_NAME
```

The logical name can be created in the SYSTEM table, in which case all processes on the computer will be able to read it. The privilege SYSNAM or SETPRV is required for this. If all the processes sharing the logical name are from the same job (created by using the SPAWN or a similar command), then the logical name can be placed in the job table. In this case no special privileges are required to share the logical name.

Data exchange is limited by the size of logical names, which is 255 characters. Multiple logical names can be used but, global sections may be more appropriate for large amounts of data. Multiple DCL command procedures can also communicate using common logical names.

7.4   GLOBAL SECTIONS

The global sections is one of the most efficient methods for sharing main memory among processes on the system. A logically contiguous piece of memory can be allocated to a global section for shared use by one or more processes. Some form of synchronization between the processes will be required to avoid multiple processes writing simultaneously to the same shared area. See the next section for a description of synchronization techniques.

Unfortunately, global sections are not available clusterwide. One node can have a common global section for all the nodes on a cluster, and the nodes access this global section when reading and writing the section. For redundancy, more than one node can have mirror images of the global section. Such redundancy has to be implemented using transaction processing techniques since a VAX might fail during the transfer of data from a global section's memory to a global section in another VAX's memory. DECnet task-to-task communications can be used to implement this scheme. Most clusters have DECnet running over Ethernet. The communications may be slow when a large amount of data is flowing between the VAXes. In this case, high-speed parallel interfaces can be used between the VAXes.

In some cases, it may be convenient to keep the data on disk files rather than in global sections. All the VAXes can have access to the common data on the disk. Since files are available clusterwide and the operating system assumes the task of accessing the same records by multiple VAXes, no special synchronization is needed by the programs running on various VAXes on the cluster. This scheme simplifies program design. Another method for sharing data in high-volume applications may be the use of electronic disks which are described later in this chapter.

Figures 7.4 and 7.5 show two programs — GLOBAL_SECTION_WRITER and GLOBAL_SECTION_READER. GLOBAL_SECTION_WRITER creates a global section of 2048 bytes. The program then reads input from the terminal and writes it to the global section, repeating the terminal input until the 2048-byte limit of the global section has been reached. The program GLOBAL_SECTION_READER reads the global section from bytes 20 to 40 every 5 sec and writes the output to its terminal. **The programs should be run from two different terminals.**

```
/* global_section_writer.c    Jay Shah   19-DEC-1990
 *
 * This program
 *  . creates a global section, GBL_SECTION_DEMO, of 2048 bytes
 *  . reads a string entered at the terminal
 *  . and writes the string to the global section.
 *    The string is repeated to fill-up the 2048 bytes
 *    of the global section.
 *
 * 2048 is a multiple of 512; global section main memory
 * is allocated in multiples of 512 bytes by the
 * operating system.
 */

#include stdio
#include descrip
#include secdef
#include ssdef

main ()
{

char global_memory[2048];
$DESCRIPTOR ( gbl_secnam, "GBL_SECTION_DEMO" );
struct memrange { char *startaddress; char *endaddress; };
struct memrange inaddress = { global_memory, global_memory + 2047 };
struct memrange retaddress;
char ident[8] = {
'\000','\000','\000','\000','\000','\000','\000','\000' };
char *tmpaddress, resp_len;

char response[80];
int status;

/* create the global section */
status = sys$crmpsc(
        &inaddress,     /* range of memory to be mapped */
        &retaddress,    /* actual memory mapped */
        0,              /* access mode. Full access by others */
        SEC$M_GBL       /* Global, not private, section */
        | SEC$M_WRT     /* Read/Write allowed */
```

Figure 7.4 Global section demonstration: the writing program.

```
                  | SEC$M_EXPREG  /* Map into available space */
                  | SEC$M_PAGFIL, /* Page file not a disk file section */
                  &gbl_secnam,
                  &ident,         /* version number 0 */
                  0,              /* first page of section to be mapped */
                  (short) 0,      /* channel for file sections */
                  4,              /* number of pages. all */
                  0,              /* first virtual block number of file*/
                  0,              /* protection. none */
                  0               /* page fault cluster size */
                  );
if (status == 1561) printf ("section created\n");
else if (status != SS$_NORMAL) lib$stop(status); /* error? */

while (TRUE)
   {
   puts("Input a string to be inserted in global section:");
   gets(response);

   /* insert the response in global memory, repeat response
    * until global memory is filled up.
    */
   tmpaddress = retaddress.startaddress;
                        /* start of global memory */
   resp_len = strlen(response);
   while (tmpaddress <(retaddress.endaddress - resp_len))
      {
      strcpy( tmpaddress, response);
      tmpaddress = tmpaddress + resp_len;
      };
   };

}
```

Figure 7.4 *(Continued)*

```
/* global_section_reader.c     Jay Shah  19-DEC-1990
 *
 * This program
 * . reads a part of the global section created by
 *   GLOBAL_SECTION_WRITER above
 * . and displays the contents on the terminal.
```

Figure 7.5 Global section demonstration: the reading program.

```
 *
 * The two programs should run from two separate terminals.
 */

#include stdio
#include descrip
#include secdef
#include signal
#include ssdef

main ()
{

char global_memory[2048];
$DESCRIPTOR ( gbl_secnam, "GBL_SECTION_DEMO" );
struct memrange { char *startaddress; char *endaddress; };
struct memrange inaddress = { global_memory, global_memory + 2047 };
struct memrange retaddress;
char ident[8] = {
'\000','\000','\000','\000','\000','\000','\000','\000' };
char *tmpaddress, resp_len;

char response[80];
int status;

/* map the process to the global section created by the
 * execution of the program, GLOBAL_SECTION_WRITER.C
 */
status = sys$mgblsc(
        &inaddress,      /* range of memory to be mapped */
        &retaddress,     /* actual memory mapped */
        0,               /* access mode. Full access by others */
        SEC$M_GBL        /* Global, not private, section */
        | SEC$M_WRT      /* Read/Write allowed */
        | SEC$M_EXPREG   /* Map into available space */
        | SEC$M_PAGFIL,  /* Page file not a disk file section */
        &gbl_secnam,
        &ident,          /* version number 0 */
        0                /* first page of section to be mapped */
        );
if (status != SS$_NORMAL) lib$stop(status);     /* error? */

printf ("Global section size is 2048 bytes.\n");
while (TRUE)
    {
```

Figure 7.5 (*Continued*)

```
    printf ("bytes 20 to 40 are: %.20s\n",retaddress.startad-
dress+19);
    printf ("waiting for 5 seconds...\n");
    sleep (5);
    };


}
```

Figure 7.5 (*Continued*)

The global section can be seen by entering:

```
$ INSTALL/LIST/GLOBAL      !List all global sections on computer
```

Global sections are allocated pages of memory. Since a page is 512 bytes, the section sizes will be multiples of 512 bytes. Disk file sections allow files to be mapped into memory. This way, a large file's contents can actually be manipulated as if it were memory locations in the program. Also, the section can be written out to disk automatically for later use.

Global sections can be created at the group or system level. Group global sections are accessible to processes within the group while system global sections are accessible to all processes on the computer. The SYSGBL privilege is required to be able to create system global sections.

Global sections can be permanent or temporary. Temporary global sections are deleted by the operating system when no process is mapping to them. Permanent global sections can be deleted by the SYS$DGBLSC system call. The PRMGBL privilege is required to create permanent global sections. Note that if multiple processes are mapping to the same global section and one of them deletes the section, the section is actually marked for delete. In this case, the section is deleted only after all the processes release the mapping.

7.5 SYNCHRONIZATION

Synchronization among processes is required when they share common resources and there is a possibility of other processes accessing the resource, which one process needs for exclusive use. Many resources like disks and printer queues do not create contention among processes because the operating system handles synchronization issues for these resources. However, resources defined or created by cooperating processes may need to be shared amicably. An example of such a resource could be a common area in memory that is used by one or more processes.

There are two main program synchronization techniques:

1. *Event flags*. These are bit flags managed by the operating system. Processes can decide to wait until an event flag is set (or reset) by another process before continuing execution. When a process waits for an event flag, the operating system puts it in a wait state until the flag is modified. Event flags are not clusterwide. If internode synchronization is required, the distributed lock manager (described later) can be used instead.

2. *Locks*. Locks are a few bytes of memory locations. These can be created by cooperating processes, and then processes can queue up to use the lock. Once a process has a lock, other processes waiting for the lock will be put in a wait state by the operating system until the lock is released by the process that has acquired it. ASTs can be used to wait on a lock and continue program execution. ASTs are described later in this chapter. Locks can be used for synchronization between processes on different nodes on a VAX cluster; locks are clusterwide.

7.5.1 Event Flags

Event flags are bit data structures within the operating system that can be set by one process and tested by the same or another process on the same VAX. They can be used to signal the completion of an event by one process, so that another process that is waiting for the event to be completed can continue execution.

Consider an example: Process 1 handles input from a terminal and stores it in a global section for processing by a "terminal command interpreter" process (process 2). Every time process 1 receives a terminal input and stores it in the global section, process 1 must inform process 2 that there is a string in the global section for processing. Of course, process 2 could continuously loop to check whether a new string has arrived in the global section, but this would be a waste of CPU time. Instead, process 2 sets a flag and waits for process 1 to zero it when there is a terminal string ready for processing. Figures 7.6 and 7.7 show two programs EVENT_FLAG_WRITER and EVENT_FLAG_READER that use event flags for synchronization.

```
/* EVENT_FLAG_WRITER.C        Jay Shah   20-DEC-1990
 *
 * This program demonstrates the use of event flags
 * for synchronization between two processes. The
 * program maps to a global section created by
 * another program, EVENT_FLAG_READER.C and then
 * reads input from the terminal. It waits for a
 * common event flag to be set by the other program,
 * puts the terminal input in the global section, and
 * resets the event flag so that the other program
 * can read the global section. The program then
 * reads more terminal input, and the operation is
 * repeated.
 *
 * See the run-time library manual for a description
 * on how to acquire an event flag using the library
 * function LIB$GET_EF.
 */

#include stdio
#include descrip
#include secdef
#include signal
#include ssdef

#define event_flag_1 65
#define event_flag_2 66

main ()
{

char global_memory[2048];
$DESCRIPTOR ( gbl_secnam, "GBL_SECTION_DEMO" );
struct memrange { char *startaddress; char *endaddress; };
struct memrange inaddress = { global_memory, global_memory + 2047 };
struct memrange retaddress;
char ident[8] = {
'\000','\000','\000','\000','\000','\000','\000','\000' };

char response[80],resp_len;
int status;

$DESCRIPTOR( evflag_cluster_name, "EV_CLUSTER");

status = sys$mgblsc(
        &inaddress,     /* range of memory to be mapped */
        &retaddress,    /* actual memory mapped */
```

Figure 7.6 Synchronization with Event flags: the writing program.

```
              0,             /* access mode. Full access by others */
         SEC$M_GBL      /* Global, not private, section */
         | SEC$M_WRT    /* Read/Write allowed */
         | SEC$M_EXPREG /* Map into available space */
         | SEC$M_PAGFIL, /* Page file, not a disk file section */
         &gbl_secnam,
         &ident,        /* version number 0 */
         0              /* first page of section to be mapped */
         );
if (status != SS$_NORMAL) lib$stop(status);    /* error? */

/* Associate this process with common event
 * flag cluster EV_CLUSTER
 */
status = sys$ascefc(
         event_flag_1,
         &evflag_cluster_name,
         (char) 0,      /* protection: group access  */
         (char) 0       /* temporary, not permanent cluster */
         );
if (status != SS$_NORMAL) lib$stop(status);    /* error? */

while (TRUE)
    {

    /* wait for event flag 2 to be set */
    status = sys$waitfr (event_flag_2);
    if (status != SS$_NORMAL) lib$stop(status);    /* error? */
    /* zero event flag 2 */
    status = sys$clref (event_flag_2);
    if ((status && 1) != 1) lib$stop(status);     /* error? */

    /* read terminal input */
    printf("Input a string to be inserted in global section:");
    gets(response);

    /* put terminal input in global section GBL_SECTION_DEMO */
    resp_len = strlen(response);
    strcpy( retaddress.startaddress, response);

    /* set event flag 1 */
    status = sys$setef (event_flag_1);
    if ((status && 1) != 1) lib$stop(status);     /* error? */

    };

}
```

Figure 7.6 (*Continued*)

```
/* EVENT_FLAG_READER.C      Jay Shah   20-DEC-1990
 *
 * This program demonstrates use of event flags
 * for synchronization between two tasks. The
 * program creates a global section and sets a
 * common event flag. Another program,
 * EVENT_FLAG_WRITER.C, puts data in the global
 * section and resets the event flag. This program
 * then processes the global section (in this case
 * it simply prints its contents out at the
 * terminal) and then sets the event flag to repeat
 * the operation.
 */

#include stdio
#include descrip
#include secdef
#include signal
#include ssdef

#define event_flag_1 65
#define event_flag_2 66

main ()
{

char global_memory[2048];
$DESCRIPTOR ( gbl_secnam, "GBL_SECTION_DEMO" );
struct memrange { char *startaddress; char *endaddress; };
struct memrange inaddress = { global_memory, global_memory + 2047 };
struct memrange retaddress;
char ident[8] = {
'\000','\000','\000','\000','\000','\000','\000','\000' };

char response[80],resp_len;
int status;

$DESCRIPTOR( evflag_cluster_name, "EV_CLUSTER");

/* create the global section */
status = sys$crmpsc(
        &inaddress,     /* range of memory to be mapped */
        &retaddress,    /* actual memory mapped */
        0,              /* access mode.Full access by others */
        SEC$M_GBL       /* Global, not private, section */
        | SEC$M_WRT     /* Read/Write allowed */
```

Figure 7.7 Synchronization with Event flags: the reading program.

```
            | SEC$M_EXPREG  /* Map into available space */
            | SEC$M_PAGFIL, /* Page file not a disk file section */
            &gbl_secnam,
            &ident,         /* version number 0 */
            0,              /* first page of section to be mapped */
            (short) 0,      /* channel for file sections */
            4,              /* number of pages. all */
            0,              /* first virtual block number of file*/
            0,              /* protection. none */
            0               /* page fault cluster size */
            );
if (status == 1561) printf ("section created\n");
else if (status != 1) lib$stop(status); /* error? */


/* create a common event flag cluster called EV_CLUSTER */

status = sys$ascefc(
        event_flag_1,
        &evflag_cluster_name,
        (char) 0,      /* protection: group access */
        (char) 0       /* temporary, not permanent cluster */
        );
if (status != SS$_NORMAL) lib$stop(status);      /* error? */

while (TRUE)
   {

   /* let other process know that it can
    * write to the global section
    */
   status = sys$clref (event_flag_1);
   if ((status && 1) != 1) lib$stop(status);       /* error? */
   status = sys$setef (event_flag_2);
   if ((status && 1) != 1) lib$stop(status);       /* error? */


   /* wait for the event flag 1 to be set by
    * EVENT_FLAG_WRITER.C. When the flag is set,
    * EVENT_FLAG_WRITER.C has placed data in
    *the global section for this process to read
    */


   status = sys$waitfr(event_flag_1);
```

Figure 7.7 (*Continued*)

```
if (status != SS$_NORMAL) lib$stop(status);      /* error? */

/* read and display contents of global section */
printf("New data in global section: %s \n ",retaddress.startad-
dress);

}

}
```

Figure 7.7 (*Continued*)

Each process has four sets of 32 event flags. Each set is called a cluster. Clusters 0 and 1 (event flags 0 through 63) are local to the process, while clusters 2 and 3 (event flags 64 to 127) are common to processes in the same UIC group. Clusters 2 and 3 have to be given a name by the process that creates them. Cluster 0 and 1 event flags are automatically available to processes, while common event flags are available only by associating the process with the cluster name (by using the $ASCEFC system service).

7.5.2 Locks

Locks can be used in place of event flags. Locks are more general than event flags; locks can be used to synchronize use of resources by multiple processes. In fact, locks are "known" across a cluster, so they can be used to synchronize processes across a cluster. Event flags can be used when there are two processes and one process is waiting for another to complete a task.

The lock facility is provided by the system, but, locks are not controlled by the system. A cooperating set of processes define and use locks in an appropriate way. A process can acquire a lock and use the corresponding resource, but this does not stop another process from using the resource. The second process should wait for the lock to be released, acquire the lock, and then use the resource.

Figure 7.8 shows a program that reads and writes to a global section. The program can be run from multiple terminals; all the processes will then read and write to the same global section. The lock, GBLSEC_LOCK, will be used for synchronization. The process acquiring the lock can access the global section.

```
/* LOCK.C              Jay Shah   22-DEC-1990
*
* This program illustrates use of the lock
* management facility on VAX/VMS. The program
* creates a global section and a lock, GBLSEC_LOCK.
* The program then acquires the lock, which allows
* it to gain exclusive access to the global section.
* The program prints the contents of the global
* section, writes new data in the global section, and
* then releases the lock. The program then waits
* a random amount of time before reading and writing
* the global section again.
*
* The program can be run from multiple terminals to
* see varying output at each terminal, depending on
* the order in which processes acquire the lock.
*/

#include stdio
#include descrip
#include secdef
#include lckdef
#include ssdef

/* variables for global section */
char global_memory[2048];
$DESCRIPTOR ( gbl_secnam, "GBL_SECTION_DEMO" );
struct memrange { char *startaddress; char *endaddress; };
struct memrange inaddress = { global_memory, global_memory + 2047 };
struct memrange retaddress;
char ident[8] = {
'\000','\000','\000','\000','\000','\000','\000','\000' };

int status;

main()
{

struct {
      short vms_cond;
      short reserve;
      int   lock_id;
      char  lock_val[16];
      } lock_status_block;
$DESCRIPTOR (resource_name,"GBLSEC_LOCK");
```

Figure 7.8 Demonstration of locks.

```
char response[80],resp_len;
char this_process_id[80];

create_or_mapto_globalsection();

/* create a string to be put in the global section */
sprintf ( this_process_id,"process id = %d", getpid() );


/* loop forever: acquire lock, read global section, write global sec-
tion, release lock.
*/
while (TRUE)
    {
    sleep ( rand() & 3);   /* random wait between 0 and 3 seconds */
    status = sys$enqw(    /* acquire exclusive access to GBLSEC_LOCK */
            35,            /* event flag */
            LCK$K_EXMODE,   /* lock mode: exclusive */
            &lock_status_block,
            0,             /* flags: none */
            &resource_name,
            0,             /* parent lock: none */
            0,             /* AST address */
            0,             /* AST parameter */
            0,             /* blocking AST routine: none */
            0,             /* access mode: default */
            0              /* nullarg: reserved */
            );
    if (status != SS$_NORMAL) lib$stop(status);    /* error? */
    printf ("Global section contains: %s \n",retaddress.startad-
dress);
    strcpy (retaddress.startaddress, this_process_id);
    status = sys$deq(          /* release lock */
            lock_status_block.lock_id,     /* lock id */
            &lock_status_block.lock_val,   /* value block */
            0,                     /* access mode */
            0                      /* flags */
            );
    if (status != SS$_NORMAL) lib$stop(status);    /* error? */
    };

};


create_or_mapto_globalsection()
{
```

Figure 7.8 (*Continued*)

```
/* create the global section (if it does not exist) */

status = sys$crmpsc (
         &inaddress,      /* range of memory to be mapped */
         &retaddress,    /* actual memory mapped */
         0,              /* access mode. Full access by others */
         SEC$M_GBL       /* Global, not private, section */
         | SEC$M_WRT     /* Read/Write allowed */
         | SEC$M_EXPREG  /* Map into available space */
         | SEC$M_PAGFIL, /* Page file not a disk file section */
         &gbl_secnam,
         &ident,         /* version number 0 */
         0,              /* first page of section to be mapped */
         (short) 0,      /* channel for file sections */
         4,              /* number of pages. all */
         0,              /* first virtual block number of file*/
         0,              /* protection. none */
         0               /* page fault cluster size */
         );
if (status == 1561)
    {
    printf ("section created\n");
    strcpy(retaddress.startaddress,"starting process");
    }
else if (status != SS$_NORMAL) lib$stop(status); /* error? */
    else
    {
    /* map to existing global section */
    status = sys$mgblsc (
             &inaddress,      /* range of memory to be mapped */
             &retaddress,    /* actual memory mapped */
             0,              /* access mode. Full access by others */
             SEC$M_GBL       /* Global, not private, section */
             | SEC$M_WRT     /* Read/Write allowed */
             | SEC$M_EXPREG  /* Map into available space */
             | SEC$M_PAGFIL, /* Page file not a disk file section */
             &gbl_secnam,
             &ident,         /* version number 0 */
             0               /* first page of section to be mapped */
             );
    if (status != SS$_NORMAL) lib$stop(status);    /* error? */
    };
};
```

Figure 7.8 (*Continued*)

Some features of locks are:

- When a number of locks are being used by a set of processes, there is a possibility of a deadlock. For example, suppose process A has lock L1 and process B has lock L2. A deadlock occurs if process A waits for lock L2 and process B waits for lock L1, since the processes will be waiting forever. VMS monitors the system for such deadlocks; if it finds that there is a deadlock, it returns a status of SS$_DEADLOCK to one of the processes. Since VMS arbitrarily decides which programs should receive this message, programs using locks must be able to process this status appropriately.

- Locks in the system can be displayed using the system dump analyzer utility (although a good understanding of VMS internals is required to analyse the output):

```
$ ANALYZE/SYSTEM
VAX/VMS system analyzer
SDA> SHOW LOCKS
```

The MONITOR utility can display a summary of lock usage on the system:

```
$ MONITOR LOCKS
```

7.5.3 The Distributed Lock Manager

The distributed lock manager is an extension of the lock manager on single-VAX computers. On a VAXcluster, all locks, even those defined and used on a single node, are available for clusterwide use.

Figure 7.9 shows a program CLUSTER_LOCK.C that loops to acquire a lock (called STUDY_LOCK), holds it for a random time interval, and then releases it. The program can be run from multiple terminals, on the same or different VAXes on a VAXcluster. The display indicates how locks can be used for synchronization among processes on different nodes on a cluster.

```
/* CLUSTER_LOCK.C        Jay Shah   22-DEC-1990
 * This program illustrates the use of the
 * distributed lock manager on a VAXcluster.
```

Figure 7.9 Demonstration of clusterwide locks.

```
*
* The program creates (if it is not already created)
* a lock called STUDY_LOCK. The program then
* acquires the lock and prints a message on the
* terminal. The program waits a random amount
* of time and then releases the lock.
*
* The program can be run from multiple terminals
* on different nodes on a VAXcluster to see
* varying output at each terminal, depending on
* the order in which processes acquire the lock.
*/
#include stdio
#include descrip
#include lckdef
#include ssdef

int status;

main()
{
struct {                    /* the lock data structure */
     short vms_cond;
     short reserve;
     int   lock_id;
     char  lock_val[16];
     } lock_status_block;
$DESCRIPTOR (resource_name,"STUDY_LOCK");

/* loop forever: acquire lock, read global section, write global sec-
tion, release lock */
while (TRUE)            /* loop until a CTRL/Y is entered */
   {
   status = sys$enqw(   /* acquire exclusive access to STUDY_LOCK */
           35,           /* event flag number, arbitrary*/
           LCK$K_EXMODE,  /* lock mode: exclusive */
           &lock_status_block,
           0,            /* flags: none */
           &resource_name,
           0,            /* parent lock: none */
           0,            /* AST address: none */
           0,            /* AST parameter: none */
           0,            /* blocking AST routine: none*/
           0,            /* access mode: default */
           0             /* nullarg: reserved */
```

Figure 7.9 (*Continued*)

```
            );
if (status != SS$_NORMAL) lib$stop(status);      /* error? */
printf ("This process has the lock \n");
sleep ( rand() & 10);  /* random wait between 0 and 10 seconds */
printf ("This process is releasing the lock \n");
status = sys$deq(        /* release lock */
        lock_status_block.lock_id,      /* lock id */
        &lock_status_block.lock_val,    /* value block */
        0,                              /* access mode */
        0                               /* flags */
        );
if (status != SS$_NORMAL) lib$stop(status);      /* error? */
}; /* while loop end */

};
```

Figure 7.9 (*Continued*)

7.6   OBJECT LIBRARIES

An object library is a file containing commonly used routines in
compiled form (not linked from). The advantage of this method is
that programmers do not have to write code to perform the functions of these routines; instead, they just link their programs with
the library. The routines can be used from a program by issuing
calls to the routines. In most other respects, the routines can be
treated as subroutines defined within the main program.

The main program must be linked with the object library. The
next set of steps shows how to create an object library of two
routines; one displays the current process identification and the
other reverses an input string. The LIBRARIAN utility is used to
create library files.

Figures 7.10 and 7.11 show the two subprograms (functions) that
will be inserted in the library.

```
/* PID.C function to print process id */

pid()
{
printf("\nProcess identification is: %d\n", getpid() );
}
```

Figure 7.10 Subprogram one for the object library.

```
/* REV.C
   function to reverse an input string
*/

revstr (instr,outstr)
char instr[], outstr[];
{
int tmp,pos;
outstr[0] = '\000';
tmp = strlen(instr);
for (tmp=strlen(instr)-1, pos = 0;  tmp=0;  tmp--, pos++ )
     outstr[pos] = instr[tmp];
}
```

Figure 7.11 Subprogram two for the object library.

To create the library, the commands are:

```
$CC  PID        ! compile the two programs
$CC  REVSTR
$LIBRARY/CREATE/OBJECT CLIB.OLB    ! Create library. File is CLIB.OLB
$LIBRARY/INSERT CLIB.OLB PID.OBJ, REVSTR.OBJ   ! Insert the mod-
ules in the library
```

The program in **Figure 7.12** calls the two routines in the object library created above.

```
/* mainpgm.c
*/

main()
{
char response[80],reversedstr[80];

pid();
printf("Input a string: "); gets(response);
revstr(response,reversedstr);
printf ("Input reversed is: %s", reversedstr);

}
```

Figure 7.12 A main program that uses the object library

The next set of commands create and run the main program image.

The library is specified in the LINK command line.

```
$CC MAINPGM
$LINK MAINPGM, CLIB.OLB/LIB, SYS$INPUT:/OPTION !Create
object module
SYS$SHARE:VAXCRTL/SHARE
<CTRL/Z>
$RUN MAINPGM
```

7.7 SHARED IMAGES

When, for example, 12 users simultaneously run the same program, the program is loaded 12 times in memory. This may cause memory to be depleted. The program can be redesigned so that only one image (of the program) is in memory while any number of other programs can use the image. In most cases the programs do not have to be rewritten; only the LINKER options have to be changed. Note that the data area must be separate for each user using the shared image (and that the shared image must be reentrant). Normally, this burden is assumed by the system. The linker creates separate sections (PSECTs) for program and data. When the shareable program image is run, the loader maps the installed shared image's code into the user's process and then creates a separate area in memory for the user's data.

An image on disk that can be installed as a shared image is called a shareable image. To avoid loading multiple copies of the image, it must be installed by using the INSTALL command.

Consider Figure 7.13, which shows a C program containing two C functions. The first function reverses a specified input string. The second function displays the process identification of the current process (which can also be displayed from DCL by $SHOW PROCESS.

```
/* File: revpid.c
 * The file contains two functions that
 * will be used to create a shareable image.
 */
```

Figure 7.13 Source program for a shareable image.

```
revstr (instr,outstr)
char instr[], outstr[];
/* the function reverses an input string */
{
int tmp,pos;
outstr[0] = '\000';
tmp = strlen(instr);
for (tmp=strlen(instr)-1, pos = 0;  tmp>=0;  tmp--, pos++ )
    outstr[pos] = instr[tmp];
};

pid()
/* display current process identification */
{
printf("\nProcess identification is: %X\n", getpid() );
};
```

Figure 7.13 (*Continued*)

These routines are used by a number of other programs. The routines can be put in an object library. However, because the code from object libraries is linked with the calling program, there is no saving in memory when a number of programs use the routines, i.e., the routines will be duplicated in each program's executable image. If the routines are put in a shareable image, other programs can still link to the routines; but the routines will be placed in memory only once. Here's how to create a shareable image of the routines.

```
$ cc revpid                  !compile the function file
$ link/notrace/share  revpid,sys$input:/option
sys$share:vaxcrtl/share
universal=pid
universal=revstr

$ copy revpid.exe  sys$share:  !move to the shareable image dir.
$ install sys$share:revpid.exe /share
```

The link command has the /SHARE qualifier so the image file is a shared image file. The options file (sys$input: in this case) contains the UNIVERSAL clause, which specifies that the function names are available to any other image linking with this image. Consider the C program in Figure 7.14.

```
/* mainpgm.c
*/
#include stdio

main()
{
char response[80],reversedstr[80];

pid();
printf("\nInput a string: "); gets(response);
revstr(response,reversedstr);
printf ("Input reversed is: %s", reversedstr);

};
```

Figure 7.14 A main program using a shareable image.

This program can be compiled and linked with the shared image by using:

```
$link  mainpgm,sys$input:/option
sys$share:vaxcrtl/share
sys$share:revpid/share
```

Here is a sample execution of the main program:

```
$ run mainpgm
Process identification is: 1057
Input a string: This is a Test
Input reversed is: tseT a si sihT
```

Note that shareable images can contain a set of commonly used routines that are similar to object libraries. The main difference is that programs link to one shared image of the common routines in memory, while routines from object libraries are included with the program. Shareable images have another advantage. They can be installed with privileges, i.e., shareable images can be designed to perform functions that require privileges not assigned to programs (processes) linking with these privileged shared images.

To see shared images that are installed in memory use:

```
$ install list
```

7.8 ASYNCHRONOUS SYSTEM TRAPS

An AST is an interruption to a program. The interruption is triggered by some event external to the program. Typically, the program services the interrupt by executing an interrupt service subprogram and continues where it left off in its normal flow of execution.

Consider a program that is required to loop indefinitely to accept a line of input from the terminal and display the line. The program is also required to display "Timer interrupt" every 5 sec on the terminal. The program in Figure 7.15 uses ASTs to achieve this.

```
/* AST.C              Jay Shah   27-DEC-1990
 * This program demonstrates use of ASTs.
 * The program loops to accept input from
 * the terminal and then display it. A
 * timer will generate an AST every 5
 * seconds and the AST routine will display
 * a message.
 */
#include stdio
#include descrip
#include ssdef

int status;
char delta_time[8];
$DESCRIPTOR(timbuf,"0 00:00:05.00");   /* 5 seconds */
int ast_routine();      /* routine declared later */

main()
{
char response[80];

status = sys$bintim(      /* convert ascii time to internal form */
        &timbuf,
        delta_time
        );
if (status != SS$_NORMAL) lib$stop(status);

/* set timer to interrupt normal program after specified time */
status = sys$setimr(
        35,                /* event flag */
        delta_time,          /* time before AST interrupt */
```

Figure 7.15 A demonstration program for ASTs.

```
             &ast_routine,              /* ast address */
             0,                  /* timer id, ignore */
             0                   /* elapsed time, not CPU time */
             );
if (status != SS$_NORMAL) lib$stop(status);

while(TRUE)      /* This loop will be regularly interrupted by the
timer */
   {
   printf("Enter any input: "); gets(response);
   printf("You entered %s\n",response);
   };

};
ast_routine()    /* This routine is invoked by timer interrupt AST */
{
printf("\nTimer interrupt\n\n");

/* rearm the timer */
status = sys$setimr(
         35,                /* event flag */
         delta_time,         /* time before AST interrupt */
         &ast_routine,        /* ast address */
         0,                /* timer id, ignore */
         0                 /* elapsed time, not CPU time */
         );
if (status != SS$_NORMAL) lib$stop(status);

};
```

Figure 7.15 (*Continued*)

To use ASTs in programs:

- The user should let the operating system know about the type of AST to enable and the subroutine to be executed when the AST condition is satisfied.

- Program execution is continued.

- When the AST condition is satisfied, the operating system will deliver the AST to your program. Effectively, execution control will transfer to the address of the subroutine. When the subroutine completes executing, normal program execution will continue. Note that once an AST has been delivered, the AST is disabled until it is "rearmed" (reenabled) by the subroutine or the program.

- Since the timing of AST delivery is not known to the program (that is why it is called asynchronous), the program and the AST routine should not make assumptions about the state of execution of each other. Specifically, common data access should be synchronized by some means such as the AST routine setting a flag when it has data ready for the main program to process.

ASTs can be used to invoke a routine on completion of some system services like $QIO, $ENQ, and $SETTIMR. In these calls, the address of the AST routine is given as a parameter. An AST routine can be explicitly invoked by the $DCLAST (declare AST) system service.

7.9 EXIT HANDLERS

A program can be interrupted during normal execution by, for example, the user entering CTRL/Y at the terminal. When a program image is stopped, the operating system performs cleanup operations such as closing files opened by the image. The operation is called winding down of the image. It may also be crucial for the image to perform its own cleanup before exiting. For example, the image may want to send a warning message to the operator terminal if it is aborted for any reason. Exit handlers are subroutines within programs that are executed if the program image is aborted. The subroutine is declared to the operating system by a SYS$DCLEXH system service call at the start of the program so that when the program aborts, the operating system calls the subroutine before deleting the image. The program image can abort because of:
- A CTRL/Y entered at the terminal from which the program is run
- A SYS$EXIT system service call from within the program
- A SYS$FORCEX call from another program (process) on the system

Figure 7.16 shows a program with an exit handler. To see the exit-handler function, abort the program by entering CTRL/Y on the terminal (followed by, for example, a DIR command so that the image rundown starts). The process identification (PID) is displayed by the $ SHOW SYSTEM command.

Note that image execution is temporarily halted when a CTRL/Y is entered at the terminal. The image execution can be continued by entering:

```
$ CONTINUE
```

If a command is entered and the command requires that a new image be run, the current image will be terminated before the new command is executed. The exit handler executes when the image is terminated and not when CTRL/Y is entered.

```
/* EXIT_HANDLER.C        Jay Shah   28-DEC-1990
 *
 * This program demonstrates the use of
 * exit handlers. When the program is
 * run, it continuously displays a string
 * on the terminal. If the program is
 * terminated by a CTRL/Y entered at
 * the terminal or by a SYS$FORCEX system
 * call from another process, the program
 * executes the exit-handler routine.
 */

#include stdio

int exit_handler(); /* exit-handler routine is at end */
int status;

/* data structure required to declare an exit handler */
int cond_val;
struct {
     int vms_reserved;
     char *ex_handler_address; /* address of exit handler */
     int argument_count;       /* optional arguments */
     int cond_val_addr;        /* condition value returned by vms */
     } descriptor_block
     = { 0, exit_handler, 0, &cond_val };
main()
{
status = sys$dclexh (&descriptor_block); /* declare the exit handler
*/

while(TRUE)      /* loop forever until program image is aborted */
   {
```

Figure 7.16 A demonstration of exit handlers.

```
  printf ("Waiting for a CTRL/Y ... ");
  sleep(2);
  };
};

exit_handler()
{
    printf ("This line printed by exit-handler routine\n");
};
```

Figure 7.16 (*Continued*)

7.10 DISTRIBUTED PROGRAMMING ACROSS VAXes

VAXes can be connected to each other by a DECnet network over Ethernet (multidrop lines), direct DDCMP (point-to-point) lines, or some other line type. VAXes could also be interconnected by a *computer interconnect* (CI) bus on a VAXcluster. All these VAXes can be used to develop distributed applications such as:

- *Distributed databases*. Data is spread on files on disks attached to the various VAXes. Programs on the VAXes communicate to transfer data and perform other data manipulations.

- *Distributed computing*. Applications can be designed so that parts of it run on individual computers for a higher overall throughput. An example is one VAX handling all terminal I/O, including input data validation, while another VAX acts as a database machine, storing, and managing data on disk.

- *Resource-sharing applications*. One server VAX may have an expensive supercomputer connected to it locally. The server VAX can allow controlled access to the supercomputer by means of appropriate task-to-task communications between the VAXes.

The following sections discuss how to write programs that interact with other programs over DECnet and VAXclusters.

7.10.1 Programming Using DECnet

This section shows how to execute command files over the network and use task-to-task communications programs.

7.10.1.1   Executing command files over the network

A command file can be executed on another machine by simply specifying the node name in the file specification. Here is a command, issued on node MAYUR:: to execute a command file NETCMD.COM on node GANGES::

```
$ @GANGES"SHAH KELTUM"::[TEST]NETCMD.COM
```

The following should be noted:

- The user name and password (SHAH and KELTUM) have to be specified as shown in the above command unless GANGES has a proxy account for user SHAH.

- The command effectively performs a login on GANGES, executes the specified command file there, and then logs off the VAX.

- Output and error messages are displayed on the source node.

7.10.1.2   Task-to-task communications over the network by command files

A command file can initiate the execution of another command file on another node. The command files can then transfer data to each other, effectively allowing communications between the nodes.

Here is an example. GANGES is on a DECnet network of VAXes and has a high-speed laser printer attached to it. Users on other VAXes wish to print files on this printer. The command file NETCMD_CLIENT.COM (Figure 7.17) can be on any node in a DECnet network. The command file NETSRV.COM (Figure 7.18) is in the login directory of user SHAH on GANGES. SHAH must have an account on GANGES. When NETCMD_CLIENT is executed, it will execute the command file NETSRV.COM on GANGES. The process name would be, for example, SERVER_0012. The file name of the file to be printed on GANGES will be prompted. The file is copied to GANGES by NETCMD_CLIENT.COM and printed by NETSRV.COM. The key command line is:

```
$ OPEN/READ/WRITE/ERROR=ERROR_EXIT NET_IO_CLIENT -
        GANGES"shah keltum"::"TASK=NETSRV"
```

Here, the open statement actually performs a network login from the current VAX to GANGES. The user name and password are specified within double quotes. After the login, the command file NETSRV.COM is run from the login directory. To see more information on the connection, use

```
$ NCP:==$NCP
$ NCP show known links
```

The command files then communicate via

- The channel specified in the OPEN statement in the client VAX. In this case the channel is NET_IO_CLIENT.

- The channel created by opening SYSNET: on the server VAX. In this case, the channel is NET_IO.

```
$!File: NETCMD_CLIENT.COM
$!
$! This command file can be used on any
$! node in a network to print a file from
$! that node on a printer attached to the
$! node GANGES::. The file NETSRV.COM must
$! be present on GANGES:: in your login
$! directory.
$!
$! The pair of command files can be modified
$! to write cooperating applications between
$! computers on a network.
$!
$ OPEN/READ/WRITE/ERROR=ERROR_EXIT NET_IO_CLIENT -
          GANGES"SHAH KELTUM"::"TASK=NETSRV"
$ IF P1 .EQS. "" THEN -
     $INQUIRE/NOPUNCTUATION P1 "File to be printed on GANGES: "
$ IF P1 .EQS. "" THEN $EXIT
$ COPY 'P1' GANGES"SHAH KELTUM"::
$ WRITE/ERROR=ERROR_EXIT NET_IO_CLIENT "''p1'"
$                !Send file name of command file to be executed
$ DISPLAY:       ! Display input from the other node
$   READ/END=END_NET/ERROR=ERROR_EXIT NET_IO_CLIENT OUTPUT_LINE
$   WRITE SYS$OUTPUT OUTPUT_LINE
$ GOTO DISPLAY
$ END_NET:
$ CLOSE NET_IO_CLIENT
$ EXIT
$!
$ ERROR_EXIT:
$ WRITE SYS$OUTPUT F$MESSAGE($STATUS)
$ EXIT
```

Figure 7.17 DECnet client command file.

```
$ !File: NETSRV.COM
$ !
$ ! This file acts as a server for network
$ ! requests from other nodes. The file
$ ! works in conjunction with
$ ! NETCMD_CLIENT.COM on other VAXes on the
$ ! network. Presently, it copies and prints
$ ! a file from the client node onto this node.
$ !
$ SET NOON
$ SET VERIFY
$
$ OPEN/READ/WRITE NET_IO SYS$NET:   !Open the channel to the process
on
$                                   !the source VAX.
$ READ/END=EXIT NET_IO FIL          !Read file name
$ DEFINE/USER SYS$OUTPUT NET_IO     !Set output for the next command
to
$                                   !go over the network to the process
$                                   !that executed this file.
$ PRINT 'FIL
$ CLOSE NET_IO
$ EXIT
```

Figure 7.18 A DECnet server command file.

A file NETSERVER.LOG will be created in the login directory on GANGES. This file will contain the output from the execution of the command file. The output is similar to that produced by executing a file using the SUBMIT command. The file can be used to debug the application.

7.10.1.3 Task-to-task communications over the network by programs

Program communication over the network is similar to command file communication described above. Here is an example where two C programs on different nodes communicate with each other. INQ_CLIENT.C (Figure 7.19) can reside on any node on a DECnet network. When its image is run, it executes the command file INQSER.COM (Figure 7.20) on node GANGES. The command file INQSER.COM is required on the server node to run the actual C program INQ_SERVER.C (Figure 7.21). The two C programs can pass data to each other. In this example, the client is asking for a table lookup in the server database.

```
/* This program, inq_client.c, performs
 * a database lookup on a server VAX on
 * the DECnet network. The server VAX runs
 * a command file INQSER.COM that in
 * turn runs a program inq_server.c, which
 * performs the database lookup based on a
 * key passed by this program and returns
 * the accessed value to this program.
 */

#include stdio
#include file

main ()
{
int net_chan, stat;     /* channel to server VAX */
char *buf;
char inp_buf[80];

/* invoke INQSER.COM on the server VAX */
net_chan = open ("ganges\"shah keltum\"::\"task=in-
qser.com\"",O_RDWR);
if (net_chan <0)
   {perror("network command file open error"); exit(SS$_NORMAL);};

buf = "7415";   /* search for this account on server VAX database */
stat = write(net_chan, buf, 4);
if (stat <0) exit(SS$_NORMAL); /*end of file*/

stat = read(net_chan, inp_buf, 80);        /* read account title sent
by server VAX */
if (stat <0) exit(SS$_NORMAL); /*end of file*/
printf ("%s",inp_buf);
if (stat == -1) exit(SS$_NORMAL); /*end of file*/

close (net_chan);
}
```

Figure 7.19 A DECnet client program

```
$! File: INQSER.COM
$! Database server for lookup of information
$! on this node by other nodes.
$ SET VERIFY
$ RUN INQ_SERVER.EXE
$ EXIT
```

Figure 7.20 A DECnet server command file.

```
/* This program, inq_server.c,is run by
 * the command file INQSER.COM that
 * is invoked by the program, inq_client.c,
 * on another VAX over the DECnet network.
 * The programs demonstrate a client-server
 * model for distributed applications on a
 * network.
 */

#include stdio
#include file
#include ssdef

main ()
{
int net_chan, chan_stat;          /* channel to client VAX */
char inp_buf[5];
char *tmp_title;

/* Create a database of account information. In practice, the data-
base would be on disk files.*/
struct acc_struct
      {
        char *no;
        char *title;
      };
struct acc_struct acc_info[5] =
             {
               { "2543", "Mary Smith"          },
               { "1234", "Peter Kak"           },
               { "7415", "James Shneider"       },
               { "8323", "John Bayer"           },
               { "9231", "Gene Cortess"         },
             };

/* Open the channel to the client VAX */
net_chan = open ("sys$net:",O_RDWR);
if (net_chan == -1) {perror("SYS$NET: open error"); exit(SS$_NOR-
MAL);};

/* Get account number from client VAX */
chan_stat = read(net_chan, inp_buf, 4);
if (chan_stat <=0 ) {perror("Error on network read");exit(SS$_NOR-
MAL);}

/* Given account number, find account title. In practice, this
   step would be a database lookup on disk. */
```

Figure 7.21 A DECnet server program.

```
tmp_title = "Account does not exist";
if (strcmp(inp_buf,acc_info[0].no) == 0) tmp_title=acc_info[0].ti-
tle;
else if (strcmp(inp_buf,acc_info[1].no) == 0) tmp_ti-
tle=acc_info[1].title;
else if (strcmp(inp_buf,acc_info[2].no) == 0) tmp_ti-
tle=acc_info[2].title;
else if (strcmp(inp_buf,acc_info[3].no) == 0) tmp_ti-
tle=acc_info[3].title;
else if (strcmp(inp_buf,acc_info[4].no) == 0) tmp_ti-
tle=acc_info[4].title;

/* Send account title to the client VAX */
chan_stat = write(net_chan, tmp_title, 512);
if (chan_stat <=0 ) {perror("Error on network write");exit(SS$_NOR-
MAL);}

close (net_chan);
}
```

Figure 7.21 (*Continued*)

The sequence of steps are:

- INQ_CLIENT.EXE is run on a VAX.

- The OPEN statement refers to another node, GANGES, so DECnet establishes a logical link with GANGES.

- The file SYS$SYSTEM:NETSERVER.COM is executed by DECnet on GANGES. This file in turn executes SYS$SYS-TEM:NETSERVER.EXE. This file, in turn works in conjunction with the process NETCAP and completes the connection. The execution of the specified command file INQSER.COM is logged in the login directory of NETSERVER.LOG.

- The device SYS$NET: on the server VAX is used to communicate back with the client VAX. This device is set up when the logical link is established.

Internode communications can be established by creating network objects. This method of communications does not require a command file to be executed on the server node, and it can offer more control of the link. For example, a network object can be set up to serve multiple nodes. Creating network objects is not discussed in this book.

7.10.2   Task-to-Task Communications within a VAXcluster

Normally, communication between tasks on a cluster is performed over DECnet. In this sense, the programs are similar to those described above. While the CI cluster connection can be used for communications, it is not recommended because the CI software and hardware is customized for cluster messages rather than arbitrary user messages. Moreover, when the cluster has HSCs, the CI is used for disk I/O between VAXes and the HSCs; using the CI for interprogram communications can degrade disk I/O performance.

7.11   DECdtm — DISTRIBUTED TRANSACTION MANAGER

Effective with version 5.4, VMS facilitates distributed-transaction processing by means of DECdtm system services. DECdtm is a software component of VMS that uses the standard two-phase commit protocol (2pc) for ensuring integrity of databases distributed on VAXes interconnected by a DECnet network. DECdtm is just a transaction manager and works in close conjunction with resource managers on individual VAXes on the network. Currently supported resource managers are *record management services* (RMS) journaling, Rdb, VAX DBMS, ACMS, DECintact, RALLY, and VAX SQL. Third-party database systems cannot be converted for distributed applications using DECdtm as the design of DECdtm is proprietary.

From a programmer's point of view, DECdtm comes into play when the following system services are used:

$START_TRANS	!Start a transaction
$END_TRANS	!Commit the transaction
$ABORT_TRANS	!Backout current transaction

Synchronous forms of the three system services can also be used:

$START_TRANSW	!Start a transaction
$END_TRANSW	!Commit the transaction
$ABORT_TRANSW	!Backout current transaction

These three services are similar to the corresponding one's shown above except that the program using a service waits until the service has completed execution, which is somewhat like the QIO and QIOW system services for I/O. Sample usage of the DECdtm system services is shown in the section of RMS journaling in the chapter on RMS.

DECdtm generates a unique *transaction identifier* (TID) for each $START_TRANS or $START_TRANSW call issued from any program on the VAX. Transactions are tracked by TIDs. Each node on the network (and VAXcluster) has a separate log file where transaction information is maintained by DECdtm. The transaction log file is created by the LMCP utility described later.

Programmers can convert current simple RMS applications on single nodes for operation in a transaction-oriented, high-availability, distributed environment by using RMS journaling. RMS journaling can be used on files across a network by specifying the node name in the data file specifications as in:

```
VAX3::database_disk:savings.account
```

Of course, Rdb or other supported systems software can also be used instead of RMS journaling.

7.11.1 Log Manager Control Program (LMCP) Utility

While DECdtm system services are available with VMS, transactions cannot be started until a transaction log file is created on the system. The LMCP CREATE command is used to create the log file. A log file must be present on each participating node on the network. The log file is used to maintain states of current transactions so that proper recovery is ensured in the event of node failures. Here is an example of a creation of a log file:

```
$ MCR LMCP
Log Manager Control Program V1.0
LMCP> CREATE LOGFILE SYSTEM$NODEA
```

Here NODEA is the DECnet node name of the VAX. The file will be   SYS$COMMON:[SYSEXE]SYSTEM$NODEA.LM$JOURNAL. The file can be created on any disk and directory, but the file name must be of the form SYSTEM$nodename. In a VAXcluster, one file must be created for each node. If a node fails, another VAX will access the file and continue processing transactions on behalf of the failed VAX.

The /SIZE qualifier can be used to preallocate blocks in the log file. The value will depend on the maximum number of currently-in-progress transactions anticipated on that node. DEC recommends a size specified by :

Log file size in blocks = Transaction start rate × transaction duration × 40

The parameters can be determined by observing DECdtm performance, using the $MONITOR TRANSACTION command. For example, if up to 10 transactions can be in progress at any time and the node takes 12 sec to process a transaction, then the log file size should be 10 x 12 x 40 = 4800 blocks. This can be specified as

```
LMCP> CREATE LOGFILE/SIZE=4800 SYSTEM$NODEA
```

In addition, a number of LMCP commands are available for dumping the contents of the log file and changing transaction states that can be useful when a node fails and later reboots.

7.11.2 Monitoring DECdtm Activity

The MONITOR command now has TRANSACTION as a new parameter. Figure 7.22 shows a sample usage.

```
$ MONITOR TRANSACTION
                VAX/VMS Monitor Utility
             DISTRIBUTED TRANSACTION STATISTICS
                 on node GANESH
              19-MAR-1991 14:35:54
                           CUR      AVE      MIN      MAX
      Start Rate           3.00     5.00     1.00     8.00
      Prepare Rate         2.00     4.00     1.00     9.00
      One Phase Commit Rate 2.00    5.00     0.00     7.00
      Total Commit Rate    4.00     6.00     0.00     9.00
      Abort Rate           0.00     0.00     0.00     0.00
      End Rate             0.00     0.00     0.00     0.00
      Remote Start Rate    0.00     0.00     0.00     0.00
      Remote Add Rate      0.00     0.00     0.00     0.00


      Completion Rate   0-1  0.00    0.00     0.00     0.00
      by Duration       1-2  1.00    1.00     0.00     2.00
      in Seconds        2-3  1.00    4.00     1.00     3.00
                        3-4  2.00    1.00     0.00     5.00
                        4-5  0.00    0.00     0.00     0.00
                        5+   0.00    0.00     0.00     0.00
```

Figure 7.22 MONITOR TRANSACTION output.

7.12   THE ROLE OF ELECTRONIC DISKS

In most major applications, there is a need to share data among processes on the system. Disk files can be shared. However, they may be too slow for high-volume on-line applications. On an independent VAX computer, the application database can be stored in global sections in main memory. This way, fairly large amounts of data, which can be efficiently accessed, can be shared by multiple processes. Of course, system failures can cause data in global sections to be erased. Moreover, global sections cannot be used for storing more than a few Mbytes of data, depending on the amount of available main memory. So most applications make judicious use of global sections and disk files.

VAXclusters do not have global sections that can be shared by processes on different VAXes in the cluster. Since disk files can be shared, most applications resort to putting shared data on magnetic disks, causing the application to run inefficiently. A simple, though possibly expensive, solution is to use electronic disks. These disk devices are accessed like any other disk on the VAXcluster. Instead of storing data on a rotating magnetic medium, these disk-devices store data in semiconductor memory that is similar to the main memory on VAX systems. The semiconductor memory is also known as *random access memory* (RAM).

Currently, DEC offers one electronic disk — the *electronic storage element 20* (ESE20). For most practical purposes, it is an ordinary RA series disk drive except that it is fast. The disk has an access time of 1.3 msec and can handle over 300 I/Os per sec. Theoretically, on a VAXcluster the electronic disk can be up to 10 times faster than a typical magnetic disk. A speedup of four-fold can be achieved with little or no changes to the applications, provided all the disk files are moved to the electronic disk.

The formatted storage capacity of the ESE20 is 120 Mbytes. The disk is compliant with *digital storage architecture* (DSA). The disk has a backup magnetic disk and a rechargeable battery power supply. In case of power failure, data in the disk's RAM memory is written on the magnetic disk. When power resumes, the data in the magnetic disk is copied back to the semiconductor memory.

Data common to processes on the VAXcluster and that require fast access by an application can be stored on the ESE20 disk. On an independent VAX computer, global sections can be accessed more quickly than electronic disks. The application designer will have to make trade-offs between using global sections, electronic disks, and magnetic disks.

7.13   THE DISK-STRIPING DRIVER

The disk-striping driver software can be used to create one large logical disk from a set of physical disks. The logical blocks are spread over the physical disks such that the first few blocks are on the first physical disk, the next few are on the next physical disk, and so on. This way, a typical file will have data blocks spread over multiple disks. The advantage here is that file access requests will be serviced by multiple physical disks, resulting in faster I/O response time. This may be important for reasons given in the previous section. Performance can significantly improve with applications that have heavily accessed, large data files if these files are placed on striped disks.

The STRIPE command is used for disk-striping operations. Here are a series of commands for mounting three RA92s as a disk striping set.

```
$ STRIPE/INITIALIZE/CHUNK_SIZE=50 -
    $2$DUA3:,$1$DUA12:,$1$DUA5:  1,2,3
    !The three volumes are volumes 1,2, and 3 in sequence.

$ STRIPE/BIND $2$DUA3:,$1$DUA12:,$1$DUA5:  STRIPE$DEV1
$ INITIALIZE STRIPE$DEV1 STRIPE$DISK1
$ MOUNT/SYSTEM STRIPE$DEV1 STRIPE$DISK1

$!Here is an example command:
$ COPY DISK$USERS:TMP.DATA  STRIPE$DISK1:TMP.DATA
```

The chunk_size qualifier specifies that the first 50 logical blocks of the stripe disk will be on physical disk 1, the next 50 will be on physical disk 2, and so on. The overall storage capacity of the stripe set volume is about three times the capacity of one RA92. Individual volumes in the stripe set can be shadowed. Disks with different geometries cannot be mixed in a stripe set. So, for example, RA90s and RA92s cannot be part of the same stripe set.

Multivolume disk-striping logical disks are not to be confused with multivolume volume sets. VMS allows a set of disks to be mounted as one large logical disk without using the disk-striping driver. This large logical disk is called a volume set. When files are created on this logical disk, any free space on a physical disk is allocated before the next physical disk is used. Overall I/O throughput will be about the same as when individual physical disks are mounted as separate logical disks.

7.14 AUTOMATIC FAILOVERS

Applications running on a cluster should be designed so that users can access the application from multiple nodes on a cluster. That way, if a VAX fails, the users can access the application from other VAXes.

Usually on a VAXcluster, terminals are connected to terminal servers on Ethernet. VAXes on the Ethernet, including those which are VAXcluster members, offer *local area transport* (LAT) services. Users access a VAX by connecting to a service offered by that VAX. The same service can be offered by multiple VAXes, in which case users connecting to the service will be connected to one of the VAXes offering the service. The VAX that the users are connected to will depend on the service rating of the VAX, which should not be of concern to the users. Typically, VAXes in a cluster will offer the same service, so users connecting to the service will be using one of the cluster VAXes. This way, if a VAX fails or a VAX is removed from the cluster, users will be able to transparently log into one of the other VAXes. Individual VAXes in the cluster can also offer their own services.

When a VAX in the cluster with logged-on users fails, the users will be able to reconnect to one of the other VAXes. This is one of the main reasons why the applications should be accessible from any VAX. Note that when a VAX fails, the sessions of logged-on users are aborted. The application must back out transactions which were left incomplete by the user.

The terminals on a terminal server can be dedicated to a particular service. In this case, when the user enters the return key, the terminal automatically connects to one of the VAXes that offer the service. If the VAX to which a dedicated terminal is connected fails, the user session aborts; on entering the return key, the terminal connects to another VAX offering the same service.

7.15 REDUNDANCY OF PRINTER AND BATCH QUEUES

VAXes on a cluster can have generic printer queues. These logical queues can point to one or more queues on the VAXes with attached printers. The output will be generated on one of the free printers. If one of the VAXes fails, further jobs sent to the generic queue are directed to the remaining queues. Jobs already in the queue of the failing VAX will not be completed and will have to be resubmitted.

Queues are also supported on printers connected to terminal servers on Ethernet. Such queues can be created, one per VAX, on all the VAXes on the cluster. The terminal server interacts with the VAXes to sequentially print the jobs. Failure of a VAX stops the jobs submitted to the queue on that VAX; other VAXes are not affected. In fact, printers on terminal servers can be shared by queues on VAXes that are not necessarily on the VAXcluster.

Batch job queues, like print queues, can be generic. Jobs submitted to these queues will actually run on a VAX that is the least "busy." If a VAX fails, the batch jobs running on that VAX will remain in the generic queue. The jobs will have to be restarted. Batch queues can also be local to a VAX, in which case the jobs submitted to these queues will execute properly irrespective of failures of other VAXes in the cluster. Note that if a job is submitted to a generic queue, the user submitting the job must have the necessary privileges to run batch jobs from any VAX to which the job can be routed. The chapter on managing VAXclusters shows how to create generic queues on a VAXcluster.

7.16   FDDI AND VAXclusters

FDDI (*fiber distributed data interface*) defines a standard for interconnecting computers and peripherals using fiber optics technology. The standard is being formulated by the American National Standards Institute (ANSI) committee X3T9.5, which was formed in 1982.

FDDI cables have a raw bandwidth of 100 Mbits/sec (in contrast to Ethernet, which has a theoretical peak bandwidth of 10 Mbits/sec and a throughput of less than 4 Mbits/sec for most practical applications). An FDDI-based LAN (local area network) can have a circumference of about 60 miles. As elaborated later, FDDI specifies a dual ring, token-passing technique for communications. A tree-structured configuration can also be designed.

A computer connects to a fiber optic cable via a concentrator. The computer (or device) connecting to the concentrator is called an attachment station. A station can be one of two types: a *single attachment station* (SAS) or a *dual attachment station* (DAS). A SAS connects to one of the dual rings (the primary ring) via the concentrator. The DAS, which is more complex and expensive, can connect to both the primary and backup rings, creating redundancy.

DEC's FDDI concentrator is DECconcentrator 500. At the time this book was written, DEC did not have a SAS or DAS module that could plug into a VAX system and directly communicate with a concentrator. Such modules will soon be announced. (FDDIcontroller 700 allows a DECstation 5000, which is a RISC computer, to be directly connected to a concentrator.) Meanwhile, the DECbridge 500 device allows Ethernet to be connected to the FDDI concentrator. The DECbridge is a SAS. Effectively, a set of Ethernet LANs can be interconnected by a FDDI backbone. Figure 7.23 shows a possible FDDI network.

FDDI specifies a token ring network. Dual rings, called the primary and backup rings, are used for redundancy. A token circulates in the primary ring. A station will receive a token from an adjacent station. The station merely repeats the token for the next station unless it wishes to transmit data. A station can transmit data only if it has obtained (absorbed) the token. Once it has absorbed the token, the station sends out the data frame followed by the token. Intermediate stations repeat the data frames and the token. The destination station reads the frame (and processes it as required by the application), sets appropriate status flags in the frame, and transmits it. The destination station then receives and repeats the token. The transmitting station reads the frame returned by the destination station, checks the status bits, deter-

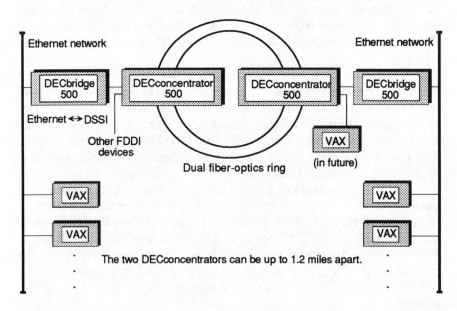

Figure 7.23 A simple FDDI network.

mines that the frame has been read by the destination station, and strips the frame off the ring. The transmitting station then receives and repeats the token. This is the basic commununication technique on FDDI.

For more efficient usage of the high-fiber optics bandwidth, FDDI allows more than one data frame to circulate in the ring. Consider a configuration where four stations A, B, C, and D are in sequence on the ring. Station A is sending a data frame to station C, and station B wants to send a frame to station D. Station B will receive a data frame and the token from station A, which station B would repeat if it did not have any data frame to transmit. But since station B has data ready for transmission, it repeats station A's data frame, receives the token, transmits its data frame, and then transmits the token. This way any station can transmit data frames when it has absorbed the token. Effectively, multiple frames can precede a token on the ring.

FDDI is an emerging technology. For VAXclusters it is likely to have the following significant impact:

- Currently, the cluster communications is performed using either Ethernet or the CI bus (70Mbits/sec bandwidth). Moreover, the maximum cluster radius in case of the CI bus is 45 meters. If, FDDI becomes the cluster communications medium, a cluster could communicate more efficiently over a much wider area.

- With an appropriate design, mirrored disks can be placed at multiple locations that are fairly distant from each other. Disk I/O can flow through the fiber optics cable. This can reduce the need for a disaster recovery procedure, and a site failure will have little impact on normal operations.

7.17 SUMMARY

The chapter discussed issues of concern to applications designers and programmers. The emphasis was on programming features unique to VAX/VMS; general programming concepts were not discussed. Most of the features discussed are available to programmers on independent VAXes and VAXclusters.

The distributed lock manager is the key component for program synchronization among programs on different nodes on a cluster. Programs on different nodes can communicate with each other by using DLM or DECnet. In the coming years, fiber optics–based networks will play a major role in VAXcluster systems. The chapter introduced FDDI and fiber optics components.

An application distributed across VAXes in a cluster is very likely to be using disk files that are common to the cluster member VAXes. The next chapter describes record management services which is a key facility on VAXclusters.

8

RMS—Record Management Services

RMS (*record management services*) is the component of VAX/VMS (and VAXclusters) that controls and manages access to disks and tape volumes. VAX/VMS supports three major types of disk files: *sequential, relative,* and *indexed* (ISAM). Tape files can only be sequential. These files and the records in these files are manipulated using RMS. Since RMS is integrated with the operating system, no commands have to be issued to use it. RMS can be used over DECnet to manipulate files on other nodes by specifying the node name in the file specifications.

VAXclusters support distributed RMS. Files on disks are available for access by any VAX on a VAXcluster. The same file can be opened from multiple nodes in a cluster. If a process on a node locks a record, distributed RMS will not allow processes on other nodes to access that record. RMS on a cluster makes extensive use of the *distributed lock manager* to ensure controlled access of files and records by processes on cluster member VAXes.

8.1 OVERVIEW

Files on disk consist of a logically sequential set of data blocks. Physically, these blocks may be scattered on the disk. Information about block usage is maintained in two files, INDEXF.SYS and BITMAP.SYS. These files are in directory [000000] on each disk.

The block size (also known as sector size) on the disk is 512 bytes. The record size can be defined to be variable or fixed when a file is created. For practical applications, files can be arbitrarily large, provided there is adequate free disk space.

Records in sequential files can be accessed sequentially from the beginning of the file. Once a record is skipped over, it can be accessed only by scanning the file from the first record. Records are created at the end of the file and cannot be deleted. Records can be updated as long as the new record's size does not exceed the size of the existing record.

Relative files, also known as random files, have fixed-size record cells. When the file is created, the cells may be defined to contain fixed- or variable-length records. Records can be accessed in any order. So record number 50 can be accessed, followed by record 10, and then record 65. Records can be inserted, deleted, or updated at any cell position.

Records in indexed files have keys. Records can be accessed randomly by specifying the key of the record. Records can also be accessed sequentially; RMS will return records sorted by keys. Keys are defined by their position and length in the record. For example, an indexed file can have records of 120 bytes and two keys, the first key of length 7 (starting at position 5) and the second key of length 25 (starting at position 50). An indexed file has at least one key called the primary key. The file can have up to 254 additional keys called alternate keys. Indexed files usually have two logical areas; one contains the data records and the other contains keys and data record pointers. The keys are stored sorted as a B-tree data structure. Actually, if an index file has more than one key, then a separate area can be created for each key.

To see file attributes of an existing file, the command is

```
$ DIR/FULL file name
```

For example,

```
$ DIR/FULL client.dat
Directory SYS$SYSDEVICE:[MAYUR.DATA]

CLIENT.DAT;15                        File ID:  (1526,286,0)
Size: 15/15                          Owner:    (200,12)
Created: 10-JUL-1988 15:20           Revised:  10-JUL-1988 15:21 (1)
Expires: <None specified>            Backup:   <No backup done>
File organization:         Indexed, Prolog: 3, Using 2 keys
File attributes:           Allocation:15,Extend:0,Maximum bucket size:2
                           Global buffer count: 0, No version limit
```

```
Record format:            Fixed length 55 byte records
Record attributes:        Carriage return carriage control
Journaling enabled:       None
File protection:          System:RWED, Owner:RWED, Group:RE, World:
Access Cntrl List:        None

Total of 1 file, 15/15 blocks.
```

The file is CLIENT.DAT, version 15. The used size is 15 blocks, and the actual allocated size is 15 blocks also. The file type is indexed and has two keys. The record attribute parameter specifies that RMS will append a carriage return (and line feed) after every record when the file is typed.

8.2   RECORD FORMATS

RMS supports four record formats:

1. Fixed length   All fixed-length records have the same length. The record length is stored in the file header.

2. Variable length Variable-length records (VARs) are preceded by a 2-byte header, specifying the length of the record.

3. VFC   Variable length with fixed-length control (VFC) records have a variable data area with a fixed-control field in the front. The control field can be used as a hidden field for storing information pertaining to the record.

4. Stream   Stream (STM) records are variable length, delimited by a terminator. The terminator is usually a carriage return, line-feed, or a carriage return and a line-feed (specified as Stream_CR, Stream_LF, or Stream).

While the maximum record size depends on file attributes, RMS supports a size of at least 16,000 bytes for any format. Relative and indexed files support variable-length records, but the maximum record size must be specified for relative files when the file is created. Since relative files have fixed-record cells, space is not

• 28-byte fixed-length records (fix:28)

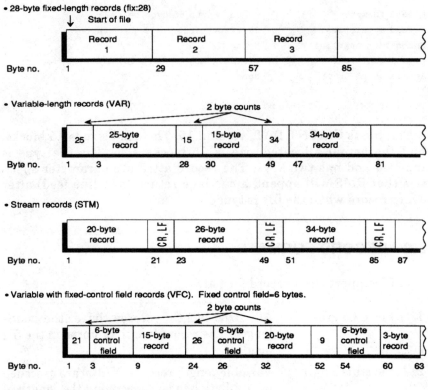

Figure 8.1 Record formats.

conserved by storing records that are smaller than the maximum size. Figure 8.1 shows various record formats.

Usually, fixed-record format incurs the least processing overhead. Variable-record formats also do not have a high overhead, but 2 bytes per record are used to store the count of characters in the record. Figure 8.2 shows some of the file characteristics.

8.3 INITIAL ALLOCATION

RMS dynamically allocates disk blocks as new records are added to files. This incurs the overhead of scanning for free blocks on disks. This overhead can be eliminated if disk blocks are allocated to the file when it is created. Also, if disk blocks are dynamically allocated, there is a chance of the disk running out of free blocks. If the number of records to be stored is known when the file is created,

File organization	Record format *	Maximum record size	Random access support
Sequential	FIX	32,767	No
	VAR	32,767	No
	VFC	32,767-FSZ	No
	STM	32,767	No
Sequential (tape)	VAR	9,995	No
Relative	FIX	32,225	Yes
	VAR	32,253	Yes
	VFC	32,253-FSZ	Yes
Indexed	FIX	32,224	Yes
	VAR	32,224	Yes

* Note: FIX = fixed-length records;
VAR = variable-length records;
STM = stream records (including STM_CR and STM_LF);
VFC = variable length with fixed-length control field records; and
FSZ = fixed-control field size of VFC records

Figure 8.2 File characteristics.

then preallocating the required number of blocks ensures that the disk will not run out of space when creating records in the file. If more blocks are required when writing to the file at a later stage, RMS allocates them dynamically.

8.4 EXTEND SIZE

When a record is being added to a file and there are no more blocks in the file, RMS allocates just enough blocks from the disk's free block list to fit the new record. This allocation overhead can be reduced by having RMS allocate more blocks at a time than required for storing the record. That way when additional records are created, RMS does not have to allocate new blocks for every record that is created. The number of new blocks that are allocated at one time is called the extend size. The extend size can be specified when the file is created.

For example, if a file has fixed-size records of 1000 bytes and the extend size is 7, then when the first record is created, RMS allocates 7 blocks (7 X 512 = 3584 bytes) to the file. No blocks are allocated when the next two records are created. A set of 7 blocks will be allocated when the fourth record is created.

Large extend sizes may cause the last extend of the file to be mostly empty. The default extend quantity is defined when the disk is initialized. This can be overridden during the disk mount. For example,

```
$MOUNT /EXTENSION=10   DUA0: VMSUSER
```

sets an extend size of 10 blocks for disk DUA0. To see the disk's extend size use the command:

```
$SHOW DEVICE DUA0: /FULL
```

8.5 DISK CLUSTER SIZE

The free-allocated information of every block on the disk is maintained in a table file called BITMAP.SYS. One entry would normally be required for each block. To reduce the size of this table, the minimum allocation quantity is a disk cluster (not to be confused with a VAXcluster), which is defined as one or more consecutive blocks. So if the cluster size parameter is 4, then the size of the cluster allocation table would be one-fourth the size of a similar table maintaining block allocation information. When a file requires more blocks, RMS determines how many blocks the file should have as determined by the extend size parameter. Just enough clusters are allocated to fit the allocated blocks. In addition to fragmentation due to overallocation of blocks in the last extend of the file, there is further disk fragmentation due to overallocation of blocks in the last cluster of the file. As a trade-off, RMS speed increases. The cluster size parameter can be displayed by

```
$SHOW DEVICE DUA0: /FULL
```

8.6 I/O BUCKETS

A bucket is a sequence of blocks used by RMS for each transfer from disk to memory and memory to disk. If the bucket size of a file is defined as 5 during file creation and a block is required to be read by RMS, then RMS will read the complete bucket containing the block. Reading 5 blocks at a time is faster than reading 5 blocks, one block at a time. Large bucket sizes are useful for sequential access in relative or indexed files since the probability is high that the next record to be accessed has already been read in memory. More physical memory is used as file buffers for larger buckets. Records cannot span across buckets. If records are accessed in random mode rather than sequentially, large bucket sizes may in fact slow down RMS. Bucket sizes can be up to 32 blocks in RMS. A default bucket size of 0 will cause the bucket size to be just large enough to hold one record.

8.7   BLOCK SPANNING

If a file contains records of size 400 bytes, the first record will fit in the first block allocated to the file, while the second record will span over from the first block to the second. In fact, many records in the file will span blocks, so that most reads and writes involve two blocks. To avoid this, the file can be defined to have no-spanning of records, which means that records cannot continue across blocks and that the maximum record size is limited to 512 bytes. (Actually 510 bytes for VAR record-length files since 2 bytes are used for storing the size of each record. Also, some more bytes may be used in index files for index information.) When a record is being created in a no-spanning file and the record cannot fit in the remaining space in the last block of the file, that space will be wasted and the record will be stored in the beginning of the next block. No-spanning reduces file I/O at the expense of unutilized fragments in the file. See Figure 8.3.

8.8   FILES AND RECORDS: SHARING AND LOCKING

Many on-line applications require a number of programs to share the same set of disk files. The first program opening a file can allow

- No access
- Read access
- Read and write access

to other programs attempting to open the file.

200-byte fixed-length records

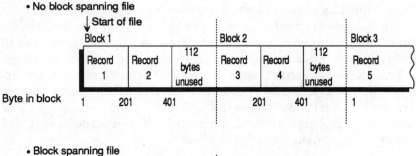

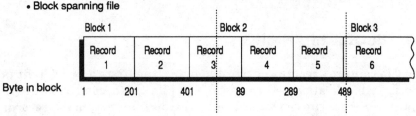

Figure 8.3 Record spanning.

When two programs share a file, there is a possibility that both of them will attempt to simultaneously update a particular record. RMS supports two methods for record locking to avoid contention:

1.   Automatic record locking

2.   Manual record locking

In the case of automatic record locking, RMS handles record locking on behalf of the program accessing the file. If the file is opened for read access, then other programs are allowed read access to any record. If the file is opened for write or update, other programs cannot access records being read by the first program. This is the default locking method.

If the first program opening a file declares manual record locking, then the programs explicitly lock and unlock records. Multiple records from the same file can be locked using this method. Any record can be locked so that other programs cannot access the record at all or can access it for reading only.

8.9   INDEXED FILE PARAMETERS

Here are some terms used in the context of indexed files.

8.9.1 Duplicate Keys

When an indexed file is created, the DUPLICATE KEY option can be specified for any key. Records with the same key value can be inserted in a file only if the DUPLICATE KEY option is specified for that key number. When accessing these records, only the first record can be retrieved by giving the key value. The other records have to be sequentially accessed.

8.9.2 Changeable Keys

When the CHANGEABLE KEY option is specified for alternate keys, existing records can be updated with new values for these alternate keys and RMS will update the alternate indexes accordingly. An update that changes the primary key has to be implemented as a DELETE followed by an INSERT of the record.

8.9.3 Areas

By default, data and keys are intermingled in the data blocks of the indexed file. For better performance they can be placed in separate areas within the same file. An area is simply an internal logical partition of the file for better performance when searching for keys. In fact each key group (specified by a key number) can be placed in separate areas. Separate areas can be specified when creating files using the EDIT/FDL utility.

8.9.4 Index Bucket Size

A bucket is an integer multiple of 512-byte blocks. Each area consists of a set of buckets. When records are inserted, keys are in key buckets. When a bucket is filled and a new key has to be inserted in the bucket, the bucket is split and the depth of the tree structure is increased by 1. This reduces CPU performance. Larger bucket sizes should be specified when the file is created. The trade-off is that when keys are searched in buckets, whole buckets are brought in memory and this in turn deteriorates performance if bucket sizes are large. Generally, bucket sizes should be increased if index depth levels exceed 1.

8.9.5   Record Key Fill Factor

Usually, a number of records are initially inserted when indexed files are created. Records are then randomly inserted in the future. If key buckets are packed (with a fill factor of 100 percent) by the initial record load, there will be many bucket splits when records are randomly inserted later. This causes a deterioration in performance. If a lower fill factor (say 50 percent) is specified when the file is created, the initial record load will fill buckets only to the specified level. Later, when records are randomly inserted, the free space in the buckets is used to store key information reducing the amount of bucket splits. The trade-off for a lower fill factor is more disk space required for the initial loading of the file.

Figure 8.4 shows a COBOL program for accessing a RMS-indexed file.

8.10   USING RMS FILES IN C AND Macro-32

In COBOL, BASIC, FORTRAN, and most other high level languages, the languages have standard constructs (statements) for accessing RMS files. C has some constructs built into the language, but these do not support many of the RMS features. For example, C has no means of accessing indexed files; VAX/VMS system service routines have to be used for this purpose. MACRO-32 uses a set of macros defined in SYS$LIBRARY:STARLET.MLB. This file is scanned during assembly of programs. To use indexed files in such cases, an understanding of RMS data structures is essential.

8.10.1 RMS Data Structures

RMS associates four data structures with every file:

1. *FAB (file access block)*. This contains file information such as file organization.

2. *RAB (record access block)* . This contains record-level information such as record number for relative files.

3. *XAB (extended access block)* . This contains additional information such as key length and position for indexed files.

```
IDENTIFICATION DIVISION.
PROGRAM-ID. INDEXED_IO.
* The program opens and populates an indexed file
* with two keys. The compilation commands are:
*      $ COBOL INDEXED_IO
*      $ LINK INDEXED_IO

ENVIRONMENT DIVISION.
INPUT-OUTPUT SECTION.
FILE-CONTROL.
   SELECT CIF-FILE ASSIGN TO "CLIENT.DAT"
     ORGANIZATION IS INDEXED
     ACCESS MODE IS DYNAMIC
     RECORD KEY IS DDA-NUMBER
     ALTERNATE RECORD KEY IS SWIFT-ADDRESS WITH DUPLICATES.
DATA DIVISION.
FILE SECTION.
FD  CIF-FILE.
01  CLIENT-INFORMATION.
    02  DDA-NUMBER            PIC X(9).
    02  CLIENT-ADDRESS        PIC X(35).
    02  SWIFT-ADDRESS         PIC X(11).

PROCEDURE DIVISION.
START-PROGRAM.
   OPEN OUTPUT CIF-FILE.
   DISPLAY "Creating and populating the CIF indexed file".
   DISPLAY "Enter OVER for DDA-NUMBER to terminate".
   PERFORM UNTIL DDA-NUMBER = "OVER"
    DISPLAY "Enter DDA number: " WITH NO ADVANCING
    ACCEPT DDA-NUMBER WITH CONVERSION
    IF DDA-NUMBER NOT = "OVER" THEN
      DISPLAY "Enter SWIFT address: " WITH NO ADVANCING
      ACCEPT SWIFT-ADDRESS
      DISPLAY "Enter client address: " WITH NO ADVANCING
      ACCEPT CLIENT-ADDRESS
      WRITE CLIENT-INFORMATION INVALID KEY
        PERFORM
        DISPLAY "Problem during write, RMS STATUS = "
            RMS-STS OF CIF-FILE WITH CONVERSION
        STOP RUN
        END-PERFORM
      END-IF
   END-PERFORM.
   STOP RUN.
```

Figure 8.4 COBOL program for accessing a RMS-indexed file.

4. *NAM (name block).* An optional block for storing complete file name specification when the FAB contains incomplete (wildcard) information. For example, the file specification in FAB may not contain the version number (the latest version assumed), but RMS will store it in the NAM block when the file is opened.

Opening a file requires creating these data structures, storing the file and record attributes in them, and issuing the RMS OPEN call. In most languages like COBOL and FORTRAN, these structures are created by the compiler when parsing OPEN statements. In C, the four data structures are defined by RMS.H and they have to be expicitly created by the programmer. The basic C RMS calls for file operations are sys$create, sys$open, sys$close, and sys$erase. These calls take the address of FAB as the only parameter and return RMS STATUS. The basic record operation calls are sysget, sysput, sys$update, and sys$delete. These calls take the address of RAB as the only parameter and return RMS STATUS.

Since the four data structures contain many fields, RMS.H provides prototypes for initializing the structures with default values. For example, the prototype to initialize the FAB data structure is cc$rms_fab. The file RMS.H is in the SYS$LIBRARY: directory. The fields of the four data blocks are described in the files NAM.H, FAB.H, RAB.H, and XAB.H within the directory SYS$LIBRARY:.

Figure 8.5 shows a C program to create an indexed file and write one record in it. The optional NAM block is not used.

```
/*      INDEXED_IO.C
 *      Program opens and populates a RMS indexed file.
 *      The compilation commands are:
 *            $ cc indexed_io
 *            $ link indexed_io,sys$input:/option
 *            sys$share:vaxcrtl.exe/share
 */
#include rms
#include stdio
#include ssdef
struct FAB fab;
struct RAB rab;
struct XABKEY primary_key,alternate_key;
int rms_status;
```

Figure 8.5 Indexed file I/O in the C language.

```
struct {                          /*Indexed file record layout*/
     char dda_number[9];
     char client_address[35];
     char swift_address[11];
     } cif_record;

main()
{

char input_buffer[512];            /*for terminal input*/

initialize("CLIENT.DAT");
                         /*open file and
                         set up fab,rab,and xab*/
rms_status = sys$create(&fab);      /*create the file*/
if (rms_status != RMS$_NORMAL)
   {
   printf("file: CLIENT.DAT create error\n");
   exit(rms_status);
   };
rms_status = sys$connect(&rab);      /*associate fab and rab*/
if (rms_status != RMS$_NORMAL)
   {
   printf("file: CLIENT.DAT open error\n");
   exit(rms_status);
   };

/* get input from user and write records to file*/
printf("Creating and populating indexed file\n");
for (;;)                          /*forever*/
   {
   printf("Enter dda number (OVER to terminate): ");
   gets(&input_buffer);
   if (strcmp("OVER",input_buffer) == 0) exit();
   strncpy(cif_record.dda_number,input_buffer,
        sizeof cif_record.dda_number);

   printf("Enter client address: ");
   gets(&input_buffer);
   strncpy(cif_record.client_address,input_buffer,
        sizeof cif_record.client_address);

   printf("Enter SWIFT address: ");
   gets(&input_buffer);
   strncpy(cif_record.swift_address,input_buffer,
```

Figure 8.5 (*Continued*)

```
              sizeof cif_record.swift_address);


    rab.rab$b_rac = RAB$C_KEY;            /*these are required*/
    rab.rab$l_rbf = &cif_record;          /*for every write   */
    rab.rab$w_rsz = sizeof cif_record;

    rms_status = sys$put(&rab);           /*write record to file*/
    if (rms_status != RMS$_NORMAL &&
      rms_status != RMS$_OK_DUP)
        {
        printf("file: CLIENT.DAT write error\n");
        exit(rms_status);
        };
    }; /*for loop end*/
} /*end of main*/


initialize(file_name)
    char *file_name;
/* This routine is required to initialize the fab,rab, and xab data
structures.*/
{
    fab = cc$rms_fab;                     /*default initializations*/
    fab.fab$b_fac = FAB$M_DEL |           /*record operations to be*/
            FAB$M_GET |           /*performed: delete,read*/
            FAB$M_PUT |           /*write and update */
            FAB$M_UPD;
    fab.fab$l_fna = file_name;
    fab.fab$b_org = FAB$C_IDX;
                              /*file organization indexed*/
    fab.fab$b_fns = strlen(file_name);
    fab.fab$l_xab = &primary_key;         /*pointer to first xab*/

    rab = cc$rms_rab;                 /*initialize rab*/
    rab.rab$l_fab = &fab;                 /*rab points to fab*/
                          /*of the indexed file*/

    primary_key = cc$rms_xabkey;          /*first xab is for*/
                              /*primary key*/
    primary_key.xab$w_pos0 = 0;           /*key position in record*/
    primary_key.xab$b_ref = 0;            /*this is primary key*/
    primary_key.xab$b_siz0 = sizeof cif_record.dda_number;
                              /*key size*/
    primary_key.xab$l_nxt = &alternate_key;
                              /*pointer to second xab*/
```

Figure 8.5 (*Continued*)

```
    alternate_key = cc$rms_xabkey;
                              /*initialize second xab which is for
the secondary key*/
    alternate_key.xab$b_flg = XAB$M_DUP;
                              /*allow duplicate keys*/
    alternate_key.xab$w_pos0 =
        (char *) &cif_record.swift_address
        -(char *) &cif_record;       /*position of this key*/
    alternate_key.xab$b_ref = 1;        /*this is key 1*/
    alternate_key.xab$b_siz0 =
        sizeof cif_record.swift_address;  /*key size*/
}; /*end of initialize*/
```

Figure 8.5 (*Continued*)

8.11 RMS UTILITIES

The utilities FDL (*file definition language*), CONVERT, and DUMP can be used to maintain RMS files. FDL is used to create specifications for RMS files and create the RMS files. CONVERT is used to copy records from one file to another of any organization. It can also be used to restructure files; e.g., to change the position of keys. The records will change to reflect the organization of the output file. DUMP is used to display file contents in ASCII, decimal, hexadecimal, and octal representations.

8.11.1 FDL

While the OPEN statement in VAX languages allows any existing file to be opened for update, not all RMS parameters can be specified when creating a file. The file definition language facility can be used to create files with most RMS parameter specification, and the file can then be opened for update by programs.

The FDL facility is also useful for modifying RMS parameters for existing files. For example, a file contains 82-byte records and a new field of 6 bytes is to be added at the end of each record. A FDL file containing the RMS parameters of the original data file is created using the ANALYZE/RMS/FDL command. The FDL file is edited to reflect the new record length of 88 bytes. This can be done using any text editor or the EDIT/FDL command. The new data file is created using the CREATE/FDL command. Records from the old file are copied to the new file using the CONVERT command. The new records can be padded with blanks to the right by using the /PAD qualifier with the CONVERT command.

The FDL facility can be accessed by three commands:

1. *EDIT/FDL*. Used to create a definition file containing specifications for RMS data files.

2. *CREATE/FDL*. Used to create an empty data file from a previously created specifications file.

3. *ANALYZE/RMS/FDL*. Used to create a FDL specifications file using the RMS parameters of an existing data file.

8.11.1.1 EDIT/FDL

The syntax for the command is

```
$ EDIT/FDL fdl-file-spec
```

The command can be used to create a new FDL file or edit an existing one. The questions that are asked depend on the responses to previous questions. Here is an example for creating an indexed file with fixed-length records of size 180 bytes and one key starting at position 4 (the fifth byte of the record) with a length of 9 bytes. Default values are specified for most answers. A question mark response to any question elicits help on that question. Figure 8.6 shows an example use of the FDL utility.

The following are some comments about the program in Figure 8.6.

- Each question shows the possible responses in parenthesis. Default values are specified in square brackets. A dash for the default value means that the value has no defaults and must be specified.

- The index depth graph shows the depth of key indexes of the B-tree structure for the number of initial load records specified and various bucket sizes. If the graph shows a depth greater than 4 for the specified bucket size then the bucket size should be increased.

- Key load fill percents should be less than 100 if records will be added randomly in the future. If initially the file is empty and all records will be added randomly in the future, then this parameter is insignificant.

```
$ edit/fdl client.fdl
          Parsing Definition File

SYS$SYSDEVICE:[MAYUR]CLIENT.FDL; will be created.

(Add Delete Exit Help Invoke Modify Quit Set View)

Main Editor Function                (Keyword)[Help]   : I


(Add_Key Delete_Key Indexed Optimize
Relative Sequential Touchup)
Editing Script Title                (Keyword)[-]      : I


Target disk volume Cluster Size     (1-1Giga)[3]      :
Number of Keys to Define            (1-255)[1]        :


(Line Fill Key Record Init Add)
Graph type to display               (Keyword)[Line]   :


Number of Records that will be Initially Loaded
into the File                       (0-1Giga)[-]      :100


(Fast_Convert NoFast_Convert RMS_Puts)
Initial File Load Method            (Keyword)[Fast]   :?


Fast_Convert:   using the VAX-11 Convert/Fast_Load option
NoFast_Convert: using the VAX-11 Convert/NoFast_Load option
RMS_Puts:       writing to a file from a High Level Language
(Fast_Convert NoFast_Convert RMS_Puts)

Initial File Load Method            (Keyword)[Fast]   :


Number of Additional Records to be Added After
the Initial File Load               (0-1Giga) [0]     :
Key  0 Load Fill Percent            (50-100) [100]    :50
```

Figure 8.6 Creating an indexed file with FDL utility.

```
(Fixed Variable)
Record Format                      (Keyword)[Var]    : FIX
Record Size                        (1-32231)[-]      : 180


(Bin2  Bin4  Bin8  Int2  Int4  Int8  Decimal  String
Dbin2 Dbin4 Dbin8 Dint2 Dint4 Dint8 Ddecimal Dstring)
Key  0 Data Type                   (Keyword)[Str]    :


Key  0 Segmentation desired        (Yes/No)[No]      :
Key  0 Length                      (1-180)[-]        : 4
Key  0 Position                    (0-176)[0]        : 9
Key  0 Duplicates allowed          (Yes/No)[No]      :
File Prolog Version                (0-3)[3]          :
Data Key Compression desired       (Yes/No)[Yes]     :
Data Record Compression desired    (Yes/No)[Yes]     :
Index Compression desired          (Yes/No)[Yes]     :

             *   |
             9   |
             8   |
Index        7   |
             6   |
Depth        5   |
             4   |
             3   |
             2   | 2
             1   |    1 1 1 1 1 1 1 1 1 1 1 1 1 1 1 1 1 1 1 1 1
             +-  + - - + - - + - - + - - + - - + - - + - - - +
                 1    5   10   15   20   25   30      32
                 Bucket Size (number of blocks)


Prolog Version       3 KT-Key  0 Type      String EM-Emphasis Flatter ( 3)
DK-Dup Key 0 Values  No KL-Key 0 Length   4 KP-Key  0 Position        9
RC-Data Record Comp 0 % KC-Data Key Comp   0 % IC-Index Record Comp 0 %
BF-Bucket Fill       100 % RF-Record Format   Fixed RS-Record Size  180
LM-Load Method Fast_Conv IL-Initial Load 100 AR-Added Records        0
(Type "FD" to Finish Design)
Which File Parameter   (Mnemonic)[refresh]  : FD
```

Figure 8.6 (*Continued*)

```
Text for FDL Title Section          (1-126 chars) [null]:
Test for learning the FDL facility
Data File file-spec                 (1-126 chars) [null]:
client.dat
(Carriage_Return FORTRAN None Print)
Carriage Control                    (Keyword) [Carr] :


Emphasis Used In Defining Default:  (      Flatter_files        )
Suggested Bucket Sizes:             (        3      3     12)
Number of Levels in Index:          (        1      1      1)
Number of Buckets in Index:         (        1      1      1)
Pages Required to Cache Index:      (        3      3     12)
Processing Used to Search Index:    (      126    126    510)


Key  0 Bucket Size       (1-63) [3]           :
Key  0 Name              (1-32 chars) [null]  :
Account number
Global Buffers desired   (Yes/No) [No]        :


The Depth of Key  0 is Estimated to be No Greater
than 1 Index levels, which is 2 Total levels.

Press RETURN to continue (^Z for Main Menu)
(Add Delete Exit Help Invoke Modify Quit Set View)
Main Editor Function         (Keyword) [Help] : exit

SYS$SYSDEVICE:[MAYUR]CLIENT.FDL;1  44 lines
```

Figure 8.6 (*Continued*)

The definition file that is created, client.fdl, is a text file. Minor changes can be made to it using a text editor like EVE. The recommended procedure for modifying the file is to use EDIT/FDL and to select the MODIFY option from the main menu. The file is shown in Figure 8.7.

```
$ TYPE client.fdl

TITLE   "Test for learning the FDL facility"
IDENT       "16-DEC-1990 12:22:32    VAX-11 FDL Editor

SYSTEM
            SOURCE                  VAX/VMS
FILE
            NAME                    "client.dat"
            ORGANIZATION            indexed
RECORD
            CARRIAGE_CONTROL        carriage_return
            FORMAT                  fixed
            SIZE                    180
AREA 0
            ALLOCATION              48
            BEST_TRY_CONTIGUOUS     yes
            BUCKET_SIZE             3
            EXTENSION               12
AREA 1
            ALLOCATION              3
            BEST_TRY_CONTIGUOUS     yes
            BUCKET_SIZE             3
            EXTENSION               3
KEY 0
            CHANGES                 no
            DATA_AREA               0
            DATA_FILL               100
            DATA_KEY_COMPRESSION    yes
            DATA_RECORD_COMPRESSION yes
            DUPLICATES              no
            INDEX_AREA              1
            INDEX_COMPRESSION       yes
            INDEX_FILL              100
            LEVEL1_INDEX_AREA       1
            NAME                    "Account number"
            PROLOG                  3
            SEG0_LENGTH             4
            SEG0_POSITION           9
            TYPE                    string
```

Figure 8.7 An FDL file.

8.11.1.2 CREATE/FDL

The file described in the above FDL file can be created by the command:

```
$ CREATE/FDL=client.fdl
```

The file that is created is client.dat, as specified in the FDL file. The file name can be overridden by giving it on the command line as:

```
$ CREATE/FDL=client.fdl test.dat
```

The file specifications for the created file are:

```
$ DIR/FULL client.dat
Directory SYS$SYSDEVICE:[MAYUR]

CLIENT.DAT;1               File ID:  (5836,18,0)
Size:     52/52               Owner:    [1,1]
Created: 16-DEC-1990 17:28    Revised: 16-DEC-1990 17:28 (1)
Expires: <none specified>     Backup:   <no backup recorded>
File organization:        Indexed, Prolog: 3, Using 1 key
                              In 2 areas
File attributes:          Allocation: 52, Extend: 12, Maximum bucket size: 3
                          Global buffer count: 0, No version limit
                          Contiguous best try
Record format:            Fixed length 180 byte records
Record attributes:        Carriage return carriage control
Journaling enabled:       None
File protection:          System:RWED, Owner:RWED, Group:RE, World:
Access Cntrl List:        None

Total of 1 file, 52/52 blocks.
```

8.11.1.3 ANALYZE/RMS/FDL

This command is used to extract the FDL specification of an existing file. The FDL file can then be modified to create a new data file that has the same RMS parameters as the original file except for the modifications performed on it. The command syntax is

```
$ ANALYZE/RMS/FDL file-spec
```

File-spec is the data file. The FDL file that is created has the same file-spec except for the file name extension, which is .fdl. For example,

```
$ ANALYZE/RMS/FDL account.dat
```

creates the file account.fdl.

8.11.2 DUMP

This command has the following qualifiers:

/ASCII	|	
/decimal	|	Specifies display data representation.
/hex	|	By default hex and ASCII values are displayed.
/octal	|	

/byte	|	
/longword	|	Specifies grouping for the displayed data.
/word	|	

/record	|	Specifies logical record display.
/block	|	Specifies display of blocks of the file. Optionally the starting record (or block) can be specified. The ending record (or block) can also be specified. Alternately, the number of records (or blocks) can be specified instead of the ending record (or block). For example:
	|	DUMP/RECORD=(START:3,END:5) client.dat
	|	DUMP/RECORD=(START:3,COUNT:3) client.dat

Figure 8.8 shows an example use of the command.

```
$ DUMP/RECORD=(START:2,COUNT:3) client.fdl

Dump of file SYS$SYSDEVICE:[TESTING.DATA]CLIENT.FDL;2
on 17-DEC-1990 12:42:12.22
File ID (6510,3,0)    End of file block 2 / Allocated 2

Record number 2 (00000002), 48 (0030) bytes

 39312D43 45442D36 31220954 4E454449 IDENT."16-DEC-19 000000
 41562020 2035333A 36323A32 31203938 89 12:26:35  VA 000010
 22726F74 69644520 4C444620 31312D58 X-11 FDL Editor" 000020
Record number 3 (00000003), 6 (0006) bytes

                        4D45 54535953 SYSTEM......... 000000

Record number 4 (00000004), 17 (0011) bytes

 4D562F58 41560909 09454352 554F5309 .SOURCE...VAX/VM 000000
                        53 S.............. 000010
```

Figure 8.8 DUMP command output.

8.11.3 CONVERT

The CONVERT command is used to convert (or restructure) a file of one organization to another. The syntax of the command is :

```
$ CONVERT/qualifiers input-file-spec  output-file-spec
```

This command has the following qualifiers:

/exceptions_file	A file of records that could not be copied to the output file because of format errors is created. It is recommended that this qualifier be always used.
/fdl=file-spec	The output file is created using the FDL specifications from the file specified.
/merge	This qualifier specifies that records are to be inserted in an existing indexed file.

/pad=x

/pad=%by

If the output file has a fixed-length record format and the input record has a smaller record size, the records are padded with the specified character. "x" is any ASCII character. "y" is a number in the base given by "b" which can be "d" for decimal, "h" for hex, or "o" for octal. For example, /pad=%h45 specifies the pad character to be hex 45 (or ASCII "E").

/statistics

This qualifier outputs summary information such as the number of converted records after the conversion is complete.

/truncate

If the output file has fixed-length record format and the input records have a larger record size, then the records are truncated to the output record size before writing.

For example, the file INPUT.DAT is sequential and contains 4 records that are to be loaded in the indexed file CLIENT.DAT created by the CREATE/FDL command above. Here is the sequence of commands:

```
$ DIR/FULL input.dat

Directory SYS$SYSDEVICE:[TESTING.DATA]

INPUT.DAT;1                        File ID:  (6497,5,0)
Size:          1/2                 Owner:    [1,1]
Created:       21-dec-1990 11:56   Revised: 21-DEC-1990  11:56 (1)
Expires:       <none specified >   Backup:  <no backup recorded>
File organization:      Sequential
File attributes:        Allocation: 2, Extend: 0, Global buffer count: 0,
                        No version limit
Record format:          Variable length, maximum 25 bytes
Record attributes:      Carriage return carriage control
Journaling enabled:     None
File protection:        System:RWED, Owner:RWED, Group:RE, World:
Access Cntrl List:      None

Total of 1 file, 1/2 blocks.

$ TYPE input.dat
```

```
SMITH A. 2547 TEST DATA 1
BEY J.   7123 TEST DATA 2
BELL A.  8213 TEST DATA 3
HOLMES K.3987 TEST DATA 4


$ CONVERT/MERGE/PAD=0  input.dat  client.dat


$ TYPE client.dat


SMITH A. 2547 TEST DATA 1000000000...
HOLMES K.3987 TEST DATA 4000000000...
BEY J.   7123 TEST DATA 2000000000...
BELL A.  8213 TEST DATA 3000000000...
```

Client.dat is sorted by the key at position 9. The padding character is 0 so each record has 0s appended to make the record size equal 180 bytes. More records can be added to client.dat by using the same CONVERT command line.

8.12 RMS JOURNALING

RMS Journaling is a layered product that minimizes the impact of *system failures, disk crashes,* and *file corruptions* on RMS files. The product is particularly suitable for on-line *transaction-processing* applications. Basically, the product keeps track of updates to data files in a separate set of journal files and uses these journal files to recover the original files in case they become corrupt. RMS journaling could be considered for use on VAXclusters when designing fail-safe applications.

8.12.1 RMS Journaling Features

Many programmers use RMS sequential, relative, and indexed files without realizing the impact of disk and system power failures on these files. RMS files, particularly indexed files, can be corrupted if, for example, the system fails when the files are being written to. Keeping critical files on shadowed disk volumes does not help since a file corruption due to power failure is a logical corruption of the internal file pointers, which implies that the file on all shadowed disks will be corrupt. See the discussion in the chapter on volume shadowing. Effective with VMS version 5.4,

RMS journaling is supported on DECnet and allows the development of robust distributed-transaction-processing systems. RMS journaling uses three techniques to safeguard data: *after image* (roll forward) journaling, *before image* (roll back) journaling, and *recovery unit* (transaction) journaling. For most transaction-processing applications, recovery unit journaling is the most important.

After image (AI) journaling allows a data file to be recovered in case the file becomes corrupt because of disk head crashes, system failures, etc.. Before image (BI) journaling allows modifications to a data file to be backed out. Modifications may need to be backed out if, for example, records have been inserted or updated incorrectly. Recovery unit (RU) journaling allows a set of operations on a set of data files to be treated as a transaction. In case the system fails while the operations are being performed, the operations are either completed when the system reboots or they are completely backed out. Effectively, database integrity is maintained by recovery unit journaling.

It should be noted that not all operations to a journaled RMS file are recoverable. For example, a RENAMEing of a journaled file is not journaled and hence cannot be redone by RMS journaling if the file has to be recovered. The RMS journaling manual should be consulted to determine exactly which RMS operations are recoverable. Usually, operations that change file contents, such as record deletes, writes, and updates, are journaled. This journaling is sufficient for data recovery. Just about any RMS file can be journaled.

It should be anticipated that journaling incurs overheads in terms of CPU time and disk space for journal files. We will now study the three journaling techniques in detail.

8.12.1.1 After image journaling

To set up a data file for after image journaling, the file must be marked as such by the $SET FILE command. The file must then be backed up using the BACKUP utility. The COPY command cannot be used since it does not set appropriate flags in the file header of the copied file. The journal file and the data file can later be used for recovery of the data file in case the original file is lost. Here is an example of journaling of a savings account file of bank customers:

```
$ SET FILE /AI_JOURNAL=(FILE=BACKUP_DISK:, CREATE) -
       database_disk:savings.account
$ BACKUP/RECORD database_disk:savings.account -
       backup_disk:savings.bck
```

Record operations to the data file database_disk:savings.account will now be journaled. The journal is in the file backup_disk:savings.rms$journal. The CREATE option in the $SET FILE command specifies that a new version of the file should be created rather than using an existing journal file. The BACKUP command must be issued after (not before) the $SET FILE /AI_JOURNAL command is used. The /RECORD qualifier notes the date and time of backup of the data file. This information is used during the recovery process. If the /RECORD qualifier is not used, the recovery process will work; but it may take more time.

In case the original data file, savings.account, is corrupt, it can be recovered by using:

```
$ RECOVER/RMS_FILE/FORWARD backup_disk:savings.bck
```

The qualifier /RMS_FILE is optional. The /FORWARD qualifier is required (/BACKWARD is used for before image recovery, which is described later). During recovery, RMS journaling automatically uses the journal file noted in the file header of savings.bck. The recovery process updates savings.bck using the journal file to re-create the contents of the original file within savings.bck. The original file can then be restored by using:

```
$ COPY backup_disk:savings.bck database_disk:savings.account
```

If the recovered data file is to be journaled, the $SET FILE /AI_JOURNAL and the $BACKUP commands must be issued again on the recovered data file.

8.12.1.2 Before image journaling

To set up a data file for before image journaling, only one command is required:

```
$ SET FILE /BI_JOURNAL=(FILE=BACKUP_DISK:, CREATE) data-
    base_disk:savings.account
```

Unlike for AI journaling, the data file does not have to be backed up.

During recovery, the /BACKWARD instead of the /FORWARD qualifier is used. The /UNTIL qualifier allows the file to be recovered up to a particular time. For example,

```
$ RECOVER/RMS_FILE/BACKWARD/UNTIL=15:30 database_disk:
  savings.account
```

will restore the contents of the data file to the state they were in at 3:30 p.m. It should be noted that the recovery is performed on the original data file by undoing (in reverse chronological order) all RMS operations after 3:30 pm.

8.12.1.3 Recovery unit journaling

A recoverable unit is a group of operations on one or more RMS files. The operations, normally performed from one program, constitute one logical transaction. This transaction is treated as one atomic operation. Recovery unit journaling ensures that these operations are either all completely performed on the data files or none are performed. RU journaling protects against loss of database integrity and consistency. RU journaling, along with the other journaling techniques, are supported on files residing on VAXes on a DECnet network, provided that RMS journaling software is loaded on all the participating nodes. This facilitates the design of distributed-database applications.

To appreciate the power of RU journaling, consider the quintessential debit-credit transaction. A bank has two RMS indexed files for customer savings and checking accounts. Suppose a customer uses an ATM connected to the VAX system and transfers $500 from his or her checking account to the customer's savings account. The program running on the VAX would subtract $500 from the balance field of the customer's record in the checking file and then add $500 to the corresponding field in the savings file. Obviously, this constitutes two separate RMS operations. If the system fails after the checking file is updated but before the savings file is updated, the files would be in an inconsistent state—the customer "loses" $500 from his or her savings account. This problem can be alleviated if RU journaling is used on these two files and the program is written appropriately. Note that AI and BI journaling does not solve the problem. To use RU journaling, the two files should be marked by:

```
$ SET FILE /RU_JOURNAL database_disk:savings.account
$ SET FILE /RU_JOURNAL database_disk:checking.account
```

The programmer then encloses the set of RMS operations that constitute a transaction within the two system service calls:

```
$START_TRANS
```

and

```
$END_TRANS
```

The RMS journaling software (working with the distributed-transaction manager—DECdtm) will consider all journalable RMS operations between the two system service calls to be one atomic operation. The system guarantees that the transaction will be either completely done or not done at all even if the system fails during the operation. As explained in the chapter on VAXcluster programming, the transaction log file is maintained by DECdtm.

Figure 8.9 shows the credit-debit program COBOL. The program can be run from a terminal and aborted with a CTRL/Y when the terminal displays "waiting for 5 seconds." The data files can be inspected to see that the two files are consistent. Try running the programs after removing RU journaling on the files by typing:

```
$ SET  FILE  /NORU_JOURNAL  database_disk:savings.account
```

```
$ SET  FILE  /NORU_JOURNAL  database_disk:checking.account
```

Aborting the program this time will cause the files to be inconsistent.

```
IDENTIFICATION DIVISION.
PROGRAM-ID. RMSJournal_DEMO.
* Transaction Processing using RMS journaling.
* Jay Shah  March 20, 1991.
* This program shows the essence of RMS journaling for
* transaction-processing databases. The program subtracts $500
* from a customer's checking account and adds $500 to the
* customer's savings account. Initially, both the checking and
* savings account files contain $2000 as the customer's
* balance. After the program is run, the customer should have
* $1500 in the checking account and $2500 in the savings
* account. If the program execution is aborted by a control-y
* entered at the terminal when the message "waiting for 5
* seconds" is displayed, the checking file update will have been
```

Figure 8.9 RMS journaling demonstration.

```
* executed but not the savings file update. The program
* should be run twice: once with no journaling on the account
* data files and once with RU journaling enabled. In both
* cases the program can be aborted when the screen displays
* "waiting for 5 seconds." When RU journaling is not used, the
* account files should be typed after the program is aborted to
* note that the checking account file has a balance of $1500
* and the savings account file has a balance of $2000 (when it
* should have been $2500).
*
*
* To create the RMS INDEXED account files use:
*
*   $ DEFINE database_disk  sys$sysdevice:[tmp]
*   $ CREATE/FDL=SYS$INPUT:  database_disk:checking.account
*   FILE
*              ORGANIZATION            indexed
*   RECORD
*              FORMAT                  fixed
*              SIZE                    13
*   KEY 0
*              PROLOG                  3
*              SEG0_LENGTH             5
*              SEG0_POSITION           0
*   $CREATE tmp.tmp        !customer 26124, balance $2000
*   2612400200000
*   $CONVERT/MERGE tmp.tmp database_disk:checking.account
*   $COPY database_disk:checking.account  -
*        database_disk:savings.account
*
* To mark the files for recovery unit journaling use:
*
*   $ SET FILE database_disk:checking.account /RU_JOURNAL
*   $ SET FILE database_disk:savings.account /RU_JOURNAL
*
*
ENVIRONMENT DIVISION.
*
INPUT-OUTPUT SECTION.

FILE-CONTROL.
* the two customer account files
   SELECT CHECKING-FILE
      ASSIGN TO "database_disk:checking.account"
      ORGANIZATION IS INDEXED ACCESS MODE IS RANDOM
      RECORD KEY IS CHECKING-NUMBER.
```

Figure 8.9 (*Continued*)

```
    SELECT SAVINGS-FILE
        ASSIGN TO "database_disk:savings.account"
        ORGANIZATION IS INDEXED ACCESS MODE IS RANDOM
        RECORD KEY IS SAVINGS-NUMBER.


DATA DIVISION.
FILE SECTION.
FD CHECKING-FILE.
01 CHECKING-RECORD.
    02 CHECKING-NUMBER      PIC 9(5)    USAGE IS DISPLAY.
    02 CHECKING-BALANCE     PIC 9(6)V99 USAGE IS DISPLAY.
FD SAVINGS-FILE.
01 SAVINGS-RECORD.
    02 SAVINGS-NUMBER       PIC 9(5)    USAGE IS DISPLAY.
    02 SAVINGS-BALANCE      PIC 9(6)V99 USAGE IS DISPLAY.


WORKING-STORAGE SECTION.
* transaction identifier used by DECdtm system services
01 TID              PIC X(16)   USAGE IS DISPLAY.
* event flag. arbitrary value of 5.
01 EVENT_FLAG       PIC 9(9)    USAGE IS COMP
                                VALUE IS 5.
* i/o status block. Ignored in this program.
01 IO_STATUS_BLOCK      PIC X(8)    USAGE IS DISPLAY.
01 CALL-STATUS          PIC S9(9)   USAGE IS COMP.
01 WAIT-TIME                        USAGE IS COMP-1
                                    VALUE IS 5.0.
PROCEDURE DIVISION.
MAIN SECTION.
*
OPEN-FILES.
    OPEN I-O CHECKING-FILE.
    OPEN I-O SAVINGS-FILE.
*
TRANSFER-FUNDS.
*
* DECdtm system service to start a transaction.
    CALL "SYS$START_TRANSW"
        USING BY VALUE EVENT_FLAG
            BY VALUE 0
            BY REFERENCE IO_STATUS_BLOCK
            BY VALUE 0
            BY VALUE 0
            BY REFERENCE TID
        GIVING CALL-STATUS.
```

Figure 8.9 (*Continued*)

```
    IF CALL-STATUS IS FAILURE
        DISPLAY "START_TRANS failed."
        STOP RUN
    END-IF.
*
* Get checking account record for customer number "26124".
*
    MOVE 26124 TO CHECKING-NUMBER.
    READ CHECKING-FILE RECORD
        INVALID KEY
            DISPLAY "No such checking account."
*
* The zero values in this and following CALLs are for DTM flags,
* AST address and AST parameters. All are unused in this program.
*
            CALL "SYS$ABORT_TRANSW"
                USING BY VALUE EVENT_FLAG
                    BY VALUE 0
                    BY REFERENCE IO_STATUS_BLOCK
                    BY VALUE 0
                    BY VALUE 0
                    BY REFERENCE TID
            STOP RUN
    END-READ.
*
    SUBTRACT 500 FROM CHECKING-BALANCE.
*
* Update the customer's checking account record.
*
    REWRITE CHECKING-RECORD
        INVALID KEY
            DISPLAY "Cannot update the customer's checking account."
            CALL "SYS$ABORT_TRANSW"
                USING BY VALUE EVENT_FLAG
                    BY VALUE 0
                    BY REFERENCE IO_STATUS_BLOCK
                    BY VALUE 0
                    BY VALUE 0
                    BY REFERENCE TID
            STOP RUN
    END-REWRITE.

    DISPLAY "Waiting for five seconds. Use control-Y to abort...".
    CALL "LIB$WAIT" USING BY REFERENCE WAIT-TIME.
*
```

Figure 8.9 (*Continued*)

```
* Get savings account record for customer number "26124".
*

   MOVE 26124 TO SAVINGS-NUMBER.
   READ SAVINGS-FILE RECORD
      INVALID KEY
         DISPLAY "No such savings account"
         CALL "SYS$ABORT_TRANSW"
            USING BY VALUE EVENT_FLAG
               BY VALUE 0
               BY REFERENCE IO_STATUS_BLOCK
               BY VALUE 0
               BY VALUE 0
               BY REFERENCE TID
         STOP RUN
   END-READ.
*

   ADD 500 TO SAVINGS-BALANCE.
*
* Update the customer's savings account record.
*

   REWRITE SAVINGS-RECORD
      INVALID KEY
         DISPLAY "Cannot update the customer's savings account."
         CALL "SYS$ABORT_TRANSW"
            USING BY VALUE EVENT_FLAG
               BY VALUE 0
               BY REFERENCE IO_STATUS_BLOCK
               BY VALUE 0
               BY VALUE 0
               BY REFERENCE TID
         STOP RUN
   END-REWRITE.
*
* End (and commit) the transaction.
*

   CALL "SYS$END_TRANSW"
            USING BY VALUE EVENT_FLAG
               BY VALUE 0
               BY REFERENCE IO_STATUS_BLOCK
               BY VALUE 0
               BY VALUE 0
               BY REFERENCE TID
            GIVING CALL-STATUS.
   IF CALL-STATUS IS FAILURE
      DISPLAY "Cannot end the transaction to transfer funds."
      STOP RUN
```

Figure 8.9 (*Continued*)

```
   END-IF.
*
CLOSE-FILES.
   CLOSE CHECKING-FILE.
   CLOSE SAVINGS-FILE.
   STOP RUN.
END PROGRAM RMSJournal_DEMO.
```

Figure 8.9 (*Continued*)

8.12.2 Other Issues

Other RMS journaling issues are:

- More than one type of journaling can be applied to data files.

- The same journal file can be used for multiple data files.

- The /UNTIL qualifier can be used during recovery for any type of journaling.

- If RU journaling is combined with AI and/or BU journaling, then transaction consistency is maintained for data files that are restored during the recovery.

- The $ABORT_TRANS system service allows a transaction started by a $START_TRANS to be logically aborted so that the transaction operations are rolled back.

- RMS journaling cooperates with DECdtm software to support distributed-transaction processing. See the chapter on VAX-cluster programming for further details.

- RMS journaling is supported on a VAXcluster where multiple nodes may update common database files.

- The DIR/FULL command applied to a data file displays journaling flags on the file. See Figure 8.10.

8.13 SUMMARY

Record management services is the file management system on VAX/VMS systems, including VAXclusters. Files can be shared by programs on different VAXes in a cluster. An instance of RMS runs on each VAX in a cluster. The distributed lock manager is used internally by RMS to ensure disk and file integrity and file access

```
$ DIR/FULL RMSJNL.TMP

Directory SYS$SYSDEVICE:[SHAHJ]
RMSJNL.TMP;1              File ID: (544,18,0)
Size:      3/3      Owner:   [1,1]
Created: 19-MAR-1991 12:05:24.38

Revised: 19-MAR-1991 12:05:27.84 (2)
Expires:   <None specified>
Backup:  19-MAR-1991 12:05:34.07
```

File organization:	Indexed, Prolog: 3, Using 1 key
File attributes:	Allocation: 3, Extend: 0, Maximum bucket size: 2
	Global buffer count: 0, No version limit
Record format:	Fixed length 18 byte records
Record attributes:	Carriage return carriage control
RMS attributes:	None
Journaling enabled:	AI, BI, RU
AI journal file:	DISK$VAXVMSRL054:[SHAHJ]RMSJNL$AI.RMS$JOURNAL;1
BI journal file:	DISK$VAXVMSRL054:[SHAHJ]RMSJNL$BI.RMS$JOURNAL;1
File protection:	System:RWED, Owner:RWED, Group:RE, World:
Access Cntrl List:	(RMS_AI_JOURNAL,JOURNAL_FILE=DISK$VAXVMSRL054:[SHAHJ]
	RMSJNL$AI.RMS$JOURNAL;1,JOURNAL_LEVEL=1,
	JOURNAL_CREATION_DATE=19-MAR-1991:12:05:26.50,
	JOURNAL_STREAM_INDEX=1,BACKUP_SEQUENCE_NUMBER=1,
	JOURNAL_CONSISTENCY_DATE=17-NOV-1858:00:00:00.00,
	JOURNALING_OPTIONS=BACKUP_PERFORMED,OPTIONS=HIDDEN+
	PROTECTED+NOPROPAGATE)
	(RMS_BI_JOURNAL,JOURNAL_FILE=DISK$VAXVMSRL054:[SHAHJ]
	RMSJNL$BI.RMS$JOURNAL;1,JOURNAL_LEVEL=1,
	JOURNAL_CREATION_DATE=19-MAR-1991:12:05:27.19,
	JOURNAL_STREAM_INDEX=1,BACKUP_SEQUENCE_NUMBER=1,
	JOURNAL_CONSISTENCY_DATE=17-NOV-1858:00:00:00.00,
	JOURNALING_OPTIONS=BACKUP_PERFORMED,OPTIONS=HIDDEN+
	PROTECTED+NOPROPAGATE)

Figure 8.10 Attributes on a file with AI, BI, and RU journaling enabled.

synchronization when multiple programs on different VAXes access the same disks and files.

Sequential, relative, and indexed files were described. File access demonstration programs are given. The file definition language utility for creating various types of RMS files was described.

The CONVERT utility, which allows files to be converted from one format to another, and the DUMP utility which allows data in files to be displayed in various formats were mentioned.

RMS Journaling supports distributed-transaction processing applications and safeguards disk data against system and disk failures. It can play an important role on high-availability VAXclusters.

Disk files can be lost or corrupted if a disk head crashes or there are other disk failures. The next chapter describes volume shadowing, which significantly reduces the probability of data loss in case of disk failures.

9

Volume Shadowing

Failures of disk drives can have catastrophic effects on many on-line applications. The volume-shadowing facility on VAX/VMS allows a logical disk to consist of multiple physical disks, with the physical disks being mirror images of each other. In case a disk fails, I/O is performed on the remaining disks. Applications using shadowed disks are not affected by such disk failures. Volume shadowing is not a requirement for VAXclusters, but, it is used at many sites that run mission-critical applications.

Version 5.4 of VAX/VMS supports shadowing without HSCs. The shadowing software is built into the operating system and any type of *digital standard architecture* (DSA) disks can be shadowed. However, this type of shadowing is not discussed here explicitly; most of the discussion applies to both types of shadowed disks.

9.1 HOW VOLUME SHADOWING WORKS

The current implementation of volume shadowing requires that the shadowed disks be connected to a *hierarchical storage controller* (HSC). The overall requirements for using volume shadowing are:

1. The cluster must have at least one VAX connected to the HSC via the *computer interconnect* (CI) bus. Usually, this requirement is met by CI-based and mixed-interconnect VAXclusters.

2. The VAX volume-shadowing system software must be installed on at least one of the VAXes connected to the HSC. Any other VAXes that access the HSC disk drives as "local" disks and take advantage of volume shadowing must also have the software installed on it. On a CI-based VAXcluster, if a common system disk is used and VAX volume-shadowing is installed on the common disk, all the VAXes will be able to use the software.

3. The disk drives that constitute a shadow set must be of the same geometry, i.e., they must have the same number of sectors per track, tracks per cylinder, and cylinders per volume. Also, the disk drives must conform to the *digital storage architecture* and *mass storage control protocol* (MSCP). Currently, all disk drives that connect to HSCs conform to DSA and MSCP.

4. The VAX volume-shadowing software license must be installed on all the VAXes that use the facility. If a cluster license is purchased, the license has to be installed only once on the common system disk for use by all the member VAXes.

Figure 9.1 shows the minimal requirements for volume shadowing.

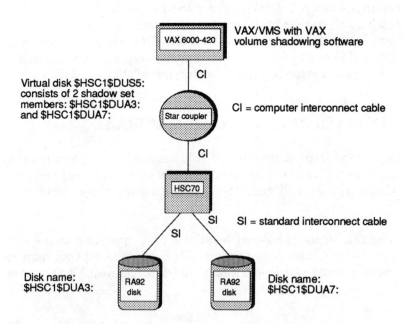

Figure 9.1 A HSC-based volume-shadowing configuration.

Programs on the VAX perform I/O to the logical disk, also called the virtual unit $HSC1$DUS5:. Usually, this I/O will be done by using high-level language statements. The I/O is routed to the *record management services* (RMS), which in turn decides which disk blocks have to be accessed. For I/O optimization, multiple contiguous disk blocks will be accessed even when a single block is to be used. We will ignore this fact in this discussion. RMS conveys the disk block I/O information to the I/O driver on the VAX, which in turn conveys the information to the HSC software. The HSC receives the disk block I/O information for the virtual unit (not a physical disk). The HSC maintains a table which lists each physical disk corresponding to a virtual unit. This table was updated when the shadow set was created by the DCL MOUNT command. If a write block operation is to be performed, the HSC writes the block to each of the physical disks that are shadow members of that virtual unit. If a read disk block operation is to be performed, the HSC reads the block from a disk that is a member of the shadow set.

Volume shadowing has little overhead on a VAX performing I/O because the VAX issues a single disk I/O command to the HSC, irrespective of whether the I/O is to a nonshadowed disk or to a virtual unit that actually consists of multiple physical disks. The HSC incurs overhead when writing to multiple disks in a shadow set. When a disk block is to be read, the HSC reads it from only one disk regardless of whether the logical disk is shadowed or not. Reads, therefore, do not incur any overhead. In fact, continuous read operations will be faster on a shadow set because the HSC's disk I/O optimizing algorithm uses the disk that has the lowest seek time among the shadow set members. As a rule of thumb, sustained I/O performance will be poorer on multiple disk shadow sets than on single disks if more than 25 percent of the I/O operations are writes.

Physical disks can be added to a shadow set after a shadow set has been operational. Disk blocks from the existing shadowed disks are copied to the new disk in the shadow set by the HSC. This has no overhead on the VAXes using the shadow set, although the HSC throughput will decrease if the HSC is heavily utilized.

9.2 WHAT VOLUME SHADOWING CANNOT DO

Hardware redundancy is required for critical on-line applications. Since disk drives are key components of most of these applications, well planned disk drive configurations and the use of the volume-shadowing facility on a cluster eliminates problems associated with disk drive (or disk) failures. Some system analysts and programmers believe that if logical disks are adequately shadowed, no special transaction-processing considerations are required when developing critical applications. This is not true.

Because of system software bugs or power supply glitches, a set of shadowed disks may be temporarily inoperational. The application must be designed so that, with minimum impact to users, it can be restarted on other disks or it can reuse the shadowed disks after they are properly functioning. A particular challenge is to ensure that integrity of the disk databases is maintained when the application recovers. Often, the application was in the process of updating a series of files and the disks failed after a few of these files were actually updated. In this case, the databases may be in an inconsistent state after the application recovers. The application must be able to back out such partial updates before the users perform any operations to the databases.

A power supply problem can cause the complete system to be brought down involuntarily. In most such situations, proper power supply is restored within a short time. In this case, when proper power supply is restored and the operating system is brought up, the application should be able to recover in a short time.

The volume-shadowing facility treats the disks as consisting of a sequence of 512-byte blocks and is oblivious of the higher level logical disk structure. Sometimes, a disk's logical file structure becomes corrupt because of software bugs and improper file design. If a disk file is corrupt, the file will be corrupt on all the disks that are members of a shadow set. Indexed files are prone to file corruption in case of power failures; volume shadowing does not mitigate the problem.

The issues mentioned here are addressed in the realm of transaction processing. A particular challenge is to develop fail-safe and resilient databases whose integrity is not compromised by various kinds of system and software failures. Currently, most critical commercial applications are written in standard languages with transaction-processing extensions. These extensions are usually calls to subroutines that are part of a separate software package. Many vendors offer such transaction-processing packages. A detailed discussion on how to design transaction-processing applications is not within the scope of this book.

9.3 IMPLEMENTING VOLUME SHADOWING

Consider Figure 9.1. The VAX has created a virtual unit, $1HSC1$DUS5:, by using the command:

```
$ MOUNT $HSC1$DUS5: -
      /SHADOW=($HSC1$DUA3:, $1HSC1$DUA7:) TESTDISK
```

Here TESTDISK is the logical name of the virtual unit. The virtual unit can be used by anyone who issues that command. If the disk is for use by everyone on the cluster, the command to create the shadow set could be:

```
$ MOUNT/SYSTEM $HSC1$DUS5: -
      /SHADOW=($HSC1$DUA3:,$1HSC1$DUA7:) TESTDISK
```

The shadow set name is $HSC1$DUS5:. It contains the two shadow set members $HSC1$DUA3: and $HSC1$DUA7:. Note that the SYSGEN parameter SHADOWING must be set to 1 if shadowing is to be used on a VAX.

The DCL SHOW DEVICES command will produce a display like:

```
$ SHOW DEVICES D !Show devices with name beginning with D
```

Device		Device	Error	Volume	Free	Trans	Mnt
Name		Status	Count	Label	Blocks	Count	Cnt
$HSC1$DUA0:	(HSC1)	Mounted	0	VMSSYSTEM	21223	194	1
$HSC1$DUA3:	(HSC1)	ShadowSetMember	0	(member of $HSC1$DUS5:)			
$HSC1$DUA7:	(HSC1)	ShadowSetMember	0	(member of $HSC1$DUS5:)			
$HSC1$DUS5:	(HSC1)	Mounted	0	TESTDISK	193560	1	1

As seen in the display, the system has three physical disks and two virtual units, one shadowed and the other nonshadowed. The shadowed disk has two shadow set members.

Once a shadow set is created, more disks can be added to the shadow set while the existing shadow sets are being used. The next command adds a third disk, $HSC1$DUA8:, to the existing shadow set created above:

```
$ MOUNT $HSC1$DUS5: /SHADOW=($HSC1$DUA8:) TESTDISK
```

Data from disks on the existing shadow set is copied block-by-block to the new disk by the HSC. Virtual disk I/O can be performed by programs while this copy operation is going on so there is no down time.

A shadow set can contain one or more members. A shadow set containing just one member does not offer any disk redundancy. However, mounting a disk as a single-disk shadow set allows for other disks to be added to the shadow set later while the disk is being used. This can be useful when the error log shows that the disk has generated recoverable errors and its performance may deteriorate. In this case, another disk can be added to the single-disk shadow set. More than two disks can be used to create a shadow set so that the cluster will tolerate more than one failure of shadow set members.

A disk can be removed from the shadow set by simply dismounting it:

```
$ DISMOUNT $HSC1$DUA7:
```

If there is only one disk in the shadow set, the disk cannot be dismounted; instead the shadow set must be dissolved. To dissolve a shadow set, the virtual unit (logical disk) must be dismounted:

```
$ DISMOUNT $HSC1$DUS5:
```

When a disk that is a shadow set member fails, the HSC recognizes the failure and sends an error message to the cluster VAXes, which display an appropriate message on the operator consoles. Normal operations continue except that the HSC does not use the failed disk. The operator may choose to add another disk to the shadow set.

9.4 SHADOWING THE VMS SYSTEM DISK

In VMS, the standard disk driver for HSC disks is called DU-DRIVER. The volume-shadowing facility uses the DSDRIVER. Examples of disk names for disks accessed by the DUDRIVER are DUA2:, DUB4:, and DJA1:. Disk names for shadow sets (which use the DSDRIVER) are DUSn:, where "n" is the shadow set number.

When volume shadowing is not used, the operating system boots from a system disk and the DUDRIVER is used to access this disk. Since this disk is mounted and accessed by the DUDRIVER, the volume-shadowing facility cannot be used to shadow the system disk. To use the DSDRIVER for the system disk, the contents of CPU register R3 have to be set before the operating system is booted. The exact value is not important here; the volume-shadowing manual explains how to set the register's value. Once this value is set, the system disk has a DUS name (like DUS2:) after the computer is booted. In the start-up command files (like SYS$MANAGER:SYSTARTUP_V5.COM), another disk can be added to the system disk single-member shadow set.

Note that the operating system boots as a single-member shadow set only. More members are added during the final stages of the complete boot by commands, for example, in SYS$MAN-AGER:SYSTARTUP_V5.COM or even later by DCL MOUNT commands.

9.5   REDUNDANT HSCs

VAXcluster systems that have disks connected to only one HSC are vulnerable to failures of the HSC. Normally, all disks connected to HSCs are dual ported and so can be connected to two HSCs. Figure 9.2 shows a configuration where two HSCs are used for redundancy.

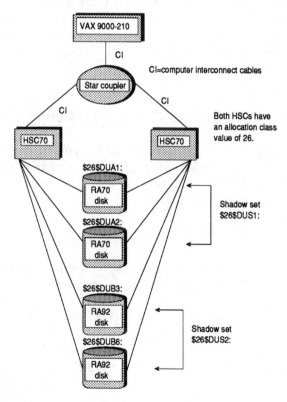

Figure 9.2 A two-HSC configuration.

The HSCs must have the same allocation class value, 26 in this example. Allocation classes are explained in the chapter on creating a VAXcluster. The disks connected to the HSCs have names preceded by 26. Two shadow sets of two physical disks each are created from the VAX by commands like:

```
$ MOUNT/SYSTEM $26$DUS1: -
        /SHADOW=($26$DUA1:, $26$DUA2:)  SMALLDISK

$ MOUNT/SYSTEM $26$DUS2: -
        /SHADOW=($26$DUB3:, $26$DUB6:)  MAINDISK
```

The HSCs are set up to be redundant; if one HSC fails, the other will handle I/O to all the disks. This will be transparent to applications running on the VAXes. An error message is displayed on the operator console so appropriate action may be taken.

Note that I/O to all the members of one shadow set is handled by only one HSC. Different shadow sets can be handled by different HSCs. If a HSC fails, the other HSC picks up and performs all the I/O on behalf of the VAXes. With the existing hardware design, three or more HSCs cannot be configured to handle more than one HSC failure. Multiple HSCs can be used, though, to accommodate more disk drives on the cluster.

9.6 VOLUME SHADOWING ON A CLUSTER

VAXes in a VAXcluster can access shadow sets in the same way that they access nonshadowed disks. The shadow set can be mounted from one VAX for clusterwide use by issuing the MOUNT command with the /CLUSTER qualifier:

```
$ MOUNT/CLUSTER $26$DUS1: -
        /SHADOW=($26$DUA1:, $26$DUA2:)  SMALLDISK
```

Note that the /SYSTEM qualifier is implicit when the /CLUSTER qualifier is used. The other VAXes do not have to mount the shadow set.

A shadow set can also be mounted from the individual VAXes that will be using it. In this case, the shadow set is accessible only to VAXes that have issued the MOUNT command.

In a mixed-interconnect VAXcluster, VAXes connected to the HSCs directly by the CI bus can serve the shadowed disks to satellite nodes. The satellite nodes must have the SYSGEN parameter SHADOWING set to 0 so that they use the standard nonshadowing driver for disk I/O. These nodes will access the shadowed disks via the CI-connected VAXes using the MSCP protocol. The satellites must mount the shadow set using the shadow set name without, however, using the /SHADOW qualifier to specify individual physical disk names:

```
$ MOUNT/SYSTEM $26$DUS1: SMALLDISK
```

The chapter on VAXcluster components and terminology gives more details on MSCP-served disks.

9.7 THE DCL LEXICAL FUNCTION F$GETDVI

F$GETDVI is used in the DCL command file to get information on devices on the computer. For example, here is DCL code to display the volume label (APPL_DEVELOP in this case) of a disk drive:

```
$ write sys$output F$GETDVI("DUA3:","VOLNAM")
APPL_DEVELOP
```

The syntax of the F$GETDVI function is:

```
F$GETDVI( device-name, item )
```

"VOLNAM" is an example of an item. The lexical function has a whole set of items that allow a variety of information on devices to be returned. Of special interest here is the items pertaining to volume shadowing. Figure 9.3 lists these items.

Figure 9.4 shows a DCL command file that displays the shadow units on a computer along with disk usage information on these units. Figure 9.5 shows a sample output created by the execution of the command file.

9.8 SUMMARY

VAXclusters, when used as high-availability systems, usually have shadowed disks. The chapter describes how volume shadowing is implemented on a VAXcluster. The system disk can be shadowed if required. The chapter describes how to obtain information on shadowed disks using the DCL lexical function F$GETDVI. The next chapter describes the low-level VAX Architecture.

item	description
SHDW_CATCHUP_COPYING	Returns "TRUE" or "FALSE," depending on whether the volume is receiving a full copy just before joining a shadow set.
SHDW_FAILED_MEMBER	Returns "TRUE" or "FALSE," depending on whether the volume has been removed from a shadow set by another VAX in the cluster.
SHDW_MASTER	Returns "TRUE" or "FALSE," depending on whether the volume is a virtual unit (the name of a shadow set).
SHDW_MASTER_NAME	Returns the value of the virtual unit name of the shadow set of which the specified device is a member. An example of a value that is returned is "_2DUS24:".
SHDW_MEMBER	Returns "TRUE" or "FALSE," depending on whether the device is a shadow set member.
SHDW_MERGE_COPYING	Returns "TRUE" or "FALSE," depending on whether the volume is receiving a merge copy just before joining a shadow set.
SHDW_NEXT_MBR_NAME	Returns the device name of the next member in the shadow set. If the device name that is specified is a virtual unit name, then the name of the member with the lowest unit number is returned.

Figure 9.3 F$GETDVI items that pertain to volume shadowing.

```
!This command file, when executed, displays a list of shadowed
$!disks and disk usage information. The list of virtual units is obtained
$!from a file (TMP.TMP) that is created by the SHOW DEVICE command
$!within this command procedure.
$!
$  SPACES       = "                                         "
$  SAY          = "WRITE SYS$OUTPUT"
$  SAY "------------------------------------------------------------"
$  SAY "                    Shadow sets on the system             "
$  SAY "                    ------------------------              "
$  SAY "                            Shadow   Max    Free    % Disk"
$  SAY "Disk drive Type Volume label  members blocks blocks    free "
$  SAY "------------------------------------------------------------"
$!
$!SHOW DEVICE (mounted virtual units) output to a file.
$!
$  SHOW DEVICE /MOUNTED /OUTPUT=TMP.TMP  DUS
$! The output looks somewhat like this:
$!
$!-----------------------------------------------------------------
$!
$
$!Device               Device Error    Volume    Free   Trans Mnt
$! Name                Status Count     Label    Blocks Count Cnt
$!$1$DUS0   (HSC002)   Mounted  0    SYSTEMDISK  850068  204   2
$!$1$DUS5   (HSC002)   Mounted  0    DEVEL_USERS 235128   1    2
$!-----------------------------------------------------------------
$!
$!Open the file to read the shadow set names, one per line
$!
$  OPEN /READ TMPFILE TMP.TMP
$!
$!ignore 3 lines; these are headers
$!
$  READ /END=EOF_TMPFILE  TMPFILE  INPUT_LINE
$  READ /END=EOF_TMPFILE  TMPFILE  INPUT_LINE
$  READ /END=EOF_TMPFILE  TMPFILE  INPUT_LINE
$NEXT_INPUT_LINE:
$!
$  READ /END=EOF_TMPFILE  TMPFILE  INPUT_LINE
$!
$!Extract disk name from the line; it is the first item in the line
$!
$  POS         = F$LOCATE( ":", INPUT_LINE )
$  SHADOW_NAME = F$EXTRACT( 0, POS+1, INPUT_LINE )
```

Figure 9.4 DCL procedure which displays shadow set information.

```
$!
$!get disk parameters
$!
$ DISK_TYPE    = F$GETDVI( SHADOW_NAME, "MEDIA_NAME" )
$ DISK_LABEL   = F$GETDVI( SHADOW_NAME, "VOLNAM" )
$ MAX_BLOCKS   = F$GETDVI( SHADOW_NAME, "MAXBLOCK" )
$ FREE_BLOCKS  = F$GETDVI( SHADOW_NAME, "FREEBLOCKS" )
$!
$!Calculate percent free space on disk
$!
$ FREE_PERCENT = F$STRING( (FREE_BLOCKS*100)/MAX_BLOCKS )
$!
$!Convert numbers to string
$!
$ MAX_BLOCKS   = F$STRING(MAX_BLOCKS)
$ FREE_BLOCKS  = F$STRING(FREE_BLOCKS)
$!
$!Pad all parameters with spaces at right
$!
$ SHADOW_NAME  = SHADOW_NAME + F$EXTRACT(0, 12-F$LENGTH(SHADOW_NAME), SPACES)
$ DISK_TYPE    = DISK_TYPE   + F$EXTRACT(0,  6-F$LENGTH(DISK_TYPE ), SPACES)
$ DISK_LABEL   = DISK_LABEL  + F$EXTRACT(0, 25-F$LENGTH(DISK_LABEL), SPACES)
$ MAX_BLOCKS   = MAX_BLOCKS  + F$EXTRACT(0, 11-F$LENGTH(MAX_BLOCKS), SPACES)
$ FREE_BLOCKS  = FREE_BLOCKS + F$EXTRACT(0, 10-F$LENGTH(FREE_BLOCKS), SPACES)
$!
$!Display the shadow set information
$!
$ SAY  SHADOW_NAME,DISK_TYPE,DISK_LABEL,MAX_BLOCKS,FREE_BLOCKS,FREE_PERCENT
$!
$!if virtual unit, display all shadow members
$!
$ SHADOW_MEM   = SHADOW_NAME
$DISPLAY_SHADOW_MEMBER:
$ SHADOW_MEM   = F$GETDVI ( SHADOW_MEM, "SHDW_NEXT_MBR_NAME")
$ IF F$EDIT(SHADOW_MEM,"COLLAPSE") .EQS. "" THEN $GOTO NEXT_INPUT_LINE
$!
$! Pad to right with spaces
$!
$ SHADOW_MEM = SHADOW_MEM + F$EXTRACT(0, 12-F$LENGTH(SHADOW_MEM), SPACES)
$!
$!display one shadow member, loop to get more members.
$!
$ SAY "                       "SHADOW_MEM'"
```

Figure 9.4 (*Continued*)

```
$!
$! Go back and check if there are any more members
$!
$  GOTO DISPLAY_SHADOW_MEMBER
$!
$EOF_TMPFILE:
$  CLOSE TMPFILE
$  DELETE /NOLOG TMP.TMP;*
$  EXIT
```

Figure 9.4 (continued)

Disk drive	Type	Volume label	Shadow members	Max blocks	Free blocks	% Disk free
		Shadow sets on the system				
1DUS0:	RA90	SYSTEMDISK		2376153	850080	35
			_1DUA0:			
			_1DUA1:			
1DUS5:	RA70	DEVEL_USERS		547041	235128	42
			_1DUA3:			
			_1DUA12:			

Figure 9.5 Output of the DCL command procedure.

10

The VAX Architecture

The VAX architecture is implemented on all the VAXes from the smallest desktop VAXes to the largest multiprocessing, vector-processing VAX-based clusters. While the architecture is the same on all the machines, the physical implementation techniques vary among the various series of VAXes. So, the VAX 9000 series *central processing unit* (CPU) uses ECL (*emitter-coupled logic*) *circuitry* with 128-kbyte *cache memory* per processor, and the MicroVAX 3900 CPU is on a single board using CMOS (*complementary metal oxide semiconductor*) circuitry with 1-kbyte cache memory. The low-end VAXes use single-bit parity main memory, while the larger machines use *error correcting* (ECC) memory. Listed below are some of the features of the VAX architecture.

1. Sixteen 32-bit general purpose registers

2. Virtual addressing of 32 bits with a total address space of 4,294,967,296 bytes

3. A total of 16 priority levels for hardware interrupts

4. A total of 15 priority levels for software interrupts

5. Demand-paged memory management hardware

6. Memory-mapped I/O

7. Four levels of privileges for CPU operations

8. Over 400 instructions

a. Instructions for switching program context in a multiprogramming environment

b. Queue instructions for linked-list manipulation

c. Bit manipulation instructions

d. Packed decimal arithmetic instructions

e. 4, 8, and 16 byte floating-point number instructions

f. Indexed and based (register-deferred) data addressing

g. Vector processing instructions

10.1 OVERVIEW

The VAX has 32-bit memory addressing, allowing the CPU to access 4,294,967,296 (2 to the power of 32) bytes of *main memory*. This address range is virtual since none of the VAXes supports that much physical memory. The memory management hardware maps the virtual memory onto physical memory (or disk) using the demand-paging technique (explained later). The large address space for programs is the basis for the name VAX, which is derived from *virtual address extension*.

The VAX is designed for multiprogramming applications. Fast context-switching instructions allow the CPU to service a number of programs with minimum overhead. To ensure that programs do not access unauthorized memory or adversely affect system resources, the CPU can operate in one of four modes of privileges: *kernel* (the most privileged state), *executive*, *supervisor*, and *user* (the least privileged state). Special interlock instructions allow multiple processes to cooperatively share system resources.

The VAX is a CISC (*complex instruction set computer*) as opposed to a RISC (*reduced instruction set computer*). The VAX has about *400 instructions* (and about *63 vector-processing instructions*). The instruction set is highly symmetric, which means that most of the instructions can be used with most of the data types and data-addressing modes. *Position independent code* (PIC) can be written using program counter-relative addressing, allowing programs to be loaded at any location in the address space. The CPU has several instructions for bit manipulation. The largest data type is 128-bit floating-point numbers.

The CPU has sixteen 32-bit *general purpose registers*. A 32-bit *processor status longword* (PSL) contains the execution state of the CPU. The lower 16 bits of the PSL are known as the *processor status word* (PSW).

Input/output (I/O) on the computer is memory mapped. There are no special instructions for I/O. Devices are controlled by means of *control and status registers* (CSRs) that are within the device but mapped to locations in the main memory (called I/O space). I/O space is set up by the operating system so that it cannot be directly accessed by user programs. Devices return status information in the status registers and optionally generate a hardware interrupt. *Hardware interrupts* have 16 levels of priority. Devices, such as disk drives, that generate interrupts at high priority are serviced before low-priority devices, such as terminals.

Vector-processing instructions allow efficient processing of DO and FOR loops. The vector-processing hardware are sets of boards that are inserted in the CPU cabinet. Currently, the FORTRAN compiler automatically generates vectorized code. The assembly language, MACRO-32, can be used to write code for the vector processor. The VMS mathematics run-time library (MTH$ routines) is modified to use the vector-processing instructions. The PPL$ library routines allow programmers to make their code parallel.

10.2   PAGES AND MEMORY MANAGEMENT

10.2.1   The Memory Translation Process

Processes on the computer can be considered to be running user programs. Processes have a large (contiguous) address space starting at location 0. Different processes' address space cannot correspond to the same physical memory locations. Each process actually has a virtual address space. When a process accesses a memory location, the location is in the process's virtual address space, which is translated by the memory management hardware into a physical address. The translation is based on a table in memory called the page translation table. The table is created and maintained by the operating system. Each element of the table is called a *page table entry* (PTE).

Memory is allocated in chunks of 512 bytes called pages. A process using 1800 bytes of virtual memory will be allocated four virtual pages. These virtual pages will be mapped into four physical pages by the *memory management hardware* (MMH). Hypothetically, two processes, each using two virtual pages, can be mapped as shown in Figure 10.1.

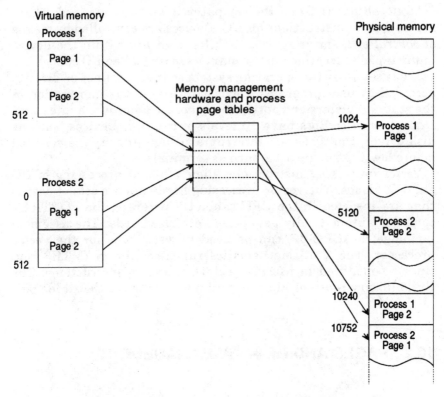

Figure 10.1 Virtual page to physical page memory translation.

In this case, if an instruction in process 1 writes into location 12, the physical memory location is 1036, while if the write is by process 2 then the physical memory location is 10764. This technique of mapping virtual memory to physical allows multiple processes to have a linear address space starting at 0.

10.2.2 Size of Memory

For example, three processes use 20 Mbytes of virtual memory each and the physical memory available for the processes is 8 Mbytes. Obviously, virtual to physical memory translation cannot map the 60 Mbytes of total virtual memory into the 8 Mbytes of physical memory. In this case the MMH has some of the virtual pages mapped into physical memory, while the operating system stores the remaining virtual pages on disk. The component of the

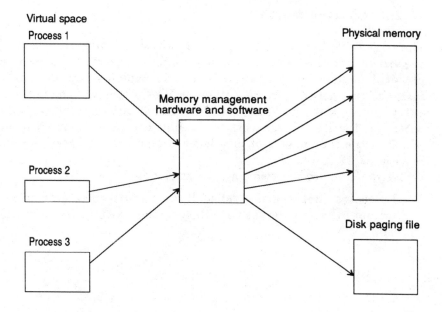

Figure 10.2 Process pages are on disk or in physical memory.

operating system that handles pages on disk is called the *pager* (see Figure 10.2).

When a process addresses a location in a page in its virtual memory and the page does not have a corresponding physical page, the MMH generates a page fault that interrupts execution of the process and the pager loads the page from disk, updates the page translation tables, and resumes execution of the interrupted process. On VAX/VMS the main paging file on the disk is SYS$SYS-TEM:PAGEFILE.SYS. This scheme of fetching pages from disk when they are required is called *demand paging*. If the disk space for paging is limited, then the operating system has various options:

1. Limit the address space of processes. (The *working set* parameters in the authorization file on VAX/VMS effectively specify maximum process size.)

2. Limit the number of processes on the computer. (SYSGEN parameter MAXPROCESSCNT specifies the maximum number of processes allowed.)

3. Crash or "hang" the system.

10.2.3 Sharing Memory

The page table entries used by MMH can be set up so that part of the virtual address space of a number of processes map to the same physical memory pages. This feature is exploited by *shareable installed images* and *global sections* in VAX/VMS. Each page table entry contains 4 bits that specify whether a process has read, write, read/write, or no access to the physical page, depending on which of the four modes of privileges the process is operating in. See Figure 10.3.

Sharing memory has two major advantages:

1. Processes that share a set of library routines consume less memory than processes that include the routines in their virtual memory.

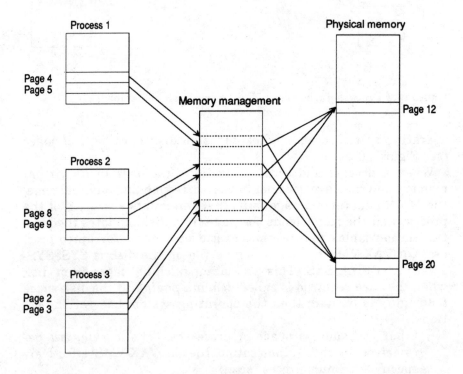

A shareable image resides in pages 12 and 20 of the physical memory. Two pages from each of the three processes' virtual memory are mapped into the shareable image, effectively allowing the processes to access the code (or data) in the shareable image.

Figure 10.3 Shareable images.

2. Memory sharing can be used for interprogram communications. Global sections are shared memory sections on VAX/VMS. Processes on the computer can map to common global sections.

10.2.4 Memory Management Details

The 4,294,967,296 (2 to the power of 32) bytes of address on the VAX is divided into two equal halves, known as the process space (or the per-process space) and the system space. Half of the system space is used by the operating system and the other half is currently unused by VAX/VMS. The process space is again divided into two equal halves, known as the P0 program region (for user program and data) and the P1 control region (for stack and process contextual information). The P0 and system space grow downwards, while the P1 space grows upwards. The virtual address space for a computer running four processes is shown in Figure 10.4. The largest user program and data cannot exceed 2 to the power of 29 (about 1 billion) bytes.

The translation from virtual to physical addresses is performed using three translation tables:

■ The *system page table* (SPT) translates addresses in system space.

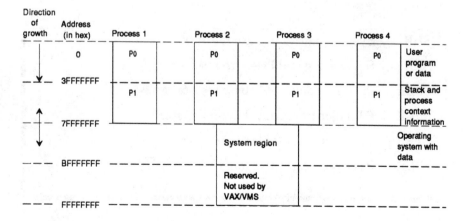

Figure 10.4 Virtual memory addressing limits.

- The *P0 process page table* (P0PT) translates addresses in P0 process space. There is one P0PT for each process.

- The *P1 process page table* (P1PT) translates addresses in P1 process space. There is one P1PT for each process.

The tables consist of 32-bit *page table entries*. The operating system creates these entries for use by the MMH. Each PTE contains information on one virtual page to physical page translation. All the translation tables are stored in system space. Each table has a base address and a specific length. The length determines the size of the virtual memory space. For example, if a P0 table has a length of 200 bytes, then the table has 50 PTEs (since each PTE is 4 bytes) and it maps 25,600 bytes of virtual space to physical memory. (Each PTE maps one page.) The starting address and length of each table are stored in base and length registers in the processor shown in Figure 10.5.

These registers are accessible to the MMH. The SPT is stored in contiguous pages of physical memory. The size of the table is fixed when the operating system is loaded. P0PT and P1PT for each process are stored in system virtual memory. The operating system maintains one set of P0PT and P1PT for each process.

10.2.5 The Translation Process

Each virtual address can be depicted as shown in Figure 10.6. Corresponding to each virtual page number (VPN) there is a PTE in one of the three types of tables. Each PTE can be depicted as shown in Figure 10.7.

SBR	System page table base register
SLR	System page table length register
P0BR	P0 region page table base register
P0LR	P0 region page table length register
P1BR	P1 region page table base register
P1LR	P1 region page table length register

Figure 10.5 CPU internal registers that define page tables.

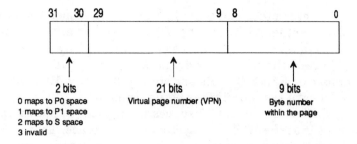

Figure 10.6 A virtual address.

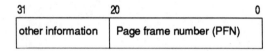

Figure 10.7 A page table entry (PTE).

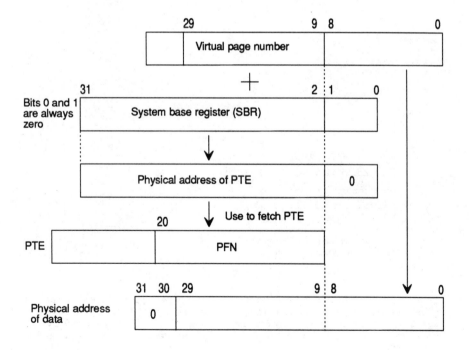

Figure 10.8 Virtual to physical address translation.

The MMH determines the table to be used by inspecting bits 30 and 31 of the virtual address. The VPN is used as an index in the page table to determine the address of the PTE. Bits 0 thru 20 of the PTE contain the *physical page number* (also called the *page frame number* or *PFN*). Details are shown in Figure 10.8, where a virtual address in system space is being translated.

The translation for P0 and P1 spaces takes place as shown in the figure except that the PTE is in system virtual space. Therefore, to derive the physical address of the PTE, one more translation in the system space is required. Figure 10.9 shows a simplified example.

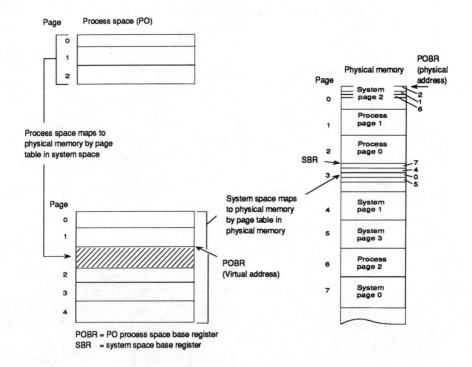

The process page table entries are in system virtual page 2. Since the system space is virtual, the process page table is, in this case, in physical page 0. Here, process virtual pages 0, 1, and 2 are mapped to physical memory pages 2, 1, and 6, respectively. System virtual pages 0, 1, 2, and 3 are mapped to physical memory pages 7, 4, 0, and 5, respectively.

Figure 10.9 Example of a process virtual memory translation.

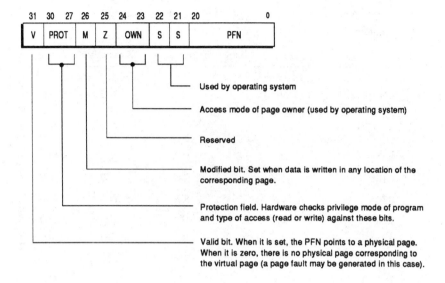

Figure 10.10 Details of a PTE.

10.2.6 The PTE

A page table entry can be depicted as shown in Figure 10.10. When a virtual page for a process is to be translated into a physical page, the hardware first determines the PTE address. The page frame number is extracted from the PTE only if two conditions are met:

1. The *protection field* of the PTE has a bit pattern that specifies the type of access (read or write) that is valid for the currently executing process. Figure 10.11 illustrates this. For example, if the protection field contains 1101 and the current process is executing in kernel privilege mode, then the process can read from or write into the page. If the process was in user mode, then a write access to the page will be invalid (the process would be terminated with an error message).

2. The *valid bit* in the PTE is set. For example, this bit is zeroed by the pager when a previously mapped page is now paged out on to disk. In this case, a translation invalid fault is generated

Protection field binary	Privilege mode of program*			
	Kernel	Supervisor	Executive	User
0000	NO †	NO	NO	NO
0001	RESERVED			
0010	RW	NO	NO	NO
0011	R	NO	NO	NO
0100	RW	RW	RW	RW
0101	RW	RW	NO	NO
0110	RW	R	NO	NO
0111	R	R	NO	NO
1000	RW	RW	RW	NO
1001	RW	RW	R	NO
1010	RW	R	R	NO
1011	R	R	R	NO
1100	RW	RW	RW	NO
1101	RW	RW	R	R
1110	RW	R	R	R
1111	R	R	R	R

> *   The privilege mode is specified in PSL.
> †   Note: R = read, W = write, NO = no access.

Figure 10.11 Access based on protection field and privilege mode.

by the hardware and the pager then retrieves the corresponding page from disk, modifies the PTE to point to the correct PFN, and sets the valid bit (and the translation continues).

The *modified bit* is set by the hardware when any of the 512 bytes in the physical page has been written into. When there is little available physical memory and the pager has to write some pages out to disk, then pages with recently set modified bits are unlikely candidates since these pages are more likely to be used soon.

The pager maintains a list of free physical memory pages. When a new process is run on the computer, the pager allocates pages from this list for the process's virtual memory. When a process terminates, all physical pages allocated to it are returned to the free page list. If there are no more free pages and a new process is created, then the pager selects a few of the allocated pages, stores their contents on the disk-paging file, updates the list of pages it has for pages on disk, resets the valid bit of the PTEs in the page tables of the processes that had owned the pages, and allocates these physical pages to the new process. In this way large amounts of virtual memory can be allocated to each process on the computer.

10.3 MEMORY-MAPPED I/O

I/O is usually handled by circuit boards in the back plane of the processor cabinet. These boards are called controllers. The controllers are connected to the CPU and memory by a bus. Figure 10.12 shows some controllers.

Four major types of buses are supported on VAXes: Qbus, Unibus, VAXBI, and XMI. Qbus is the slowest of the four and is used on the MicroVAXes, while XMI is the fastest and is used on the larger machines like the 6000 and 9000 series VAXes.

I/O is memory mapped so some physical memory is actually within the controllers. Commands to controllers and status or data information received from them are placed in system virtual memory and pass through the memory management hardware. Most controllers can also generate hardware interrupts to gain the attention of the CPU.

On the VAX/VMS operating system I/O is handled by system software called device drivers. User programs access I/O devices by means of standard high-level language statements (like OPEN and WRITE in COBOL) or by using operating system calls generically known as queued I/Os (QIOs). See Figure 10.13.

10.4 EXCEPTIONS AND INTERRUPTS

Programs consist of instructions that specify the flow of execution. Typically, the processor will sequentially execute instructions un-

Controller name	Bus supported	Function
DSSI	DSSI	Controls RF series drives
KDA50	Qbus	Controls up to four RA series drives
KDB50	VAXBI	Controls up to four RA series drives
KDM70	XMI	Controls up to eight RA series drives and TA series tape drives
UDA50	Unibus	Controls up to four RA series drives
DELQA	Qbus	VAX to Ethernet interface
DELUA	Unibus	VAX to Ethernet interface
DEBNI	VAXBI	VAX to Ethernet interface
CIBCA	VAXBI	VAXcluster interface
DMB32	VAXBI	Eight asynchronous lines (can be used for terminals) plus one synchronous line (can be used for a SDLC connection)

Figure 10.12 Examples of controllers.

less a branch is specified, in which case the instructions are executed starting at another location in the same program. This flow of execution is interrupted under certain conditions. For example, if the program attempts to execute an instruction that involves division by 0, control passes to the operating system, which then aborts execution of the program with an error message. This type of program interruption is called an exception. Program execution also stops temporarily when a device interrupts the CPU to signal completion of an output operation. In this case the operating system performs housekeeping operations for the device and allows the interrupted program to continue. This type of program execution is called an interrupt.

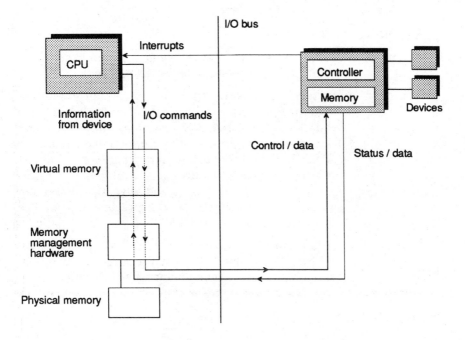

Figure 10.13 The I/O subsystem.

Exceptions are interruptions that occur during the executing process, while interrupts are interruptions caused by events external to the executing process. There are three kinds of exceptions: aborts, faults, and traps. Figure 10.14 explains them.

10.5 REGISTERS

The VAX processor has sixteen 32-bit registers available to non-privileged and privileged programs. The registers are labeled R0 through R15. While these are called general purpose registers, actually a number of them are dedicated for specific use (see Figure 10.15). By convention, R0 is used by subprograms to return values or status information to calling programs.

The processor status longword contains a collection of fields defining the current execution state of the processor. The low-order 16 bits are called the processor status word. These bits are set or reset as a side effect when many of the instructions are executed. The high-order 16 bits are available to programs running in

Exception	Description
Abort	This leaves registers and memory in unpredictable state. The processes must be terminated.
Fault	Interruption occurs during instruction execution. The process can continue after the fault condition has been corrected. For example, an access to an inaccessible page (i.e., the protection field in the PTE indicates that the current process has no access) will cause an access control violation fault. The operating system can change the protection field to allow access to the process and let the process continue execution.
Trap	Interruption occurs after instruction execution. Process execution can continue after the trap. An example is the integer-division-by-zero trap.

Figure 10.14 The three types of exceptions.

the kernel privilege mode (usually this is the operating system). See Figure 10.16.

The VAX processor also has a number of registers that can be accessed *only by processes in the kernel privilege mode*. The registers hold information for use mainly by the system software. These registers are shown in Figure 10.17. The registers are also known as internal processor registers.

The registers can be accessed by two instructions:

1. MTPR Move to processor register

2. MFPR Move from processor register

For example,

```
MTPR    R1,P0LR    ;move contents of general
                   ;register R1 to processor
                   ;register P0 process-space
                   ;Length Register.
```

When the CPU is to be allocated to a new process, the registers marked PROCESS in the table have to be loaded. The system

Usage

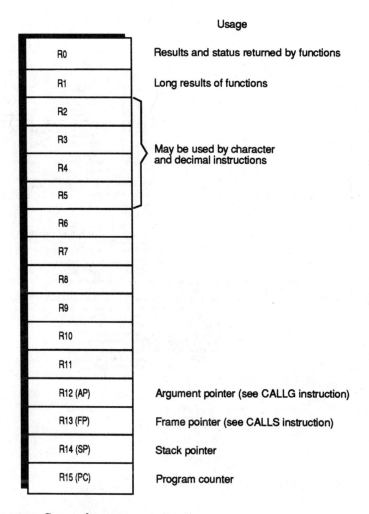

R0	Results and status returned by functions
R1	Long results of functions
R2	
R3	May be used by character
R4	and decimal instructions
R5	
R6	
R7	
R8	
R9	
R10	
R11	
R12 (AP)	Argument pointer (see CALLG instruction)
R13 (FP)	Frame pointer (see CALLS instruction)
R14 (SP)	Stack pointer
R15 (PC)	Program counter

Figure 10.15 General purpose registers.

software can load these registers using only one instruction: *load process context* (LDPCTX). The operating system maintains a *process control block* (PCB) for each process. Part of this PCB is called hardware PCB, which contains the registers shown in Figure 10.18.

When the CPU is to be allocated to a new process, the operating system, among other tasks, loads the address of the Hardware PCB of the process into the *PCB base register* (PCBB) and executes the LDPCTX instruction. The CPU is then set to execute the new process. The *save process context* instruction (SVPCTX) saves the

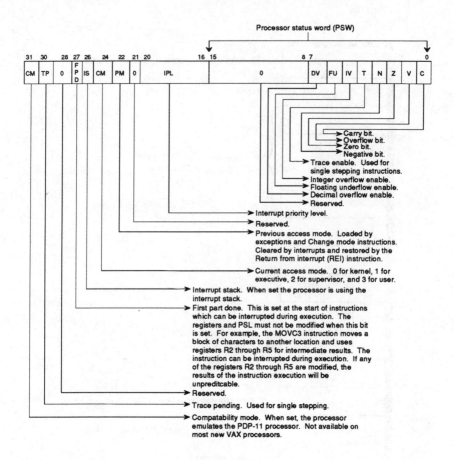

Figure 10.16 Processor status longword.

context of the hardware PCB from the processor to memory. The two instructions facilitate fast switching of the CPU among running processes.

10.6 PROGRAMMING THE MACHINE

10.6.1 The Assembly Language

While machine language can be used for low-level programming, for most purposes the assembly language is more convenient. The

Name	Symbol	Type*
Kernel stack pointer	KSP	Per process
Executive stack pointer	ESP	Per process
Supervisor stack pointer	SSP	Per process
User stack pointer	USP	Per process
Interrupt stack pointer	ISP	System
P0 base register	P0BR	Per process
P0 length register	P0LR	Per process
P1 base register	P1BR	Per process
P1 length register	P1LR	Per process
System base register	SBR	System
System length register	SLR	System
Process control block base	PCBB	System
System control block base	SCBB	System
Interrupt priority level	IPL	System
AST level	ASTLVL	Per process
Software interrupt request	SIRR	System
Software interrupt summary	SISR	System
Time of year	TODR	System
Memory management enable	MAPEN	System
Translation buffer invalid:		
All	TBIA	System
Single	TBIS	System
System identification	SID	System
Translation buffer check	TBCHK	System

* The per process registers are loaded when a process is switched for execution. Registers present on specific VAXes are not listed here.

Figure 10.17 Privileged processor registers.

	Bit 31		Bit 0
Longword			
00		Kernel mode stack	
01		Executive mode stack pointer	
02		Supervisor mode stack pointer	
03		User mode stack pointer	
04		Register R0	
05		Register R1	
06		Register R2	
07		Register R3	
08		Register R4	
09		Register R5	
10		Register R6	
11		Register R7	
12		Register R8	
13		Register R9	
14		Register R10	
15		Register R11	
16		Argument pointer	
17		Frame pointer	
18		Program counter	
19		Processor status longword	
20		Program region base register	
21	//////// 1 //////	Program region length register	
22		Control region base register	
23	2 ////////////	Control region base register	

Bits: 31 27 26 24 23 22 21 ... 0 0

NOTES:
1. Asynchronous trap pending field.
2. Enable performance monitor field.

Figure 10.18 The hardware process control block.

VAX assembly language is called Macro-32 or simply, Macro. A Macro program consists of assembler directives and VAX instructions. Assembler directives are used by the assembler during the assembly phases. No code is generated by the directives. The VAX instructions are mnemonic forms of the machine language instructions.

10.6.2 Assembler Syntax

Here is a simple assembly language program.

```
        .TITLE    Sample Program
        .ENTRY    DEMO,^M<>;Start of main program
        MOVL      #24,R2    ;Register2 = 24
TLABEL: INCL      R3        ;Register3 = Register3 + 1
        ADDL      R2,R3     ;Register3 = Register2 + Register3
        .END
```

The format of an assembler statement is:

```
Label:  Operator  Operand(s)     ;Comment
```

The fields are:

- *Label*. This defines the current location in a program.

- *Operator*. This specifies a machine instruction operation code or an assembler directive.

- *Operand(s)*. This specifies zero, one or more argument(s) for the machine instruction or assembler directive.

- *Comment*. This specifies program documentation that is ignored by the assembler.

10.7   DATA TYPES

Consider the statement

```
        MOVL  #16,R2     ;Register2 = 16
```

The instruction is manipulating longwords. A longword is a 32-bit integer. The VAX instructions support various other data types. Figure 10.19 describes them and Figure 10.20 describes the format of floating-point numbers.

10.8   INSTRUCTION FORMATS

Consider the *clear* (CLR) instruction. It zeroes the contents of the location specified by the operand. The operand can be specified in various ways. Here are some examples:

```
    CLRL   #1000        ;Clear the longword at memory
                        ;location 1000.
```

Data type	Mnemonic	Representation or precision	Size bytes	Range of values	
				Low	High
		Integers			
Byte	B	Signed	1	-128	127
		Unsigned		0	255
Word	W	Signed	2	-32,768	32,767
		Unsigned		0	65,635
Longword	L	Signed	4	-2,147,483,648	2,147,483,647
		Unsigned		0	4,294,967,295
Quadword	Q		8		
Octaword	O		16		
		Floating-point numbers			
F_Floating	F	7 digits	4	0.29×10^{-38}	1.7×10^{38}
D_floating	D	16 digits	8	0.29×10^{-38}	1.7×10^{38}
G_Floating	G	15 digits	8	0.56×10^{-308}	0.9×10^{308}
H_Floating	H	33 digits	16	0.84×10^{-4932}	0.59×10^{4932}
Variable-length bit-field	V		0-32 bits		
Packed decimal string	P		0-16		
Queue					
Character strings			0-65,535		

Figure 10.19 Data types (excluding vector data types).

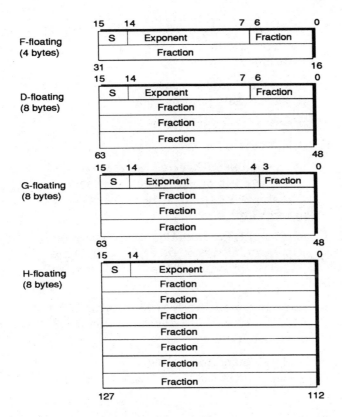

Figure 10.20 The floating-point numbers.

CLRL   @1000   ;Clear the longword at the memory
                  ;location whose address is in
                  ;memory location 1000.

CLRL   R2   ;Clear register R2.

CLRL   (R2)   ;Clear the longword at the memory
                  ;location whose address is in
                  ;register R2.

The various ways in which operands can be specified are called operand addressing modes. Figure 10.21 summarizes these modes.

Here are some examples of usage of the addressing modes. The instructions should be read in the sequence given since the operations performed by preceding instructions may be relevant to the current instruction.

```
MOVL   3000,R2    ;Operand 1: Program Counter Relative Addressing
                  ;Operand 2: Register Addressing
                  ;R2=3000.

CLRL   @1000      ;Program Counter Relative Deferred Addressing
                  ;Clear memory location 1000.

CLRB   (R2)       ;Register Deferred Addressing
                  ;Clear byte at location 3000.

CLRW   (R2)+      ;Autoincrement Deferred Addressing
                  ;Clear word at location 3000. Increment
                  ;register 2 by two (since the operand is
                  ;a longword).

MOVL   4000,(R2)  ;Operand 1: Program Counter Relative Addressing
                  ;Operand 2: Register Deferred Addressing
                  ;Move the longword value 4000 to memory
                  ;location 3000.

CLRQ   @(R2)+     ;Autoincrement deferred addressing
                  ;Clear quadword (8 bytes) at location 4000
                  ;and then R2=4008.

CLRW   24(R2)     ;Displacement Addressing.
                  ;Clear word at location 4032 (4008+24).

MOVL   3000,R5    ;

CLRB   14(R2)[R5] ;Indexed Addressing. The base is using
                  ;Displacement Addressing.
                  ;R2 contains 4032, R5 contains 3000.
                  ;Clear byte at location 7046 (4032+3000+14).
```

10.9 THE INSTRUCTION SET

Instructions are classified in the following groups:

- Arithmetic and logical instructions
- Character string instructions
- Control instructions
- Procedure call instructions
- Queue instructions
- Variable length bit field instructions
- Miscellaneous instructions

Addressing mode	Format	Description
Literal	#Literal	The literal value is part of the instruction. An example is: MOVL #20,R3
(Program counter) relative	Address	The address can be prefixed with B^, W^, or L^ that specifies the size of the literal in the instruction. An example is: CLRL W^2000. The longword at location 2000 is zeroed.
(Program counter) relative deferred	@Address	The address points to a location, which in turn contains the address of the operand. This is also known as indirect addressing.
Register	Rn	The operand is the contents of the register.
Register deferred	(Rn)	The operand address is in the register. Example: CLRL (R3). If R3 contains 2121, the contents of location 2121 are zeroed.
Autodecrement	-(Rn)	The register content is decremented by the size of the operand (specified by the instruction mnemonic). The operand address is then the register contents. Example: CLRW -(R3). If R3 contains 2121, the instruction decrements it by 2 (since the operand is a word) to make it 2019. The memory location 2019 is then zeroed.
Autoincrement	(Rn)+	The operand address is in the register. The contents of the register are incremented by the size of the operand after the operation.
Autoincrement deferred	@(Rn)+	The operand address is in the memory location whose address is in the register. The contents of the register are incremented by the size of the operand after the operation. This addressing mode is useful when a single operation is to be performed on each element of an array. Note that autodecrement deferred does not exist. (Why?).
Displacement	Disp(Rn)	The content of the register is added to the displacement to derive the effective address. This addressing mode is useful when elements of record structures have to be accessed. Example: CLRL 14(R3). If R3 contains 2121 then the effective address is 2135. The longword at 2135 is zeroed.

Figure 10.21 Operand addressing modes.

Displacement deferred	@Disp(Rn)	The content of the location derived by adding the register contents and the displacement is the address of the operand. The displacement can be specified as byte, word or longword. Example: CLRL @W^14(R3). As in the previous example, the location 4270 is derived. This location's content is used as an address for the longword operand to be zeroed.
Index	Base(Rn)	Used for array indexing. The base (of the array) is formed by one of the other valid addressing modes. Register Rn is then multiplied by size of each base element and added to the base to form the effective address. Example: CLRL W^2100[R5]. If R5 contains 6 then the effective word address is 2112. The real (byte) address is 4224. The longword at location 4224 is zeroed.

Figure 10.21 (*Continued*)

A real instruction is formed using the generic instruction, operand data type, and the number of operands. For example,

```
MULL2   M1,M2   ;M2 = M1 * M2
```

is formed from the generic instruction MUL (for multiply), the operand data type L (for longword), and the number of operands, which is 2 in this instruction. The instructions are listed here in their generic form along with a brief description.

10.9.1 Arithmetic and Logical Instructions

ADAWI Add aligned word interlocked. Adds two words and prevents other processors in a multiprocessor system from executing a similar operation. The destination must be aligned on a word boundary.

ADD   Add.

ADWC   Add with carry.

ASH   Arithmetic shift.

BIC   Bit clear. A mask specifies the bits to be zeroed.

BIS   Bit set. A mask specifies the bits to be set.

BIT   Bit test.

CLR   Clear. Zeroes the operand.

CMP   Compare.

CVT   Convert. Converts data from one form to another, e.g., packed decimal to string.

DEC   Decrement. Decrement operand by 1.

DIV   Divide. Returns the quotient.

EDIV   Extended divide. Returns the quotient and remainder.

EMOD Extended multiply and integerize. Multiplies two floating-point numbers and stores the integer and fractional parts of the result in separate operands.

EMUL Extended multiply. Multiplies two longwords and forms a quadword result.

INC   Increment. Increment by 1.

MCOM Move complemented. Moves the 1s complement of the source operand to the destination.

MNEG Move negated.

MOV   Move.

MOVZ Move zero extended. The source, with 0s padded at the left, is moved to the destination, which is greater in size than the source.

MUL   Multiply.

PUSHL Push longword (on the stack).

ROTL Rotate longword. Rotate a given number of times.

SBWC Subtract with carry.

SUB   Subtract.

TST   Test. Modifies condition codes.

XOR   Exclusive OR.

10.9.2 Character String Instructions

CMP   Compare two character strings.

LOCC Locate character. Locate a given character in a string.

MATCHC Match character. Search for a substring in a main string.

MOVC   Move character. Block data movement.

MOVTC   Move translated character. Moves characters from a source string to a given destination after translating each character, using a translation table. Used, for example, to convert ASCII characters to EBCDIC.

MOVTUC Move translated until character. Similar to MOVTC except that the translation and movement stops when the specified escape character is encountered as the translated character.

SCANC   Scan characters. Every byte in the specified string is used to look up a character in the specified 256-byte table. The character from the table is logically ANDed with a specified mask. The operation continues until the result of the AND operation is nonzero or the input string is exhausted. The instruction can be used, for example, to search for the position of the first nonalphanumeric character in a string.

SKPC   Skip character. Used to search for the first character in a string not matching a given character.

SPANC   Span characters. Similar to SCANC except that the operation continues until the result of the AND operation is 0.

10.9.3 Control Instructions

Branch and jump instructions on the VAX are different. A branch instruction contains the displacement of the branch location from the current location. The displacement is a byte or word value. The jump (and call) instruction contains the longword address of the jump location. Branches are usually more efficient than jumps.

ACB   Add compare and branch. Operand 2 is added to operand 3 and the result is placed in operand 3. The branch is performed if the absolute value of operand 3 is less than or equal to the absolute value of operand 2. This instruction efficiently implements the DO and FOR loops of high level languages.

AOB   Add 1 and branch.

B   Branch (on condition). The branch is performed depending on the value of the condition codes.

BB   Branch on bit. The branch is performed if a particular bit is set in the base operand.

BB   Branch on bit (and modify without interlock). The branch is performed if a particular bit is set or clear. Regardless of whether the branch is taken or not, the bit is set or cleared as specified.

BB   Branch on bit interlocked. This is similar to the above instruction except that the operation is an atomic one. This instruction is useful when multiple processes are implementing common semaphores.

BLB   Branch on low bit. Bit 0 is tested and the branch is performed if the bit is set or cleared as specified in the instruction.

BR   Unconditional branch. The displacement is stored in a byte or word so a branch to a location further away must be implemented using the JMP instruction.

BSB   Branch to subroutine. The program connector (PC) is pushed on the stack and the branch taken.

CASE   Case. Implements the CASE and SWITCH statements of high-level languages.

JMP   Jump. Similar to BR except that the jump can be to any location in the address space.

JSB   Jump to subroutine. Similar to BSB except that the jump can be to any location in the address space.

RSB   Return from subroutine. Used to return from subroutines called by the BSB and JSB instructions.

SOB   Subtract 1 and branch.

10.9.4 Procedure Call Instructions

These instructions implement subroutine calls and returns and adhere to the VAX procedure-calling and condition-handling standard.

CALLG   Call procedure with general argument list. The address of the list of arguments that is passed is given in the instruction. The instruction, when executed, stores the AP (Register 12) on the stack and stores the argument list base address in AP. The subroutine accesses the arguments via the AP. The instruction also saves specified registers on the stack.

CALLS   Call procedure with stack argument list. The arguments are passed on the stack. The stack pointer, SP, is stored in the Frame Pointer, FP, for use by the RET instruction to restore the stack pointer after the subroutine is executed. The instruction also saves specified registers on the stack. The instruction is particularly useful for recursive programming.

RET   Return from procedure. The instruction restores the state of the FP, SP, AP, and saved registers to their pre-CALL state.

10.9.5   Queue Instructions

A *queue* on the VAX is a circular, double-linked list. Each queue entry has a forward-pointing address, a backward-pointing address and zero or more bytes of data. While linked lists can be implemented using other instructions, the VAX has hardware instructions for efficient list manipulation. The basic queue operations are inserts and deletes of entries. All queue operations are interlocked to avoid concurrent access by multiple processes or processors.

INS   Insert entry into queue, interlocked. The entry can be inserted at the head or tail of or in between the queue.

REM   Remove entry from queue, interlocked. The entry to be removed can be at the head or tail of or in between the queue.

10.9.6   Variable-Length Bit Field Instructions

These instructions are useful for efficient bit manipulation. The size of a bit field can be from 0 to 32 bits (yes, up to 33 bits). The *branch on bit* (set or reset) instructions described above are also used for bit manipulation.

CMP   Compare field. Compare a bit field with a longword. Used to set condition codes.

EXT   Extract field. Move the given bit field to a longword location.

FF   Find first. Find the position of the first bit set (or reset, if specified in the instruction) in the given bit field. The search starts at the least significant bit and proceeds left.

INSV   Move as many bits as required to fill up the bit field from a longword.

10.9.7 Miscellaneous Instructions

BPT   Break point fault. Along with the T-bit in the processor status longword (PSL), the instruction is used for program tracing.

BUG   Bug check. Used to generate a fault. These instructions are inserted at points where the code should never be reached.

CHM   Change mode. Change mode to kernel, executive, supervisor, or user.

CRC   Calculate cyclic redundancy check. The CRC of a specified string of data is calculated using a specified polynomial.

EDITPC Edit packed to character string. The source string is edited using a specified pattern. The instruction is useful for output formatting of data (like in the PICTURE clause of COBOL).

HALT   Halt. Halts the processor.

INDEX   Compute index. Used to compute the address of an element in an array.

LDPCTX Load process context. Loads processor registers from memory. Used for rapid switching of processor from one process to another.

MTPR   Move to processor register. Used to load processor registers (like the memory management registers), excluding the general purpose registers.

NOP   No operation.

POLY   Polynomial evaluation. Accepts a table of polynomial coefficients and an argument (X value) to evaluate the polynomial. All numbers are floating point.

POPR   Pop registers (on the stack). The registers are specified in the operand.

PROBE   Probe accessibility. Checks read or write accessibility of a memory region.

PUSHR   Push registers (from the stack). The registers are specified in the operand.

REI   Return from exception or interrupt.

SVPCTX Save process context. Saves processor registers to a specified memory address. Used for rapid switching of processor from one process to another.

XFC   Extended function call. Used to implement customer-defined instructions.

10.10 VECTOR PROCESSING

Special instructions for efficient vector arithmetic now augment the normal instruction set. These instructions are implemented in hardware and extend the basic instruction set explained above. Vector processing is currently supported on the 6000 and 9000 series VAXes; it is not supported on the 3000 and 4000 series VAXes. Currently, the FORTRAN compiler automatically vectorizes programs to utilize the vector processor.

The vector processor is a coprocessor to the basic processor. A single computer can have multiple vector processors. Each vector processor has a speed of about 45 double-precision MFLOPS (*mega floating-point operations per second*) on a VAX 6000 model. From the programmer's view point, the normal machine-level instruction set is augmented with a set of vector-processing instructions.

The vector processor has *16 vector registers*, V0 to V15. Each vector register has *64 elements*. Each element is *64-bits wide*. An element can be looked upon as a simple scalar register. There are also a set of vector control registers and vector internal processor registers.

Typically, the vector processor is used as follows:

- A set of numbers are moved from main memory to the vector registers.

- A set of operations such as add and multiply are performed using the vector instructions. Since the instructions operate in parallel on a set of vector registers, the execution is fast.

- The output is moved from the vector registers back into main memory.

In MACRO, many of the vector-processing instructions start with the letter V. An example instruction is:

```
VVADDL  V4, V2, V7
```

When this instruction is executed, the longword contents of each of the 64 elements of vector register V4 are added with their corresponding 64 elements of register V2 and the results (64 values) are put in the corresponding 64 elements of register V7. Note that one instruction effectively performs 64 additions. The vector control registers can be modified so that a selected set of elements (of the vector registers), rather than all 64 elements, participate in the addition.

Here is a list of some of the vector instructions:

VLDL	Load longword memory data into vector register
VSTQ	Store (quadword) vector register data into memory
VVADDL	Vector vector integer add
VVCMPL	Vector vector integer compare
VVMULL	Vector vector integer multiply
VVSUBL	Vector vector integer subtract
VSBISL	Vector scalar bit set longword
VSSLLL	Vector scalar shift left logical longword
VVADDF	Vector vector add F_floating (32 bits)
VVDIVD	Vector vector divide D_floating (64 bits)

10.11 SUMMARY

The VAX has over 400 instructions and uses 32-bit addressing. The CPU has sixteen 32-bit general purpose registers. Virtual memory is mapped into physical pages by the memory management unit, and each page is 512 bytes. The chapter discussed the underlying architecture of VAX computers. As mentioned in previous chapters, VAXclusters consist of individual VAX computers that run the VAX/VMS operating system.

Vector processing is a recent extension of the basic VAX architecture. Additional cards have to be installed in the CPU cabinets to support vector processing. Vector processing was introduced in this chapter.

Relevant SYSGEN Parameters

The VAX/VMS operating system can be customized and tuned by changing a set of system parameters called SYSGEN parameters. These parameters are read from the file SYS$SYSTEM:VAXVMSSYS.PAR when the VAX is booted. The parameters can be modified by placing new values in the file SYS$SYSTEM:MODPARAMS.DAT and running the AUTOGEN procedure to create a new version of VAXVMSSYS.PAR. Currently, VAX/VMS has about 230 SYSGEN parameters of which a few that are of interest to the VAXcluster manager are mentioned here.

```
ALLOCLASS        Range: 0 to 255   Default value: 0
```

Allocation classes allow for fault tolerance on the system. In an Ethernet-based VAXcluster, disk and tape drives local to a VAX can be served to other VAXes in the cluster. For redundancy, the drives can be connected to two VAXes. Then the VAXes in the cluster can access the drives via either one of the two server VAXes. To achieve this, the two VAXes must have the same allocation class value. For example, a disk drive DUA3: can be attached to two VAXes in a cluster each having the ALLOCLASS SYSGEN parameter set to 3. The VAXes in the cluster can access the disk by the name 3DUA3:. The clustering software will use either one of the two VAXes to serve the disk I/O requests; if one of the two VAXes fail, the clustering software will automatically use the other VAX for disk I/Os.

VAXes on a CI-based VAXcluster can access a disk attached to a *hierarchical storage controller* (HSC). The disk is considered local to each VAX, and the allocation class defaults to 0 on each VAX and the HSC. However, if the disk is attached to two HSCs (for redundancy of the HSCs), the two HSCs must have the same nonzero allocation class value. The allocation class parameter on the HSC can be set from the HSC console; it is not considered a SYSGEN parameter.

```
DEADLOCK_WAIT      Range: number     Default value: 10
```

A lock may be acquired by a process. When another process makes a lock request for the same lock via the distributed (or local) lock manager, the system queues up the request. If the lock is not granted to the requesting process within the time period specified in seconds by the DEADLOCK_WAIT parameter, the system initiates a deadlock search. If no deadlock is found, the lock request remains in the queue. If a deadlock is found, one of the lock requests (not a granted lock) is released with a return status of SS$_DEADLOCK. A lower value for DEADLOCK_WAIT parameter aids in faster detection of deadlocks. As a trade-off, more frequent deadlock searches are performed, incurring CPU overhead.

```
DISK_QUORUM      Range: ASCII     Default value: "    "
```

This parameter value specifies a quorum disk, which contributes votes to the cluster quorum calculation. Normally, a quorum disk is used in a two-VAX cluster. In a two-VAX cluster without a quorum disk, if a VAX fails, the other VAX will not have a quorum to operate and the cluster will be down. (If a single VAX can operate as a cluster, then each of the two VAXes can operate independently as a cluster, effectively partitioning the cluster.) A quorum disk in a two-VAX cluster can allow a single VAX that is using the quorum disk to operate as a cluster; effectively the two-VAX cluster can operate even if a VAX fails. Note that the quorum disk cannot be shadowed.

```
EXPECTED_VOTES     Range: 1 to 127   Default value: 1
```

This parameter value is used to calculate an initial quorum value when a VAX boots. The value is normally set to the sum of all the votes contributed by all the VAXes and quorum disks in the cluster.

```
LOCKDIRWT      Range: 0 to 255    Default value: 0
```

This parameter value specifies the amount of distributed lock manager directory that will be handled by a VAX. The value is calculated when an AUTOGEN is performed and, normally, this value should not be changed.

```
MSCP_LOAD        Range: 0 or 1      Default value: 0
```

This parameter value determines whether the MSCP (mass storage control protocol) server is loaded when the operating system is being loaded. The MSCP server is used to serve local disk and tape drives to other VAXes in the cluster. Drives are normally served only on Ethernet-based (but not on CI-based) VAXclusters. The parameter value is set appropriately depending on the response to questions that are asked when the operating system is first loaded or customized by the CLUSTER_CONFIG procedure.

```
MSCP_LOAD_ALL    Range: 0, 1 or 2   Default value: 0
```

This parameter is effective only if MSCP_LOAD is set to 1. The possible values and interpretations are:

```
-----------------------------------------------------
Value     Interpretation
  0       Do not serve any disks.
  1       Serve all available disks.
  2       Serve local disks but not HSC disks.
-----------------------------------------------------
```

In a mixed-interconnect VAXcluster (where cluster nodes are on the CI and Ethernet buses), if a HSC-attached disk is to be served by multiple VAXes, these VAXes must have the same allocation class.

```
NISCS_LOAD_PEA0  Range: 0 or 1      Default value: 0
```

This parameter value determines whether PEDRIVER is loaded during a system boot. PEDRIVER emulates SCS functionality (and is required) for an Ethernet-based VAXcluster. The parameter value is set appropriately, depending on the response to questions that are asked when the operating system is first loaded or customized by the CLUSTER_CONFIG procedure.

```
QDSKVOTES        Range: 0 to 127    Default value: 1
```

This parameter value specifies the number of votes contributed by the quorum disk. The parameter is effective only if the QUORUM_DISK value is nonblank.

```
SCSSYSTEMID        Range: number     Default value: 0
```

This parameter value is an unique identifier for each node on the cluster. It is derived from the DECnet node number by adding the value of ((DECnet area number) X 1024) to the value of DECnet node number. For example, if the DECnet address for the node is 1.8 then the SCSSYSTEMID is 1032. The parameter value is set appropriately, depending on the response to questions that are asked when the operating system is first loaded or customized by the CLUSTER_CONFIG procedure.

```
SCSNODE            Range: ASCII      Default value: "   "
```

This parameter value is the SCS system name for the VAX and should be the same as the DECnet node name. The parameter value is set appropriately, depending on the response to questions that are asked when the operating system is first loaded or customized by the CLUSTER_CONFIG procedure.

```
VAXCLUSTER         Range: 0, 1 or 2   Default value: 1
```

This parameter value determines how to load the clustering software when the operating system is being loaded. The possible values and interpretation are:

```
-----------------------------------------------------
Value    Interpretation
  0      Do not load clustering software.
  1      Load if SCSLOA is loaded.
  2      Load SCSLOA and the clustering software.
-----------------------------------------------------
```

For a VAXcluster, this parameter must be 1 or 2.

```
VOTES              Range: 0 to 127   Default value: 1
```

This parameter value specifies the number of votes contributed by this node towards the cluster quorum. The votes and quorum scheme is used to ensure that the cluster does not get partitioned into two or more subclusters.

Glossary

Abort An exception during process execution that leaves registers and memory in an unpredictable state. The process will be terminated by VMS. Also see exceptions.

Access control entry (ACE) Each entry in an ACL table is called an access control entry.

Access control list (ACL) A protection table associated with an object. The table specifies the users and the type of access allowed. Objects are files, devices, logical name tables, queues, and globalsections.

Access control string A string specifying a user name and password that is used when accessing another node on the network. For example: $ DIR GANGES"SHAH TIPJAM"::.

Addressing mode The method of specifying addresses of operands in an assembly language (MACRO) statement. Examples of addressing modes are immediate value, where the operand is part of the instruction, or register deferred, where the operand is in the location pointed to by the specified register.

ALL-IN-1 An office automation software package. Supports word processing, document management, and time management among other functions.

Allocation class Allocation classes allow the VAXcluster to automatically route disk and tape I/O traffic through other routes if a route fails.

Two VAXes can be connected locally to one disk drive. The two VAXes can serve the disk to other VAXes on the cluster if they both have the same allocation class. The allocation class is a value from 0 to 255. If one of the VAXes fails, the disk I/O is performed by the remaining VAX.

Two HSCs on a cluster can be connected to one disk drive. In this case the HSCs should have the same allocation class. If an HSC fails, the other HSC will perform disk I/O.

Ancilliary control program (ACP) A process interfacing between user processes and an I/O device driver. The ACP process performs higher level functions than those handled by drivers. An example is the NETACP process, which handles network functions.

Area Areas are logical subdivisions in a DECnet Phase IV network. They are created for efficient routing of packets. Nodes that can route packets within an area are level 1 routers, and nodes which can route packets from one area to another are level 2 routers.

Areas in an indexed file are subsections of the file. Each subsection contains logically related data. For example, keys can be in one area while actual records can be in another area.

Asynchronous system trap (AST) A software interrupt to a program by the operating system. The normal flow of execution is suspended, a previously specified routine (within the program) is executed, and then execution resumes at the point where it was suspended.

Autoconfigure On power up and system boot, the device drivers for all attached devices are loaded by VMS. If new devices are connected later, the SYSGEN AUTOCONFIGURE command can be used to load the new drivers.

Autogen The command file SYS$UPDATE:AUTOGEN.COM is used to resize all system parameters when some parameters are modified by specifying them in SYS$SPECIFIC:[SYSEXE]MOD-PARAMS.DAT.

Automatic failovers The process of a VAX accommodating users from a failed VAX on a VAXcluster.

Backup Utility for copying files or complete disks to another device.

Balance set Set of processes resident in memory as opposed to processes swapped out to disk.

Block spanning The concept of file records on disk continuing from one block to the next. Block size is 512 bytes.

Bucket An area of up to 63 blocks in memory used as a buffer by RMS (record management services) for storing data from an open relative or index file. It is the smallest subdivision (quantum) of I/O when performing disk data read and write operations.

Buffer management A function of the system communication architecture (SCA), which manages buffers for all cluster traffic either over the CI bus or the Ethernet.

Buffered I/O I/O (e.g., to terminals or mailboxes) that use system pool buffer for data that is being transferred. Contrast this with direct I/O.

Capacity planning and modeling The process of simulating a system for a different work load or future growth.

Captive account A user account that limits the set of operations the user can perform on the system. The user will not be able to execute DCL commands directly.

CI controller The hardware that interfaces a VAX or HSC to the CI bus.

CI-based VAXcluster A cluster formed over the computer interconnect bus as opposed to a cluster formed over the Ethernet (which is an NI-based VAXcluster).

CISC Acronym for complex instruction set computer. The VAX is a CISC. The term is normally used for comparision with RISC, which is an acronym for reduced instruction set computer.

Cluster See VAXcluster.

Cluster transition The process of a node entering or leaving a cluster.

CMOS Acronym for complementary metal oxide semiconductor. The chip technology used on modules of some of the low-end VAX systems.

CMS Acronym for code management system. A software package for managing source files and project tracking.

Command file A file containing a set of DCL (digital command language) commands that can be executed by specifying the file name preceded by an @ sign.

Command line interpreter (CLI) The interface between the user and the operating system is called a CLI. A CLI accepts and parses user commands before notifying the corresponding components of VMS. DCL is the usual CLI on VMS.

Computer interconnect (CI) bus The hardware that interconnects VAXes on a CI-based VAXcluster. The bus has a bandwidth of 70 Mbits/sec.

Connection management The process of managing virtual circuit links between nodes of a VAXcluster by the SCA.

Connection manager A VAXcluster internal software application that maintains cluster integrity using the quorum and votes scheme and that updates VAXcluster internal databases, describing which nodes are currently cluster members.

Console terminal The terminal on a VAX that communicates with the CPU even when VMS is not running. An operator console is any terminal that has been enabled to receive operator messages by the REPLY/ENABLE command. Each VAX on a cluster has a separate console terminal.

Context switching The action of setting up CPU registers and performing other house-keeping functions by VMS when switching the CPU from one process to another.

CPU access mode One of the four modes in which the CPU can operate: kernel, executive, system, or user. Kernel is the most privileged, and user is the least privileged.

Credits The number of SCA cluster messages a node on a VAXcluster can send to another node.

CSMA Acronym for carrier sense multiple access. The technique used for sending data on the CI bus at the lowest level. A CI controller waits for the CI bus to be quiet (carrier sense) before sending data. The CI bus is "multiple access" because multiple controllers can send and receive data over the bus.

CSMA/CD Acronym for carrier sense multiple access/collision detection. The technique used for sending and receiving data on Ethernet at the lowest level.

CSR Acronym for control and status register. A memory location within the VAX that is also a register on a device controller on that same VAX. Programs can control the device and get status information from it by writing and reading this memory location.

Data block transfers Transfer of blocks of data from the memory of one node to that of another. On a CI-based cluster, these transfers are performed by the CI controllers without CPU intervention.

Datagrams Packets of data used for cluster communications. A datagram has a size of 576 bytes. A node sending out a datagram does not wait for an acknowledgment from the node that is supposed to receive it. Delivery of datagrams is not guaranteed. Noncritical status messages and similar information is transmitted using datagrams.

DDCMP Acronym for digital data communications protocol. This point-to-point protocol is used when VAXes are networked using communications lines.

DECforms The current form management system for the VAXes. It supercedes FMS and TDMS.

DECnet The networking component of VAX/VMS.

DECserver A communications controller that allows terminals and printers to be connected to Ethernet. The terminals and printers can then communicate with systems on the Ethernet.

DECtp A transaction processing system from DEC.

DECwindows DEC's implementation of windowing system, using X-windows that was developed at MIT.

Delta time Time specified as a difference of two absolute times. For example, 5 days and 10 hours is specified as "5-10:00:00." Usually, wherever the time has to be entered, an actual time followed by plus or minus a delta time is acceptable. For example, the next two times are equivalent:
27-JAN-1991:17:55:00
15-JAN-1991:14:30:00 +12-3:25:00
Both lines specify January 27th, 1991, 5:55pm.

Demand zero paging A page initialized to 0 when it is allocated during a page fault. The page is not written to the disk-paging file during a write operation if the page has not been modified. This way, disk space is conserved and page faults are serviced faster.

Detached process A process that has no owner process. Normally, these are the top processes of process trees. The process created when a user logs in is a detached process. Detached processes can be created by the RUN/DETACH command or the $CREPRC system service.

Device independence The process of using logical names for devices and accessing the devices via these logical names rather than the device names. This way, if a device is replaced by another, just the logical name needs to be changed, and the programs using the logical name will automatically access the new device.

Digital command language (DCL) The user interface with the operating system.

Direct I/O I/O (e.g., to disks) where data is transferred directly from the process memory to the device. Contrast this with buffered I/O.

Directory services A service offered by a node in a VAXcluster to all the nodes on the cluster. The service allows applications within the VAXcluster software to determine what applications are running on other nodes.

Distributed file services Distributed file services is the cluster software on each node that manages disk and file sharing. It also controls and manages record locking by users on the cluster. It is a form of distributed RMS for file access.

Distributed job controller The component of systems software that manages clusterwide print and batch queues.

Distributed lock manager Distributed lock manager is used to synchronize operations between nodes in a cluster. It is used by other cluster software like the distributed file service and distributed job controller. It is a superset of the lock manager on individual VAXes. Users can synchronize clustered applications by using $ENQ and $DEQ system calls.

DMA Acronym for direct memory access. The CI controllers access memory without CPU intervention when transferring blocks of disk data over the CI bus between a VAX and the HSC.

DTM Acronym for DEC test manager. A software package for performing regression tests on an application.

ECC Acronym for error-correcting code. The type of memory error checking used on most of the high-end VAXes.

ECL Acronym for emitter-coupled logic. The chip technology used for some of the VAX system modules.

EEPROM Acronym for electrically erasable programmable read-only memory. Customized boot commands and some other parameters can be stored in the EEPROM connected to the CPU on some VAXes. The EEPROM does not lose data on power failure, so the commands can be used to quickly bring up the system when power resumes.

Ethernet Ethernet is one of the communications standards used by DECnet. Ethernet has a maximum theoretical bandwidth of 10 Mbits/sec. It can be used for local area networks and, with the use of LAN bridges, for wide area networks. The Ethernet physical layer specification is defined in the IEEE 802.3 standard.

EVE Acronym for extensible VAX editor. EVE is a screen-oriented text editor programmed using the text processing utility (TPU). The editor can be enhanced for customized functions.

Event flag A bit used to indicate completion of an event either by the system or by a process. Event flags are typically used for synchronization, either within a program or among programs.

Exceptions Exceptions are interruptions caused in the context of the executing process, while interrupts are interruptions caused because of events external to the executing process. There are three kinds of exceptions: aborts, faults, and traps.

Executor The node on which NCP commands will be executed. NCP, and acronym for network control program, is a component of DECnet.

Exit handler A routine that is executed just before an image exits. The handler normally performs clean-up tasks. It executes even when the image terminates abnormally, for example, by a CTRL/Y entered at the terminal.

Fault This is an interruption that occurs during instruction execution. A process can continue after the fault condition has been corrected. For example, an access to a virtual memory location that is not mapped to actual physical memory will generate a page fault. The operating system will decide the further course of action. Also see exceptions.

Fault tolerant systems Systems that can continue normal operations when a software or hardware component malfunctions.

File access block (FAB) A data structure used by RMS to store file-related information.

Folder Located within the MAIL utility, this is a directory that contains mail messages.

Foreign tape This is a tape mounted with the /FOREIGN qualifier (or the equivalent when using the $MOUNT system service). ANSI standard label processing is bypassed by the system.

Generic queue A print or batch queue pointing to one or more queues. Generic queues are useful when a user can use one of a set of identical resources.

Global section A set of memory pages whose contents can be accessed by one or more processes.

Hierarchical storage controller (HSC) A hardware device on a VAXcluster that efficiently utilizes attached disks and tape drives on behalf of the cluster. HSCs can be used with nonclustered VAXes also, but a CI bus interconnection is required.

Heterogeneous VAXcluster When VAXes on a cluster do not boot off the same system disk, the cluster is called heterogeneous (as opposed to homogeneous). Such clusters can have VAXes running different versions of the operating system. Also known as multiple-environment VAXclusters.

High availability systems Systems like VAXclusters that have a high level of redundancy but do not support complete fault tolerance.

Homogeneous VAXcluster When VAXes on a cluster boot off the same system disk, the cluster is called homogeneous (as opposed to heterogeneous). In such clusters, all the member VAXes run the same version of the operating system.

Identifier See rights identifier.

Interrupt See exception.

Interrupt priority level (IPL) This has a value that ranges from 1 to 31. Software interrupts have a priority of 1 through 15, and hardware interrupts have a priority of 16 thru 31. A low-priority interrupt-processing routine can be preempted by a higher priority interrupt, but not vice versa.

LANBRIDGE A hardware component that connects two separate Ethernet segments.

LAVc A VAXcluster using Ethernet for cluster communications rather than the CI bus. LAVcs are also known as NI-based clusters (NI is an acronym for network interconnect).

Layered products Products that are not bundled with the operating system. Typical products are language compilers, CASE tools, and database management systems.

Lexical functions A set of functions that can be called from DCL at a terminal or from DCL command files. For example,

```
$ imagename = f$getjpi("SHAH","IMAGNAME")
```

returns the name of the image currently being executed by the process SHAH into the symbol imagename.

License The authorization to use a (software) product. The product license has to be registered in VMS before the product can run.

Line A physical link from a node to a DECnet network.

Link A session between two nodes over DECnet. A number of links can use one circuit.

Local area VAXcluster See LAVc.

Local disks A disk directly accessible to a VAX as opposed to a disk that is MSCP-served by another VAX.

Lock Locks are a VMS supported synchronization mechanism. Locks on a cluster are clusterwide even if they are created and used only on one node.

Logical names A name that, when used, is translated to a string of characters by VMS. VMS searches logical name tables for the translation. Logical names can be created by the DEFINE command.

Login directory The default directory when a user logs in. The logical name SYS$LOGIN created by VMS for each process points to this directory.

LSE Acronym for language sensitive editor. The product is an editor that automatically creates language statement templates and allows compilations from within the editor.

Mailbox A software device that can be used for (stream-oriented) communications by two or more processes. Mailboxes are node specific even on a cluster.

Mass storage control protocol (MSCP) server A VAX that serves a local disk to other VAXes on the cluster.

Mixed-interconnect VAXclusters A VAXcluster using both Ethernet and the CI bus for communications. Such a VAXcluster can support a wider range of VAXes than a NI-based or CI-based VAXcluster.

MMS Acronym for module management system. A software package for maintaining source file interdependencies, which can be used for regenerating an application when some source files are modified.

MONITOR A system utility for monitoring system resource usage.

MOTIF A windowing interface developed using X-windows as a basis.

MSCP Acronym for mass storage control protocol. Supported by most disk drive controllers for disk I/O operations.

Named-buffer transfer services A function of SCA. It is used for efficient transfer of blocks of data from one node in a VAXcluster to another. On CI-based clusters this transfer is performed by the hardware controllers, which transfer data from one node's memory to another's without the intervention of the host CPUs. The service is used mainly for disk I/O transfers between VAXes or between VAXes and HSCs.

NI-based clusters A cluster formed over Ethernet as opposed to a cluster formed over the CI bus (which is a CI-based VAXcluster).

Null device A software device, NL:, that accepts and discards data sent to it and returns an End-Of-File when accessed for input.

On disk structure-2 (ODS-2) The disk structure for FILES-11 disks on the VAX. ODS-1 is an older version of disk structure, which is also used on some PDP-11 computers.

OPCOM A process that accepts and processes messages sent to the operator by users or other processes. Users can send a message to the operator by the DCL REPLY command; programs can do the same with the $SNDOPR system service routine.

Options file A file used by the LINKER that specifies files and other parameters to be used during a link operation.

P0 space Virtual memory region where program code and data resides for a process.

P1 space Virtual memory region where stack, DCL, and process contextual information reside for a process.

PADRIVER The software driver used by VAXes for cluster communications over the CI bus. Also see VAXport drivers.

Parallel processing system A system with multiple CPUs that share memory and execute code in parallel. For example, the VAX 6540 is a four-CPU system that runs a single copy of VAX/VMS. The PPL$ library routines can be used to generate parallel code for faster execution on such systems.

Password encryption The process of storing user passwords in the authorization file using a one-way encryption algorithm. This way, even privileged users cannot determine the password of another user, although they can change it.

PCA Acronym for program coverage analyzer. A software package that displays the execution profile for a program that has been run. PCA displays information such as the CPU time spent at each source statement in a program.

PEDRIVER The software driver used by VAXes for cluster communications over the Ethernet. Also see VAXport drivers.

Priority A value ranging from 0 thru 31 assigned to each process on the system for CPU scheduling.

Privileges A set of values, one or more of which can be "owned" by each process on the system. Each privilege permits the owning processes to perform a set of operations that would not be possible if the processes do not own the privilege. For example, if a process has the READALL privilege, it can read any file on any disk.

Procedure calling standard A standard method used by all VMS software products for calling subprograms in the run-time library and system services and within modules written in any VMS language. The standard defines parameter types, parameter passing mechanisms, and conventions for returning status values. The standard also allows programs written in one language to call routines written in other languages.

Process An independent, executable entity running under VMS. The two major software components on the system are the operating system and processes. Processes either run DCL or program images.

Process identification (PID) A unique eight hexadecimal digit number assigned to each process on the system. On a cluster, this number is unique to each process on the cluster.

Processor status longword (PSL) A 32-bit register in the CPU.

Proxy account A proxy account on a VAX allows a user on another VAX to access the first VAX without having to specify passwords.

PSL See processor status longword.

Qbus A 16-bit data bus that is used on many microVAXes.

Queued Input/Output (QIO) A generic term that is used for all user-level I/O under VMS.

Quorum A quorum is an integer that determines whether the VAXes in a cluster have sufficient votes to allow the cluster to operate.

Quorum disk A disk that contributes votes in a cluster. The quorum disk cannot be shadowed.

Record access block (RAB) A data structure that is used by RMS to store record-related information such as the maximum record size for a file.

Record management services (RMS) The file management system on VAXclusters and independent VAX systems.

ReGIS Acronym for remote graphics instruction set. It is a set of commands used to display graphical output on some DEC terminals and printers.

Requestor A controller card within the HSC.

Rights identifier A rights identifier is a name stored in the rights database, SYS$SYSTEM:RIGHTSLIST.DAT. A rights identifier is used for protecting objects against unauthorized access. Users can hold one or more of these identifiers. Objects can be protected so that they can be accessed only by holders of a specific identifier.

RMS See record management services.

Run-time library (RTL) This is a set of VMS utility routines that can be called from programs.

Save set A (container) file that contains a set of RMS files. Save sets are created by BACKUP utility commands.

SCA Acronym for system communication architecture. SCA is used on VAXclusters and is somewhat like DEC network architecture (DNA) for network communications.

SCSI Acronym for small systems computer interface. SCSI is an I/O bus used on some of the MicroVAXes (and VAXstations).

Screen Management Routines (SMG) A set of utility routines for performing terminal-independent screen-oriented output and keyboard input.

SCS Acronym for system communication services. SCS is a layer of software within the system communication architecture (SCA), which is responsible for cluster communications between nodes in a cluster.

Security alarm A message sent to the operator console and the security audit log file when there is a security event (such as a security breach).

Sequenced messages Packets of cluster communications information that are guaranteed to be delivered, as opposed to datagram packets whose delivery to the destination is not guaranteed.

Shareable images Executable images that can be installed in memory. When installed, users accessing the image share one copy in memory. This saves memory.

SIXEL graphics A form of bit-image graphics used on some DEC terminals and printers.

Spawn The command used to create a subprocess of the current process.

Spinlock In a multiprocessor VAX like the VAX 6000-420, a spinlock is a software lock shared by multiple CPUs. This lock is not to be confused with the locks used for interprocess synchronization and communications. When one CPU has access to the lock, another CPU wishing to acquire the lock will loop until the lock is released—hence the term spinlock. A spinlock can simply be a bit in main memory.

Star coupler A junction box in a VAXcluster where the CI cables from all the nodes on the cluster are interconnected.

String descriptor A data structure that is used for passing string parameters from one program to another. The descriptor consists of a string address, string size, and string type.

Symbiont A process that interfaces between a user process and record-oriented devices such as printers and card readers.

Symbol A DCL variable.

Symmetric multiprocessing The technique of scheduling code to be run on any available processor in a multiprocessor CPU. On asymmetric multiprocessing computers, each processor has a dedicated function. For example, in a two-processor computer, one processor may handle I/O while the other executes non-I/O code. The VAX multiprocessor computers such as the VAX 6000-540, are symmetric multiprocessing computers.

SYSAPs This term is derived from system applications. Cluster software applications on a node which communicate with their counterparts on other nodes in the VAXcluster are SYSAPs. SYSAPs are components of the SCA software.

SYSGEN parameters A set of operating system parameters that can be changed for customizing and tuning a system.

System communication architecture (SCA) See SCA.

System communications services (SCS) SCS is the software on each node of a VAXcluster that implements communications on a cluster. SCS makes use of the VAXport drivers.

System services A set of VMS utility routines that can be called from programs.

Terminal server A hardware device that allows a number of terminals to access VAXes over Ethernet using an efficient protocol called LAT.

TPU Acronym for text processing utility. A programming tool for manipulating text oriented data.

Trap A type of exception where interruption occurs after instruction execution at the machine level. Process execution can continue after the trap. An example is integer division by zero trap. Also see exceptions.

Unibus A 16-bit I/O bus used on older VAXes.

User authorization file (UAF) An indexed file containing security- and quota-related information on all users who can access the system. The file is SYS$SYSTEM:SYSUAF.DAT and is normally accessed by the AUTHORIZE utility.

User environment test package (UETP) A set of programs that are bundled with VMS for testing VMS software and hardware components.

User identification code (UIC) A UIC consists of two numbers: a group and a member number. Each user on the system is assigned a UIC. UICs are used in the VMS protection scheme.

User profiles Accounts within the AUTHORIZE database files.

VAX units of processing (VUP) A unit of measure of VAX CPU speed. One VUP is the CPU speed of a VAX 11/780.

VAXBI An I/O bus used on some of the 6000 and 8000 series VAXes and some other VAXes.

VAXcluster One or more VAXes interconnected to form one synergetic system.

VAXcluster alias A DECnet node name and/or address that is used by one or more nodes in a VAXcluster. A node using the alias node name (or address) will be connected to any one of the VAXes that have that alias defined in their DECnet database.

VAXcluster console system (VCS) A VAX, typically a DECwindows-based VAXstation and associated software that allows all the individual consoles of VAXes in a cluster to be monitored and used from a single terminal.

VAXELN A real-time operating system based on VAX/VMS.

VAXft system A fault-tolerant VAX system. The system has duplicate hardware so that the system continues normal operations even if a component such as the CPU fails. The system runs the standard operating system, VAX/VMS.

VAXport drivers Software drivers that are used for cluster communications from one node to another. Currently there are two drivers; PADRIVER that is used on a VAX clustered via the CI bus and PEDRIVER that is used on a VAX clustered via Ethernet.

VAXsimPLUS A software tool for diagnosing system malfunctions.

Vector processing A hardware extension of the VAX CPU that increases throughput for number-crunching applications.

Volume shadowing The concept of maintaining multiple disks all containing the same data. Also known as "volume mirroring." Volume shadowing reduces the probability of data loss due to disk failures.

Votes A value contributed by each VAX in a cluster that is used to determine if the cluster is valid. See quorum.

VUP See VAX Units of Processing.

Working set The number of physical memory pages being used by a process.

X-windows A graphical display system developed by MIT.

XMI An I/O bus used on the 6000 series and 9000 series VAXes. It is the fastest of all the buses on VAXes.

XQP Acronym for extended QIO processor. This is the software that handles file I/O from a VAX to disk and tape devices on a VAXcluster.

Multiple VAXes on a cluster may open the same set of records on a disk file. XQP, using the distributed lock manager, manages such concurrent file accesses. It also manages file cache concurrency issues when multiple nodes open the same set of files. XQP supercedes ACP, which is the older file handler. ACP is an acronym for ancillary control program.

Bibliography

Basic documentation for VMS consists of the following kits:

- Base set. Includes overview of VMS, basic commands, system management, and license management.
- General user subkit. Includes VMS basics, DCL, editors, and system messages.
- System management subkit. Includes system maintenance, security, performance, and networking.
- Programming subkit. Includes programming utilities (like debugger and linker), system routines, file system, system programming, device support, and MACRO.

Other VMS documentation iinclude obsolete features and (new version) release notes. Each VAX has system-specific installation and operations manuals. Some other manuals describe RMS journaling, volume shadowing, parallel programming, and layered product development. The manuals are not listed here.

Each software-layered product has its own set of manuals that usually include an installation guide, product guide, and product reference set. Hardware products also have separate manuals.

There are a number of third-party software and hardware products not mentioned in this book. Information on these products can be found in trade magazines such as DEC Professional, Digital News, and Digital Review.

Anagnostopoulos, P. C., *VAX/VMS: Writing Real Programs in DCL*, Digital Press, Bedford, Mass., 1989.

Association of Computing Machinery, "VAXclusters: A closely coupled distributed system," *ACM Transactions on Computer Systems*, May 1986, pp.130-146.

Bynon, D. W. and T. C. Shannon, *Introduction to VAX/VMS*, 2d ed., Professional Press, Spring House, Pa., 1987.

The DECconnect Communications System Handbook, Digital Equipment Corporation, Maynard, Mass.

Diamondstone, J., *ERI Training with Jan Diamondstone, Using VAX/VMS*, Prentice-Hall, Englewood Cliffs, N.J., 1988.

Digital Press, *Digital Technical Journal*, Issue 3: Networking Products, Maynard, Mass., 1986.

Digital Press, *Digital Technical Journal*, Issue 5: VAXcluster Systems, Maynard, Mass., 1987.

Digital Press, *Digital Technical Journal*, Issue 6: Software Productivity Tools, Maynard, Mass., 1988.

Digital Press, *Digital Technical Journal*, Issue 7: CVAX-based Products, Maynard, Mass., 1988.

Digital Press, *Digital Technical Journal*, Issue 8: Storage Technology, Maynard, Mass., 1989.

Digital Press, *Digital Technical Journal*, Issue 9: Distributed Systems, Maynard, Mass., 1989.

Digital Press, *Digital Technical Journal*, vol 2, no 2: VAX 6000 Model 400 Systems, Maynard, Mass., 1990.

IEEE Computer Society, "Fault-tolerant systems," *Computer*, July, 1990.

Goatley, H., "SDA: The ultimate management tool," *VAX Professional*, Professional Press, Spring House, Pa., August, October, and December 1989.

Goldberg, R. E., Kenah, L. J., and S. F. Bate, *VAX/VMS Internals and Data Structures (Version 4.4)*, Digital Press, Bedford, Mass., 1988.

Goldberg, R. E. and L. J. Kenah, *VMS Internals And Data Structures - Version 5 Update XPRESS*, vol. 1–5, Digital Press, Bedford, Mass., 1989 and 1990.

Hubbard, J. R., *A Gentle Introduction to the VAX System*, TAB Professional and Reference Books, Blue Ridge Summit, Pa., 1987.

Leonard, T. (ed), *VAX Architecture Reference Manual*, Digital Press, Bedford, Mass., 1986.

Levy, H. M. and R. H. Eckhouse, *Computer Programming and Architecture: The VAX*, 2d Ed., Digital Press, Bedford, Mass., 1989.

Malamud, C., *DEC Networks and Architectures*, McGraw-Hill, New York, N.Y., 1989.

Peters, J. F. and P. J. Holmay, *The VMS User's Guide*, Digital Press, Bedford, Mass., 1990.

Sawey, R. M. and T. T. Stokes, *A Beginner's Guide to VAX/VMS Utilities & Applications*, Digital Press, Bedford, Mass., 1989.

VAX Architecture Handbook, Digital Equipment Corporation, Maynard, Mass.

VAXcluster Systems Handbook, Digital Equipment Corporation, Maynard, Mass.

VAX Professional Magazine, Professional Press, Spring House, Pa.

VAX Vector Processing Handbook, Digital Equipment Corporation, Maynard, Mass.

VAX/VMS Hardware Handbook, Digital Equipment Corporation, Maynard, Mass.

Index

Abort, 273, 274
Addressing mode, 281
After image journaling, 234
Allocation class, 97, 125
Ancilliary control program (ACP), 91
Area, RMS, 217
Assembly language, 276
Asynchronous system trap (AST), 188
Automatic failovers, 204

Batch and print job queues, 116
Before image journaling, 234
Block spanning, 215
Bucket, 214, 217
Buffer management, 84

Capacity planning and modeling, 146
CI-based VAXcluster, 61, 91
CLUSTER_AUTHORIZE.DAT, 113
CLUSTER_CONFIG procedure, 111
Common system disk, 108
Compilers, 10, 46
Computer interconnect (CI) bus, 57, 86
Connection management, 84
Connection manager, 91
Control and status register, 5
Controller, 5, 6, 272
CONVERT utility, 231
Credits, 84
CSMA, 87
CSMA/CD, 87

Data block transfers, 86

Data types, 280
Database systems, 13
Datagrams, 80
DDCMP, 66
DECbridge 500, 206
DECconcentrator 500, 206
DECnet, 14
DECtp, 13
DECwindows, 16
Device independence, 44
Devices, 6, 32, 40
Digital command language (DCL),
    9, 20
Directory aliases, 109
Directory services, 85
Disk striping driver, 203
Distributed file services, 91, 192
Distributed job controller, 94, 116
Distributed lock manager, 93, 181
Distributed transaction manager
    (DECdtm), 199
Distributed transaction processing,
    74, 192
DSSI bus, 5
Dual attachment station, 205
DUMP, 230

EDT, 11
Electronic disks, 202
Ethernet, 65
EVE, 10
Event flags, 172
EVL, 37

Exceptions, 271
Exit handler, 190
EXPECTED_VOTES, 95
Extended access block (XAB), 218

F$GETDVI lexical, 253
Fault tolerant systems, 69, 70
Fault, 274
FDDI controller, 205
Fiber distributed data interface, 205
File access block (FAB), 218
File definition language, 223
File sharing, 215
Files, 33

Generic queue, 116
Global sections, 158

HELP, 20
Heterogeneous VAXcluster, 61
Hierarchical storage controller (HSC),
    5, 58, 88, 98, 123, 251
High availability systems, 69
Homogeneous VAXcluster, 61
HSC backup, 126

I/O bus, 4
Input/output, 4
Installing VMS, 104
Instruction formats, 281
Interrupt, 271

Journaling, 10, 233

LANbridge, 66
LAT service, 121
Layered products, 12
LINK, 51
Local area network, 103
Local area VAXcluster (LAVc), 60, 62,
    103
Lock, 93, 172

Log manager control program (LMCP),
    200
Logical names, 42, 158

Mailbox, 158
Mass Storage Control Protocol (MSCP),
    94, 246
Memory management, 39, 261
Mixed-interconnect VAXclusters, 61, 63
MONITOR utility, 131
MSCP, 94

Name block (NAM), 220
Named-buffer transfer services, 86

NI-based clusters, 61, 91

Object Libraries, 183

P0 space, 265
P1 space, 265
PADRIVER, 90
Page table entry, 269
Pair and spare architecture, 76
Parallel processing, 64, 66
PEDRIVER, 90
Print queues, 116
Privileged register, 277
Privileges, 35
Process identification (PID), 37
Process, 35
Processor status longword (PSL), 276
Programs, 10, 46, 157, 191

Qbus, 4
Queued input/output (QIO), 271
Quorum, 95
Quorum disk, 97

Record access block (RAB), 218
Record formats, 211
Record management services (RMS), 209

Recovery unit journaling, 234
Register, 2, 273
Requestor, 124

RMS journaling, 233

Satellite nodes, 112
SCSI, 4
Search lists, 45
Security alarm, 151
Security audit, 150
Sequenced messages, 85
Shareable images, 185
SHOW CLUSTER command, 127
Single attachment station, 205
Star coupler, 58, 88
Stratus systems, 76
Synchronization, 171
SYSGEN parameters, 293 – 296
SYSMAN, 148
System applications, 82
System block, 83
System communication architecture
    (SCA), 79
System communication services
    (SCS), 80, 90

Tandem NonStop computers, 72
Terminals, 23
Token absorption, 206

Trap, 274

ULTRIX, 8
UNIBUS, 4
User authorization file (UAF), 115

VAX arcitecture, 259
VAX performance analyzer (VPA), 133
VAX Units of Processing (VUP), 3
VAX/VMS, 1, 19, 37
VAXBI bus, 4
VAXcluster alias, 118
VAXcluster console system (VCS), 121

VAXcluster password, 113
VAXft system, 70
VAXport drivers, 90
VAXset, 11
Vector processing, 2, 64, 290
Virtual to physical memory
    translation, 266
Volume shadowing, 245
Votes, 95
VT terminals, 23

X-Windows, 16
XMI bus, 4
XQP, 92

Zones, 71

ABOUT THE AUTHOR

Jay Shah has been working in VAX environments since
1983. Mr. Shah holds an M.S. in Technology Management,
and is presently employed as a senior software engineer at
Chase Manhattan Bank in New York City.